STUDIES IN ECONOMIC HISTORY

Editor:
Professor F. M. L. Thompson
Bedford College
University of London

Already published:

Eric J. Evans *The Contentious Tithe*

In preparation:

Anne Digby *Pauper Palaces*
Richard Perren *The Meat Trade in Britain 1840-1914*

LAND AND PEOPLE IN
NINETEENTH-CENTURY
WALES

LAND AND PEOPLE IN NINETEENTH-CENTURY WALES

DAVID W. HOWELL

Department of History
University College of Swansea

ROUTLEDGE & KEGAN PAUL
London, Henley and Boston

First published in 1977
by Routledge & Kegan Paul Ltd
39 Store Street,
London WC1E 7DD,
Broadway House,
Newtown Road,
Henley-on-Thames,
Oxon RG9 1EN and
9 Park Street,
Boston, Mass. 02108, USA
Printed in Great Britain by
Redwood Burn Ltd
Trowbridge and Esher
© David W. Howell 1977

British Library Cataloguing in Publication Data

Howell, David W.

Land and people in nineteenth-century Wales.
—(Studies in economic history).
1. Wales—Economic conditions 2. Wales—Rural conditions
I. Title   II. Series
330.9'429'081   HC257.W3   77-30122

ISBN 0 7100 8673 3

Owing to production delays
this book was published in 1978

CONTENTS

ACKNOWLEDGMENTS

I am indebted to many institutions and individuals for their help.
I owe thanks to the University of Wales for the award of the Dr
Samuel Williams fellowship which enabled me to pursue full-time
research between 1965 and 1968. The staffs of many record offices
and libraries have kindly assisted throughout: I owe particular
thanks to Major Francis Jones, former archivist of Carmarthenshire,
and to the members of the MSS department at the National Library of
Wales, Aberystwyth. The greater part of chapter 6 and some of
chapter 7 have appeared as articles in 'The Welsh History Review',
vol.6, no.3 (1973) and vol.7, no.1 (1974). I gratefully acknowledge
the permission given by the editor of 'The Welsh History Review',
Dr Kenneth O. Morgan, to reproduce in this book material which
originally appeared in those articles.

I owe a special debt to Professor A.H. John who supervised my
research and to Professor David Williams whose scholarship first
kindled my interest in this subject. Others whose help has been of
particular value include Professor F.M.L. Thompson, Professor G.E.
Mingay, Dr Kenneth O. Morgan and Mr Roscoe Howells. More recently,
several colleagues at Swansea have been generous with their comments;
in particular Professor Alun Davies and Dr D.J.V. Jones opened up
new perspectives. The final manuscript has benefited from the careful reading of Professor Glanmor Williams and Dr Michael Barker.
Mrs Ann Frey kindly typed the manuscript.

Finally, I owe the greatest debt to my parents and my wife, without whose encouragement this book would not have been written.

Swansea
September 1976   David W. Howell

NOTE ON ABBREVIATIONS

'Ag. Hist. Rev.'	'Agricultural History Review'
'Arch. Camb.'	'Archaeologia Cambrensis'
C.R.O.	Carmarthen Record Office
'Econ. Hist. Rev.'	'Economic History Review'
H.L.R.O.	House of Lords Record Office
H. of C.	House of Commons
H. of L.	House of Lords
'Jnl of the Bath and West of England Soc.'	'Journal of the Bath and West of England Society'
'Jnl of the Merioneth Hist. and Rec. Soc.	'Journal of the Merioneth Historical and Record Society'
'J.R.A.S.E.'	'Journal of the Royal Agricultural Society of England'
'Jnl of the Royal Welsh Ag. Soc.'	'Journal of the Royal Welsh Agricultural Society'
'Montgom. Colls'	'Montgomeryshire Collections'
N.L.W.	National Library of Wales
'N.L.W. Jnl'	'National Library of Wales Journal'
'P.P.'	'Parliamentary Papers'
P.R.O.	Public Record Office
'R.C.'	'Royal Commission'
'S.C.'	'Select Committee'
'Trans. Caerns. Hist. Soc.'	'Transactions of the Caernarvonshire Historical Society'
'Trans. Cards. Antiq. Soc.'	'Transactions of the Cardiganshire Antiquarian Society'

'Trans. Cymmr. Soc.'	'The Transactions of the Honourable Society of Cymmrodorion'
'Trans. Rads. Hist. Soc.'	'The Transactions of the Radnorshire Historical Society'
'T.R.H.S.'	'The Transactions of the Royal Historical Society'
'W.J.A.'	'Welsh Journal of Agriculture'
'Welsh Nat. Ag. Soc. Jnl'	'The Welsh National Agricultural Society Journal'

The extensive use of Parliamentary Papers necessitates harsh abbreviation. After citing the title of a Royal Commission or a Select Committee in full, further references to it will quote the Parliamentary Paper volume number and year only.

INTRODUCTION

At the opening of the nineteenth century Wales was a remote, largely
inaccessible, poor and backward region lying on the western fringes
of the British Isles. Its population of nearly 600,000 (about one-
fourteenth of that of England) was thinly but (unlike England's)
fairly evenly spread across the whole region, although there were
concentrations of people in the mineral producing areas of Anglesey,
Caernarvonshire, Flintshire, Glamorgan and Monmouthshire. Understandably, the upland core, which stretched right across the principality from north to south, was particularly sparsely populated,
many of its hundreds containing fewer than fifty persons per square
mile. As yet there was little urbanisation; in 1801 only thirteen
towns had over 3000 inhabitants and only seven had 5000. Across the
country as a whole on average more than three-quarters (and sometimes substantially more) of the occupied population were engaged in
agricultural pursuits. Each rural community was largely self-
contained. The predominantly pastoral population was scattered
among isolated farmsteads and cottages or in small hamlets. Communications were atrociously bad, the few improved turnpike roads form-
ing only a small proportion of the entire road system. In particular, many upland farmsteads could be approached only along sheep-
tracks or bridle paths.

The nineteenth century witnessed a fast growth of industry in the
southern counties of Glamorgan, Monmouth and, to a lesser extent,
Carmarthen. Population increase and distribution within Wales
reflected this new phenomenon; here, in the south-eastern valleys,
and increasingly so as the century progressed, more and more Welsh
people found work and composed a frontier society of proletarians.
Agriculture came to play a dwindling role in the principality's
economic life. Nevertheless, farming remained vital in rural areas
as an important source of food supply and employment, and local
farms continued as essential props to the people's existence (many
not directly engaged in farming) within each community. Furthermore,
hunger for farms remained intense throughout; labourers, not farmers, migrated in swarms to the towns, and had there been enough
farms to go round there would have been far less rural exodus.

A number of specialised published works are already available on
Welsh agriculture and its peasant population in the nineteenth

century. The agrarian discontent of the early decades down to the
1840s has claimed the attention of many historians both Welsh and
non-Welsh, the two most important studies to emerge being 'The
Rebecca Riots' by David Williams and 'Before Rebecca' by David Jones.
The major agrarian protest in the second half of the century was the
'tithe war' which has recently been subjected to close scrutiny in
J.P.D. Dunbabin's 'Rural Discontent in Nineteenth-Century Britain'.
Turning from the subject of rural unrest, a sociological study of
seminal importance is 'The Agricultural Community in South-West
Wales at the turn of the Twentieth Century' by David Jenkins. He
demonstrates the way in which an isolated rural community was
ordered to work the land before the advent of machinery. The more
purely agricultural history is to be found in a small number of
works, notably in 'Agriculture in Wales during the Napoleonic Wars'
by David Thomas which deals with cropping patterns and the physical
lay-out of farms, in 'The Agriculture of Wales and Monmouthshire' by
A.W. Ashby and I.L. Evans which contains a statistical survey of
agriculture from the 1870s but is mainly concerned with the years
after the First World War, and in the various books by Geraint
Jenkins on types of farm implements and rural crafts.

It will be apparent that all these studies pertain to particular
topics, areas and times. They do not attempt to present the whole
picture of agriculture and the farming community within the entire
country over the whole century. This general survey is intended to
fill such a gap. Its title 'Land and People' is meant to stress
that the study is an economic history with a strong emphasis on
human factors; how, on the one hand, relationships between tenants
and landlords and also peasant attitudes crucially impinged on agricultural development rendering it even more backward than the natural constraints imposed by climate, soil and geographical remoteness
could have been expected to make it and, conversely, how agricultural resources and organisation directly affected the nature of
social relationships within the community. Extensive use of landowners' private papers (a hitherto largely neglected source) has
afforded a whole new perspective on the conditions of life and
outlook of the Welsh peasantry.

To some extent Welsh agricultural history in the nineteenth century forms a part of that of a wider area known to geographers and
archaeologists as the 'highland zone'. (1) This region lies roughly
north-west of a line drawn from the mouth of the river Tees to the
mouth of the river Exe. Thus the relief of Wales and Monmouthshire
comprises mainly a highland bloc fringed by a narrow belt of coastal
lowland, which sometimes stretches as river valleys into the central
massif: 27 per cent of the total area lies above 1000 feet and a
further 32 per cent above 500 feet (see figure 1). The consequent
high rainfall, the restricted number of sunshine hours and the relatively low temperatures have always been the most important factors
limiting agricultural practice in the principality as within the
highland zone as a whole. Such conditions favour pastoral farming
and so the region is differentiated from the sunnier, cereal-
producing 'lowland zone' to the south-east of the line.

In common with the other areas of the highland zone, Wales in the
nineteenth century had a high incidence of family-farms. Resources
were limited and advanced technology was generally absent (though

of course, inputs like artificial feeds and fertilisers were far
less vital than in arable areas). Besides their shortage of capital,
such family-farmers were often ill-educated, wanting in enterprise,
wedded to traditional methods and suspicious of change. When compared with the substantial tenants of the large farms of the south-
east and southern Midlands of England it clearly emerges that these
family-farmers really belonged to the labouring class. They were
essentially peasant-tenants who practised semi-subsistence farming.

The farming systems within the highland zone as a whole were
shielded from the acute depressions which periodically occurred on
the heavy clays. The prevalence of mixed farming, with a concentration on livestock and dairying, reduced the risk of total collapse
in times of depression. Truly horrible indeed was the season that
hit this kind of farmer in all branches of his enterprise. Furthermore, many farmers in the highland zone were used to living frugally
and parsimoniously at the best of times; they were thus temperamen-
tally more willing and better able to suffer privation in difficult
years than were the large tenants of the lowland zone. (Such a
trait emphasises the stark poverty which unleashed the angry, desperate upsurge of Rebecca.) These small tenants of the highland
zone were, then, far better protected from the pressures of the
great nineteenth-century depressions than were the substantial
farmers of the arable areas.

The pressures on the highland-zone farmer sprang rather from
poverty, over-population and demand for holdings. Such pressures
were remorseless and unabating. Welsh agricultural history thus far
blends with the wider upland, pastoral, region. But the separate
socio-cultural characteristics of the principality imposed distinctive constraints on agricultural development. Such factors as land
hunger, the availability of men of capital from outside the region
and the ignorance of tenants about new ideas on improved farming
were all additionally influenced by their Welsh context. To a certain extent, also, the rift between the anglicised, Anglican and
Tory landowners and their Welsh speaking, Nonconformist and (from
around mid-century) Liberal tenants handicapped development. No
such division obtained on English estates, and Welsh Radical leaders
identified the cleavage as the key to the problems of the Welsh
tenantry. Whereas in England, claimed the parliamentary champion of
the Welsh farmers, T.E. Ellis, there was a 'community of feeling and
of interest' between landlords and their tenants, in Wales the cultural and political antipathies rendered such feelings impossible.(2)
Landlords were castigated by Ellis and others for mercilessly ex-
ploiting over-population and peasant land hunger in order to extract
the highest rents possible, for raising rents on tenants' improvements and for capriciously evicting them from their takings for
political and religious reasons. Tenants, it was argued, understandably felt insecure and lived in terror. The picture drawn of conditions in Wales thus bore a striking resemblance to some of the worst
features of the land system in Ireland.

Harsh landlordism was obviously an attractive explanation for
agricultural backwardness to the leaders of Welsh Radicalism. Significantly, Gladstone took the same line in a speech made in Snowdonia.
The contemporary anti-landlord indictment has generally been sympa-
thetically accepted by Welsh historians, many of whom have been

nurtured in a Nonconformist culture. (3) For them, as indeed for
all democrats, it is ideologically satisfying and has a certain
naive plausibility. We shall see that there was some substance to
the allegations; but that, equally, there was bias and misrepresen-
tation.

There is no mistaking the Welsh tenants' unwillingness to adventure capital. The explanation will constitute a major theme of
study. It will be argued that the conditions of tenure, although
often far from satisfactory, were considerably less important in
producing a reluctance to invest than was the peasant mentality
which stubbornly believed that the farmer's well-being depended upon
his rent remaining stationary and at a level charged in the past.
This attitude, more so even than the chronic shortage of capital at
the tenants' disposal, lay at the heart of Welsh farming difficulties.

Such peasant attitudes, it might be expected, would have changed
in the face of the new opportunities which the railways brought for
cheap and speedy marketing of produce. In particular, the south
Wales industrial market was brought within easy reach of many Welsh
farmers. If enclosures, then, by their very nature did not constitute an important chapter in Welsh agricultural history, surely the
railways would usher in a new era of improved farming methods? This
central problem of the response of Welsh farmers to the south Wales
industrial market and large consumer centres of demand elsewhere
will form a vital part of the discussion.

As hinted earlier, it will be stressed that the nature of the
rural community was closely bound up with the type of farming practised. Thus the close knit communities, the 'neighbourhoods', so
characteristic of Welsh rural areas despite the pattern of dispersed
settlement, are not to be explained primarily by kinship and community ties arising from cultural factors. The close intimacy of personal relationships sprang fundamentally from the interdependence of
farm and cottage, which was imposed in turn by the isolation, backwardness and relative poverty of the region. Such close knit communities were to have an important bearing on the extent and nature
of protest within rural society.

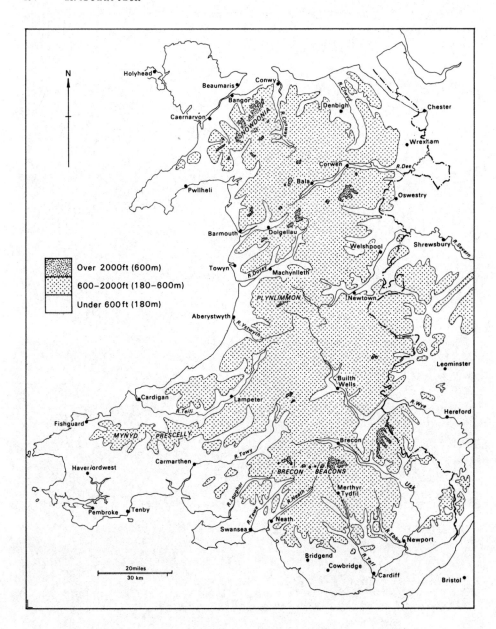

Map of Wales

CHAPTER 1

THE HISTORICAL PERSPECTIVE

I

Over the course of the nineteenth century the role of farming in the
Welsh economy, as for that of Britain as a whole, was a declining
one. (1) One index for measuring this decline is the labour force.
The population of Wales rose rapidly in the nineteenth century, multiplying between three and fourfold between 1801 and 1911 from under
600,000 to over two million. Table 1.1 shows that the increase was
not shared evenly across the principality. Although the population

TABLE 1.1 Population growth in Wales (1000)

Counties	1801	1851	1911
Glamorgan and Monmouth	116	389	1,517
Other Welsh counties	471	774	510
Total: Wales and Monmouth	587	1,163	2,027

rose sharply in all Welsh counties up until 1841, thereafter the
rate of increase slackened noticeably in the rural counties while in
the industrial counties of Glamorgan and Monmouth there was a great
acceleration in population growth. (2) The two phenomena were
closely inter-related, for of the net migration of 388,000 people
from rural Wales over the sixty years 1851-1911 there was over the
same period a net inflow of 320,000 people into the Glamorgan and
Monmouthshire coalfields from the Welsh countryside. (3) The immen-
sity of the change in population distribution is shown by the fact
that whereas at the start of the nineteenth century over 80 per cent
of the Welsh people lived in rural, non-urbanised areas by 1911
fewer than 20 per cent occupied the countryside.
From the 1840s, and even earlier, a trickle of farm-workers were
migrating from the rural farmsteads to the iron-works at Merthyr.(4)
Only from mid century, however, did this migration quicken significantly. Reasonably reliable statistics for the distribution of
the British labour force are provided in the Census Returns from

1851 onwards and they show that the numbers involved in Welsh agriculture fell by 45.8 per cent between 1851 and 1911. Indeed the
full extent of the fall is somewhat camouflaged by the rise in numbers of agriculturalists between 1901 and 1911 and if we measure the
drop between 1851 and 1901 the figure is even higher at 51.4 per
cent. By way of comparison the numbers engaged in agriculture, forestry and fishing in Britain as a whole fell by some 24 per cent
between 1851 and 1911. (5)

More useful, of course, in depicting the declining role of agriculture within the Welsh economy is a statement of the proportion of
the occupied population engaged in agriculture over the years 1851
to 1911 (see table 1.2). While nearly a fifth of the Welsh labour

TABLE 1.2 Proportion of the Welsh labour force employed in agriculture, forestry and fishing*

Year	No. of persons in agriculture, forestry and fishing	Total labour force	Percentage of labour force	Percentage of national labour force of people in agriculture, forestry and fishing in Britain**
1851	216,635	1,118,914	18.2	21.7
1861	191,567	1,312,834	14.6	18.7
1871	143,041	1,421,670	10.1	15.1
1881	112,641	1,577,559	7.1	12.6
1891	110,672	1,347,663	8.2	10.5
1901	105,371	1,538,007	6.9	8.7
1911	117,497	1,865,857	6.3	8.3

*   Figures from the Census Returns. Figures for 1891 onwards for
     fishing are separate in the Returns but are included here to
     conform with the earlier data.
** From Deane and Cole, 'British Economic Growth'(Oxford,1967), p.143.

force was occupied in agriculture around mid century, by the close
just over a twentieth were similarly engaged. Not only did the numbers working in Welsh agriculture decline but also the agricultural
sector shared none of the general increase in the labour force arising from the growth in population. The agriculturalists' importance
to the total labour force in the Welsh economy had decreased by
three-quarters between 1851 and 1911. A similar downward trend
occurred over Britain as a whole, though from table 1.2 we see that
the proportion of workers in agriculture in Britain was slightly
higher throughout these years.

Agriculture, however, retained an importance in the public mind
out of all proportion to its dwindling role in the economy. Until
the third quarter of the century it had, for reasons of transport
costs and technology, to provide the fast-growing home population

with the bulk of its food. Also, down to the 1870s and even beyond, ownership of land was all important in achieving political and social position. Landowners continued to dominate politics in Wales until the celebrated election of 1868 which made the all-important inroads into the old order. Their power at the local level, where it was most keenly felt, was only finally removed with the County Council Act of 1888. (6)

Throughout the period the character of farming throughout Wales was mixed, with the emphasis on livestock and dairying. Regional variations of course occurred within this general pattern. In north Wales the western counties of Anglesey, Caernarvon and Merioneth were cattle-rearing counties whereas the eastern counties of Denbigh, Flint and Montgomery concentrated far more on butter and cheese manufacture. Sheep were almost exclusively reared on the mountain farms of over 1400 feet in both the north and south. Within the mixed husbandry of the Vale of Glamorgan and south Monmouthshire there was an emphasis on arable both for corn and roots for live-stock fattening. Elsewhere in south Wales the breeding and rearing of store animals and the manufacture of butter and cheese prevailed. The mixed nature of Welsh farming became more dominantly pastoral from the 1870s. This balance between livestock and arable shielded the Welsh farmer from the drastic fluctuations in farming fortunes felt in certain areas of England. At times of high corn prices Welsh farming was limited in its ability to grow more grain while in times of slump there was no need for panic contraction. In this way Welsh farming throughout the century did not experience to any sig-nificant extent the 'selective' depressions which occurred in Eng-lish farming in the quarter century or so after 1815 and again from 1876 to the mid 1890s. In December 1887 the 'Cambrian News' ex-plained the relative immunity of the Welsh farmer from depression partly on the grounds that Welsh agriculture was more mixed than English farming and therefore the season had to be extremely bad to ruin him beyond recovery. (7)

When considering the Welsh small family-farm type economy it is tempting to underplay the importance of the market. The farmer's system of living was indeed largely a self-contained one: for the most part, particularly in the first half of the century, he pro-duced practically all the basic requirements of life, in food and clothing, on his holding. There was not much to sell and little to buy. While the Welsh farmer thus persisted in the peasant attitude that he should produce everything needed at home there was neverthe-less a compulsion to market in order to meet the demands of the rent, tithes, local taxation and labourers' wages. Semi-subsistent farm-ing therefore prevailed. The biggest element in farm income in most areas of Wales was in the sale of intermediate products in the form of store cattle and store sheep. Income from this source went to pay the rent while the dairy, principally butter but also cheese, poultry and eggs, brought in ready money to meet current expenses.

Prices for store animals were affected by a number of factors. The state of industry and of English pasture grazing were equally crucial in influencing demand. In the 'high farming' years animals were also in demand for manure towards increasing corn crops. Com-petition from Irish and Scottish stores and, from the 1880s, from foreign meat imports, again had an obvious bearing on Welsh store

prices. Demand for final products like butter, cheese, wool and
corn was influenced first by the prosperity or otherwise of industry.
In 1882, for example, it was reported that sheep prices in Brecknockshire had fallen because of the depression in the south Wales iron
and coal industries and that farmers in Caernarvonshire were suffering because of the depression in the local slate industry. (8)
Second, the development of improved communications linking farming
areas with urban centres was all-important in determining demand for
final products. Thus in 1845, before the railway was constructed
through south Wales, prices of provisions were as much as 12 per
cent lower in Carmarthen than in the mining districts of Glamorgan
and Monmouthshire and 'as the distance increased the difference increased'. The reason for these low prices in the western areas was
the absence of a speedy and economical means of communication with
the industrial market to the east. (9) Again, by way of illustra-
tion, it was stated in 1844 that the Welsh tithe-owner was forced to
moderate his demands to the defective husbandry and 'lower markets'
of the principality. (10) After the opening up of the country by
railways in the third quarter of the century Welsh corn prices and
those of other farm produce came more into line with those prevailing in the kingdom as a whole. And here, the superior transport
facilities linking south Wales with the London market meant that
prices in the markets of the south coincided more closely with
London's than did those ruling in the markets of mid and north Wales.
(11) Prices for final products were also influenced on the supply
side by factors like the weather and foreign competition from the
1870s. Such competition also meant that no longer could farmers be
compensated for bad seasons by high prices.

Welsh farmers, like their counterparts elsewhere in Britain, pros-
pered from the high prices of the Napoleonic War years. These dizzy
levels arose from the interaction of an abnormal run of bad harvests,
inflationary finance and, to a lesser extent, the difficulties in
obtaining imports. (12) The depression after 1814 was intermittent,
not continuous right down to the accession of Queen Victoria, as
Lord Ernle once erroneously, albeit convincingly, led us to believe.
(13) Furthermore, this depression was mainly felt by the wheat farmers of the heavy clays, thus establishing a precedent for the later
depression following 1873. (14) The movement of Welsh corn prices
shown in Appendix 1 followed the overall British trends. After the
first drastic post-war fall of between 50 and 60 per cent, Welsh
corn farmers, like their English counterparts, experienced a number
of short but sharp crises within an otherwise higher run of prices
even if substantially below their war-time level. Such crises
occurred between 1821-3, caused by good harvests and large imports
in 1818 (the sharp contrast of these years with the famine prices of
1817-18 emphasising the failure of the Corn Laws of 1815 to keep
home prices at a stable level), and again between 1832-6 due to
bountiful harvests. (15) As in English markets Welsh corn prices
between 1815 and 1846 ruled on average above their pre-war levels.(16)

For the most part, however, corn prices were of little concern to
the Welsh livestock farmer, although the fact that down to the late
1850s the home demand for wheat was constant, owing to the cost of
transport from English areas and the uncertainty of foreign supplies,
meant that small quantities of wheat were marketed off many Welsh

farms well into the third quarter of the century. (17) Having
stated this, the important fact remains that the basic pastoral
nature of Welsh farming meant that the clamour by the agricultural
interest in 1815 and afterwards for the maintenance of high corn
prices did not arouse much attention in Wales outside the Vale of
Glamorgan and other primarily corn-producing areas. Welsh corn
growers had one special reason for supporting protection, namely the
inferiority of their corn to that which was now being imported. (18)

The drop in post-war stock and dairy produce prices was much more
serious for the Welsh farmer. Cattle and sheep prices in Britain
rose considerably in 1813 and 1814 but during 1815 a marked fall set
in owing to the long summer drought which forced farmers to sell
their stock in large quantities. (19) It was stated in 1816 that in
south Wales cattle were selling at a third of their former price and
sheep at a half. At the same time it was reported of north Wales
that compared with 1814 horses and pigs were reduced in price by a
half, milch cows by a third and other horned cattle by more than a
half. (20) On 3 February 1816 E. Jones wrote to his brother from
Garthmyl, Montgomeryshire: 'I have Horses and Cattle upon my hands
which it is quite ruin to sell at the present times.' (21) Salted
butter had sold at 6d. a pound in south-west Wales before the war,
but by 1811 it was selling in Carmarthen market at an average of
11½d. a pound. (22) By 1816 its value had so fallen that it was
being sold to chandlers as common grease. (23) The following years
1817 and 1818 were worse and livestock farmers were forced to sell
their stock at any price. (24)

The situation improved between 1819 and the summer of 1821 when
once again livestock prices slumped. (25) Markets throughout Wales
continued very low until 1823. Richard Humphreys of Landawke farm
in south-west Carmarthenshire wrote to his landlord, Lord Kensington,
on 13 July 1822:

The prices of everything that a Farmer has to sell is not even
/sic/ very low, but without demand also. I have 150 sheep that I
should be glad to sell for 10s. per head but cannot get a person
that will offer me anything for them as yet. These are similar
sheep my Lord would sell for at least 30s. per head when I took
the farms. Cattle has also sunk in value at least two-thirds.(26)

Conditions once again improved for the livestock farmer in 1824 and
good harvests in 1825 kept prices up. (27) Reaction to the commercial and banking crisis of 1825 led to a fall in prices in the following year but by June 1827 livestock were once more selling at a
profit. At the Carmarthen June Fair, for example, cattle prices
were 30 per cent up on the previous year. (28) Wet summers and poor
harvests from 1828 to 1830 saw a return of crisis in the store
cattle industry between 1829 and 1832, but conditions picked up
somewhat in the middle years of the decade. (29)

In the years immediately before 1830 sheep husbandry, according
to Youatt, continued in 'the most prosperous state in the lower districts of every part of Wales'. This prosperity was shattered by
the serious outbreak of sheep rot in the seasons of 1830 and 1831
when, Youatt informs us, in many areas of Wales 'whole flocks were
swept away'. (30) The consequent scarcity led to high prices, in
south-west Wales 'much higher in proportion to other stock'. (31)
The same observation was made by a Carmarthenshire land agent who

wrote in 1833 'the hill farmers were the best off last year, sheep and wool being high and in demand'. (32) The prosperity for the Welsh, as for the English, sheep farmer continued down to the late 1830s. A.D. Jones, writing from Montgomeryshire in April 1836 informed his brother that 'Lamb sells well in the country - Couples were sold on Tuesday last at Pool at such a price as they have not known for years.' (33)

Farming conditions in Wales at the opening of the 1840s merit special scrutiny, for these were the years of the Rebecca Riots, a tenant farmers' revolt confined in the main to south-west Wales. (34) The three seasons from 1839 to 1841 were so atrocious that farmers everywhere, including corn-growing Pembrokeshire, were forced to buy corn at famine prices for their own use. Sheep prices between 1839 and 1842, and butter prices between 1837 and 1841, were high, but store cattle prices were exceptionally low in 1839 and 1840, a marked recovery occurring, however, in 1841. (35) A general fall in prices came only in 1842 and 1843 and partly accounts for the Rebecca Riots occurring precisely in these years. In October 1842 cattle prices at the Borth great cattle fair, the 'Ballinasloe' of Anglesey and Caernarvonshire, were 25 to 30 per cent down on their 1841 levels. Cattle prices similarly slumped in south-west Wales. It was reported in October 1842: 'Such is the depreciation in the neighbourhood of Carmarthen that few or no sales can be effected at any price.' The blame for this fall was directed at Peel's tariff measures of 1842 which reduced the duties on live cattle to £1 a head and lowered the duty on imported meat. Butter and fat pig prices also fell in 1842. The harvest of that year was the best seen in Wales for many years and corn prices fell steeply. (36) While hurting the corn farmers this did little to benefit livestock producers through introducing cheaper feed costs (a marginal factor at any rate in the Welsh situation where animal food was produced on the farm), for in 1843 butter and pig prices tumbled further and those of store sheep fell drastically. (37) Farm prices in south-west Wales at this time were increasingly influenced by the state of the iron industry in Merthyr, and a slump in the trade from the autumn of 1841 onwards had a harmful influence. The fall-off in demand from the mining population is illustrated by the fact that a large farmer of Newcastle Emlyn, north Carmarthenshire, who normally carried over two cwts of butter a fortnight to Glamorgan could scarcely sell this same quantity in 1843 at a reduced price once a month. (38) A general, if brief, recovery in prices set in from the middle of the decade.

After the repeal of the Corn Laws in 1846 the landed interest did not suffer the disaster that had been gloomily prognosticated. Despite the depressed years between 1848 and 1852, and recognising that the amount of grain imported increased significantly over the next twenty years, the thirty years after Repeal were not unprosperous ones for corn farmers. In this period Britain was artificially protected from heavy foreign imports by war, high transport costs, and technical problems. Only wheat entered Britain in sufficiently large quantities to offset entirely the growth of home demand and thereby depress prices. Barley and oats prices rose under the stimulus of this growing demand from industrial centres now more easily reached by railways. (39) Price movements were as follows: in the thirty years after Repeal the price of wheat in England and Wales and in Wales alone averaged 52s.8d. and 52s.4d. respectively, the former price being only 5s. a quarter less, and the latter only 3s., in their respective areas than the average prices ruling in the last twenty-six years of Protection. Barley prices in Wales rose by 22 per cent between 1848-57 and 1867-77 and oats by 27 per cent over the same years. (40)

Livestock farmers in Britain, with the exception of wool producers, fared even better once the short but acute depression of the years 1848-52 were behind them. Prices of livestock and butter in Wales slumped after the brief recovery of the mid 1840s, Welsh store cattle prices being determined, as always, by the state of the English cattle market. Store cattle, for example, met with hardly any demand at the Carmarthen September Fair of 1849 for very few drovers were sufficiently optimistic to attend after having suffered from the low prices of the Barnet Great Fair held previously. (41) Gwynne Vaughan Bowen of Ffynnon y Derwyddon noted in his Journal that the 1849 September fair at Haverfordwest was the 'cheapest fair I ever was'. (42) But from 1853 until the late 1870s Welsh livestock farmers shared in the growing prosperity of meat and dairy producers in Britain generally. This period saw pastoral prices rise markedly in response to the growth in home demand. Welsh store cattle prices between 1856-8 and 1876-8 rose by 56 per cent while those for fat cattle rose by 29 per cent over the same years. Mutton prices rose between 1855-6 and 1872-3 by 42 per cent and those of fat pigs by 19 per cent between 1858-61 and 1874-8. The relatively greater rise in livestock and dairy than in cereal prices is seen in a comparison of butter prices with those of barley and oats. Between 1847-57 and 1867-77 butter prices rose by 37 per cent compared with 22 per cent for barley and 27 per cent for oats. (43)

The detailed price history as between each commodity differed during the 'golden age' but in most cases peak prices were reached in the early 1870s. In 1872 it was written of north Wales: 'Never, perhaps, before, have such high prices been realised for horses, cattle and sheep as during the past summer, and as this is essentially a breeding district we have made excellent returns under these heads.' (44) Wool prices did not entirely conform to the general pattern of rising prices. An overall rising tendency from the mid 1850s to the mid 1860s gave way to a downward one owing to large imports of foreign wool. The Welsh sheep farmer, however, was rather less affected by this than at first might seem to have been the case for he was generally more dependent on sales of store sheep and mutton than on wool for his livelihood. (45)

Only in intermittent years were there set-backs arising from adverse weather conditions. The drought of 1868 pushed store cattle prices downwards. Lord Cawdor's land-agent wrote to him from Carmarthen in that year: 'All the tenants complain of is the difficulty of parting with stock.' (46) Their complaints were justified for at the August fair at Carmarthen there 'was no demand for store cattle owing to the great scarcity for grass'. The droughts of 1867-8 similarly affected store sheep prices which fell disastrously between 1867-9. In 1874 shortage of feed once again led to a slack demand for lean cattle with consequent low prices. (47)

The prosperous farming years of the third quarter of the century,

as already mentioned, were based on shaky foundations. The artificial protection afforded British farmers came to an end by the
early 1870s for by this time the elevator system, railways and the
revolutionised steam-ships permitted the import of foreign produce
at low costs. (48) The large inflow of corn depressed prices markedly from the mid 1870s and conditions were all the more severe from a
run of bad harvests in 1878-9 and again in 1893-4. The low and poor
yields were no longer offset by the advantage of higher prices now
that imported grain flooded the market. (49)

The first effects of the 'great depression' in British farming
were felt by the corn producers, who were also to bear the greatest
losses throughout its duration from 1873 to 1896. With its propor-
tionately low acreage under corn Wales was not nearly so adversely
affected as the considerable corn-growing areas of England by the
steep fall in grain prices. (50) Indeed, those livestock farmers in
Wales as elsewhere who had to purchase feed-stuffs for their farms
benefited from low corn prices, although most Welsh farmers produced
their feed requirements at home. Nevertheless, the relatively important corn-growing areas of Flintshire, Denbighshire, the Vale of
Glamorgan, and south Pembrokeshire suffered from the fall in corn
prices throughout these two decades or so. In 1879 Lord Cawdor's
agent wrote from the corn producing area of Stackpole, south Pembrokeshire, that his tenants 'must have experienced great losses
during the last 3 or 4 years, owing to the bad seasons and the low
price of corn'. (51) The downward trend began in Wales in 1874-5 in
wheat and barley prices and a year later in those of oats, and continued, with intermittent years of higher prices, until 1896. The
fall was worst in wheat and least in oats prices: between 1867-71
and 1894-8 wheat fell by 51 per cent, barley 42 per cent and oats
37 per cent. (52)

Corn farmers were not alone in their suffering from foreign competition in the last quarter of the century. With the perfection of
refrigerating techniques imports of frozen and chilled meat increased from the mid 1880s. Furthermore, dairy farmers from the
1870s were experiencing growing competition from imported butter,
cheese, bacon and eggs from Europe, and cheese from America. But if
all these imports increased in this period such was the growth in
home demand, stimulated by the rising population and higher living
standards, that home production also increased. In this situation,
therefore, the price fall in cattle and dairy produce was 'plainly
more a product of lower costs and increased productivity than of
import competition'. (53)

The depression in Welsh livestock and dairy farming only really
began in the mid 1880s for the general collapse in prices in 1879-80
was only a temporary one, prices recovering their former high levels
in the early 1880s. A slump came in the mid 1880s and save for a
temporary recovery at the close of the decade prices remained at a
low level until 1896. The overall falls in Welsh markets have been
calculated as follows: between 1877-80 and 1894-7 store cattle
prices fell by 20 per cent, fat cattle 19 per cent, store ewes 6
per cent, fat sheep 18 per cent and fat pigs 18 per cent. Butter
prices dropped 12 per cent between 1867-71 and 1894-8. Growing
imports of wool, combined with inclement seasons, meant that wool
prices fell much more steeply, dropping by 45 per cent between

1872-4 and 1891-2. (54) These years saw depression in a crisis sense, therefore, only in corn and wool prices. The Welsh hill farmer must have keenly felt the drop in wool prices, although his emphasis on store sheep for the grazier considerably eased his condition.

Prices gradually improved after 1897. The high prices of the mid 1870s, though, were not to be realised again before 1914. The new level was around that of the mid 1860s. The peak years of the mid 1870s were exceptional and in making comparisons with the prices of those years contemporaries often exaggerated the intensity of depression in the following decades.

II

If the concentration on store livestock within mixed farming was limited in its profitability because of the slow turnover and the minimum amount of labour expended on the product, nevertheless, as already shown, this type of farming meant that the drastic fluctuations in the level of prosperity experienced in England were largely absent in Wales. The Welsh problem was rather that of the typical peasant economy - poverty, over-population and land hunger, aggravated to some extent in Wales by a cultural and political divide between landowners and the rest of the farming community. Pressure for land engendered mistrust and feelings of insecurity amongst the tenant community on the small, though not on the large, estates, and everywhere led to the taking of farms with too little capital. Land hunger, too, meant a tendency to stabilise or to increase rents although, as later discussion will show, on the large estates rents were not consciously charged at a competitive price.

The extent of the general rise in rents on Welsh estates, as on English ones, during the Napoleonic War years differed from one estate to another and, indeed, from farm to farm on the same estate. On the Picton Castle estate in Pembrokeshire rents rose by 77 per cent between 1790 and 1820. Rents increased by 60 and 62 per cent respectively between 1795 and 1823 on the Llandeilo and Llanarthney sections of the Cawdor estate in Carmarthenshire. The continuance of long leases on these south-west Wales estates often prevented rent adjustments on certain tenements and so the real increases on the other holdings are camouflaged. On the Llanarthney estate, for example, the rise occurring on adjusted rents amounted to 167 per cent. Rents increased by 60 per cent between 1790 and 1815 on the Merioneth portion of the Wynnstay estate. (55) On the Gregynog estate in Montgomeryshire rents rose by 138 per cent between 1796 and 1815. There was an increase of 200 per cent in the rental of the Nanteos estate, Cardiganshire, between 1790 and 1820 while on the Crosswood estate in the same county the increase between 1801 and 1814 was 232 per cent. (56) Where such rent increases were made upon the expiration of leases for lives, as frequently happened, some of the increase was a necessary adjustment of previously uneconomic levels of rent.

The fall in prices after 1814 was not accompanied in Wales by a corresponding reduction in rents. Walter Davies wrote to the Board of Agriculture in 1816: 'Rent should be reduced, or rather restored

to, its proper level, universally and immediately, whilst the remaining farmers have any capital left.' (57) Davies later noted in
his Journal for June 1821: 'land let too high, according to the war
scale of former years'. (58) The fast-growing population, together
with a lack of alternative employment, saw intense competition for
farms, and this largely explains why farm rents were maintained or
even increased. The large owners did not consciously exploit this
land hunger. It was rather the smaller ones who were guilty of such
conduct. Again, many estates were so 'involved' or encumbered that
their owners' hands were tied and there was no possibility of a
reduction. (59) One other factor played an important part in influencing many sharp rises between the close of the wars and the mid
century. Tenements whose lives leases did not end during the wars
underwent substantial rent increases upon their expiry in the decades that followed. Such increases arose naturally out of a situation where the previous rent, fixed sometime in the eighteenth century, was often greatly undervalued. In contrast, those holdings
whose rents were adjusted during the wars and continued as yearly
tenures underwent only small rent increases, if any at all, in the
years before the 1850s. That undervaluation of old lives leases
necessitated substantial increases is illustrated by the policy of
the steward of the Derwydd estate, Carmarthenshire, who in 1826 drew
up the proposed 'improved' rents on holdings 'under lease' and 'at
will' respectively. On the leased tenements, upon expiration, an
increase of 153 per cent was considered appropriate while on those
from year to year, a mere 23 per cent was proposed. The same principle is reflected in the observation of John Hughes, agent for the
Nanteos estate, when he wrote on 25 March 1833: 'In all probability
before the expiration of 10 years there will be an increase of £1000
in Cardiganshire by the falling in of leases of farms.' (60) Rent
rises, then, were not simply a matter of 'screwing up' rents to
ceiling levels in response to raging land hunger.

While rents were not reduced as a general policy after 1814 some
qualifications are necessary. In the first place, as indicated, not
all farms, particularly in the south-west, were under war-time rents;
some, under leases unchanged since pre-war days, continued at low
rents well into the first half of the century. Second, it will be
shown that certain landlords attempted to alleviate hardship either
by allowing tenants to mount up arrears or by making temporary abatements. Neither expedient, however, really solved the tenants'
problems.

Unrealistic rent levels, together with a sharp rise in local
rates and taxes, weighed heavily on the Welsh peasant-tenant community up to mid century. At times of particularly low prices, and
during the banking crises of 1816, 1825-6 and 1832 which diminished
the valuation of paper money and denied farmers the 'customary
credit', conditions were desperate. (61) Thus throughout Wales the
years 1816-17 saw an unprecedented number of distresses made upon
farmers for non-payment of rent followed by sales of their livestock
and other property by auction. (62) Other tenants made off with
their stock overnight. (63) A few tenants on parts of the Wynnstay
estate who got into heavy arrears and were distrained upon in 1817
were by 1820 reported as being day labourers. (64) In 1821-3, again,
general failure to meet rents and other debts was reported among

both corn and livestock farmers. (65) Arrears of rent mounted. On
the Gregynog estate, Montgomeryshire, for example, these increased
from just over £7000 on the rental of £10,000 in 1820 to £12,000 on
virtually the same rental in 1823. On the Wynnstay estate 1823 and
1824 once more saw tenants fail and become day labourers; others
fell upon the parish, while occasionally the parish, if the farmer
had many children, would engage to pay the future rent; still
others left the country for America. (66) The low prices at the
close of the 1820s saw tenants once again hard pressed. (67)

The peak of early-century rural distress came in the late 1830s
and early 1840s. Farmers in south-west Wales took the law into
their own hands in 1839 and, more drastically, in 1842-3, in order
to remedy intolerable social and economic conditions. The spark
which ignited the Rebecca Riots was the multiplication of toll gates
along the various Trust roads which made the vital carriage of lime,
in particular, unbearably expensive. This was the final irritant,
but the farmers of the area had other grievances. At a time of
acutely depressed prices they were deeply resentful of high rents,
increasing taxation, the amount and mode of levying the fees for
magistrates' clerks, and of the new demands for ready money brought
by the new poor law and the commutation of the tithes. (68) The
traditional community bonds had been loosened in the eighteenth century with the alienation of the native squirearchy from their native
culture. In the absence of a middle class in the countryside the
vacuum of leadership was increasingly filled in the early nineteenth
century by the Nonconformist ministers. In 1843 William Day, a poor
law commissioner, wrote of the situation in south-west Wales:

> The landlords are most of them of the old Church and King school
> - the tenantry are almost all Dissenters, with a spice of the
> fanaticism of the Covenanters about them. Still there is - or
> rather has been - a sort of feudal deference existing between the
> parties - but I suspect it to be the result of habit, rather than
> of feeling resulting from conviction, and which may readily be
> put aside on a change of circumstances. There is moreover an-
> other class more powerful perhaps than even the Landlord - and
> this is the Preachers - and the great bulk of the population are
> as much in their hands as the Papists of Ireland in the hands of
> their priests. (69)

Nonconformity - especially the Baptist and Independent denominations
- doubtless played an important part in shaping the discontent of
the tenant community. Thus dislike of tithes and church rates
stemmed as much from religious principle as financial hardship.
Welsh Nonconformity, strongly averse to state interference of any
kind, also accounted for some of the hostility towards the Poor Law
Amendment Act. On the other hand, it is important to stress that
the Riots were not an ideologically inspired anti-landlord movement.
They were rather an attack on what the peasant farmers considered
were particular injustices and abuses of the old society. These
accumulated grievances between 1839 and 1843 had stretched deference
to breaking point, but with the reform of the toll system in the
summer of 1843 and the farmers' revulsion against growing violence
with the absorption of new social elements, the riots came to an
end. (70) An uneasy deference - a mix of habit, fear, ignorance and
genuine feelings of loyalty - once more bound society together.

The mid-century depression, too, saw hardship, and the farming community was greatly unsettled. Requests by tenants for time to settle their rents and for rent allowances were common. The owner of the Slebech estate in Pembrokeshire wrote to his solicitor in May 1850:

We, like all others, have had many notices to quit at Lady Day – not that any of them really mean to go but that they expected thereby to get at once a reduction of rent. If pressed, we are sure, many would leave, though they themselves would be quite aware that they would not better themselves - yet such is the temper of the farmers down here at the moment, and we might, as in the time of 'Becca', have many farms on hand. (71)

Vacant farms in a land hungry peasant-tenant society as Wales denoted an extremely serious situation.

Agricultural conditions in Wales improved from the mid 1850s. Landowners invested increasing sums in improving their properties and farmers now benefited from better markets for their products. Railways were vital in opening the hitherto remote countryside to the growing centres of urban demand. The relatively faster rise in livestock than in corn prices from the mid 1850s was also favourable to the Welsh farmer. South Wales farmers were particularly fortunate in having a ready market for their beef and mutton, dairy produce, clover-hay and wheat-straw in the mining valleys of Glamorgan and Monmouthshire. This improvement in economic conditions led to the rentals of many Welsh estates being revalued from mid century down to 1879-80. Rent increases ranged from 5 to 30 per cent depending on such variable factors as elevation and fertility of the land, proximity to railways and markets, and the previous level of rent. (72) Important, too, in determining rent levels was the extent of demand for farms, and in Wales land hunger persisted throughout the century. On the smaller estates of less than 3000 acres, covering roughly 56 per cent of the cultivated area, rents were charged at higher than the true value of the land. The large hereditary owners, on the other hand, did not run their estates along strictly commercial lines and did not consciously take an unfair advantage of the demand for holdings. Those increases in rents on large estates that occurred from the 1870s may have had something to do with political factors. One landowner claimed that such increases stemmed from the repercussions of the Secret Ballot. Hitherto, he argued, owners had deliberately charged low rents in order to ensure the ready support of their tenants at parliamentary elections. (73)

How did Welsh tenants fare in these years of good prices? Farmers with capital occupying sizeable holdings and whose landlords charged fair rents did well. Accounts are extant for the large 215 acres farm of Trefayog in the parish of St Nicholas, north Pembrokeshire, for the years 1867 to 1881. (74) The farm income came mainly from store cattle and butter. Thus in 1872, of a total income from farm sales of £602 some £88 16s.7½d. only came from sales of corn. The rent was raised in January 1873 from £126 to £156 a year, representing an increase of 24 per cent. On 21 March 1873 the credit in favour of Trefayog was £146 6s.11d., on 23 July 1874, £196 16s.8d., on 23 December 1875, £308 11s.5½d. and on 19 November 1877, £586 12s.3d. Most farms, however, were far smaller, averaging fifty or so acres in the last quarter of the century. Their occupiers

were usually short of capital and this, together with their unwillingness to improve, meant that even in good times and with moderate
rents they could hardly flourish. Some did manage to save down to
the close of the 1870s but this is explained 'by their careful and
parsimonious living, more than by the profits of their farming'.(75)
Tenants of small-sized farms on the smaller estates were in the
worst position. Their rents were charged on a competitive basis and
their landlords invested negligible amounts in the upkeep of their
holdings.

Although livestock and dairy prices, with the exception of wool,
did not fall so steeply as corn prices, and although contemporaries
misleadingly compared the fall in Welsh pastoral prices in the 1880s
and early 1890s with the peak prices of the early 1870s, Welsh farmers nevertheless suffered hardship during the depression years. On
the small estates rents were kept up all too frequently and tenants
were sometimes forced to leave their holdings either voluntarily or
after receiving notices to quit. (76) Large owners brought some
relief by granting temporary abatements in rent ranging from 5 to 20
per cent, 10 per cent being the most representative figure for the
whole of Wales. Permanent reductions, however, would have given the
tenants more certainty. In the granting of such abatements, together with other forms of help, the large owners made laudable
efforts to cushion their tenants from the worst effects of depression. Such assistance, alongside the small labour bills of these
family-worked holdings, meant that tenants on the large estates felt
the pinch but were not greatly distressed.

The difficulties of Welsh tenants on large and small estates
alike in the very low price years in meeting their rents were recognised by the agents in their letters to their employers. An experienced Pembrokeshire agent, T. Rule Owen, for example, wrote to
the owner of Picton Castle estate, Pembrokeshire, in 1886:

I can quite understand your wishing for remittances to your
credit, but I candidly tell you what I tell other landlords that
you may have to wait till fairs improve .... I keep driving away
at the tenants who owe Michaelmas rents but it's very heartless
work having to repeat the entreaties and threats so often. (77)
The arrears of rent on the Nanteos estate in Cardiganshire show that
in the years of low cattle prices, arrears mounted. Expressed as a
percentage of the total rents due, the incidence of arrears on this
estate were as shown in table 1.3. (78)

TABLE 1.3 Arrears on the Nanteos estate

Year	%	Year	%	Year	%
1880	20	1888	15	1896	22
1881	23	1889	14	1897	21
1882	-	1890	14	1898	19
1883	17	1891	18	1899	21
1884	29	1892	22	1900	20
1885	30	1893	25	1901	19
1886	24	1894	22	1902	18
1887	15	1895	27	1903	11
				1904	6

III

The 'cultivated' land in Wales in 1894 amounted to 59.8 per cent of
the total geographical area while in England it was 76.4 per cent
and in Scotland 25.1 per cent. (79) Although readily available figures do not exist before 1867 it is clear that the proportion of
'cultivated' land in Wales was considerably smaller at the opening
of the century. Between 1867-9 and 1912-14 there was a rise of 10.8
per cent in the 'cultivated' areas in Wales and Monmouthshire. Different factors operated towards extending the area under cultivation
including the enclosure of commons, the rise in the level of industrial demand and the construction of railways. Climate and physical
configuration dictated, as already stressed, that while most farms
were mixed, the greatest proportion of the land was given over to
pasture farming with an emphasis on store animals and the dairy.
    The precise extent to which arable and animal husbandry was pur-
sued at a given time was determined by economic factors. During the
Napoleonic Wars the high price of corn crops led farmers in lowland
Wales to bring more and more land under the plough. (80) Even in
upland areas lands were ploughed up to produce crops of wheat and
barley. (81) The acreage under corn in certain areas contracted
with the slump in prices. This was so, for example, in Montgomeryshire where between 1801 and 1870 the growth of cereal crops 'dropped
considerably', the decline in the arable land being largely confined
to this group. (82) But this was not immediately the case in south
Wales where the 'stupendous copper works and large iron mines, the
numerous collieries and Dockyard' increased the demand and led to a
growth in corn acreage between 1816 and 1849. (83) Although the
Agricultural Returns show an increased acreage under corn crops in
Wales between 1867 and 1872 this more than likely came after a
period of decline from the late 1850s. (84) The relatively higher
prices in the livestock sector from the mid 1850s no doubt inclined
farmers throughout Britain towards grass and away from the plough.
(85) There is evidence of this trend in Wales. It was reported in
1868 of the Union of Kington in Radnorshire: 'The tillage in the
district is rather diminishing; farmers find stock pay so much
better.' (86) Similarly Mr Price of Maesgwyn, Disserth, observed of
the Builth Union, Radnorshire: 'Very little land is in corn because
we find raising stock pay better.' (87) In 1869 the relieving officer of the Carmarthen Union testified that 'A good deal of arable
land has been laid down to grass in my district on account of the
great rise in the price of butter and milk, and the labour has been
reduced.' (88) This last reference to labour is important for the
higher labour rates now being paid consequent upon the reduction in
labour supply because of migration meant that Welsh farmers were
converting from tillage to grass. It was reported in 1872 that certain farmers in south Wales, because of the labour question and the
inducements offered for sheep breeding, were converting arable lands,
wherever suitable (as, for example, on the lowlands of north Glamorgan), to sheep pastures. (89) Again, in 1875, before the onset of
depression, it was claimed that in the region about Carmarthen: 'The
labour question has driven farmers from corn to stock and dairy produce.' (90)
    The Agricultural Returns show how changing economic conditions

influenced basic adjustments in Welsh agriculture from the 1870s
onwards (see table 1.4). The total area under cultivation remained

TABLE 1.4   Area (1000s acres) of arable and permanent grass 1870-2
to 1912-14

Area	1870-2 '000 acres	% of total cultivated area	1912-14 '000 acres	% of total cultivated area
Total cultivated area	2820.5		2990.4	
Area under permanent grass	1616.4	57.3	2248.0	75.2
Area under arable	1204.1	42.7	742.4	24.8

fairly steady but important changes occurred in the acreage under
permanent grass and arable. The area under permanent grass increased between 1870-2 and 1912-14 from 57.3 per cent to 75.2 per
cent of the total cultivated area while over the same years there
was a decrease in arable from 42.7 per cent to 24.8 per cent of the
total cultivated area. Except for the relatively insignificant
acreage under bare fallow, the fall in acreage under corn crops was
greater than that for any other component making up the arable
sector. This was the basic feature of Welsh farming in the late
nineteenth century and was the direct response to high labour costs
and relatively higher livestock prices. The permanent pasture was
increased almost wholly by the conversion of land under the plough
to grass, a tiny portion only of the 39.1 per cent rise between
1870-2 and 1912-14 being caused by the enclosure of open grazings.
It is also clear from the Returns that the late nineteenth-century
adjustment to market conditions was not only a move away from tillage crops and temporary grass into permanent grass. This was, of
course, the basic phenomenon but accompanying it between 1890 and
1902, and as part of the same process, there was a greater importance attached to the growing of temporary grass within the arable
sector at the expense of tillage, especially corn crops. From 1892,
however, there occurred a slowing down in this overall trend towards
grass in response to a policy of further adjustment on the part of
Welsh farmers to strike a new balance between grass and tillage.
    Within the arable sector only comparatively small acreages of
wheat were grown throughout the century because the high average
rainfall in Wales was unsuitable to its growth. Very little wheat
could thus be grown above 600 feet. But over the principality as a
whole wheat was grown only to a small extent because it was not
really suited to a pastoral economy with its demands for livestock
feed centring on oats and barley. (91) The preponderance of oats
and barley over wheat at the opening of the century is revealed in
the 1801 Crop Returns. From these returns David Thomas has constructed a crop-rank order for the whole of Wales. (92) The crop
which most commonly took first place in the overall parish spread
was oats, and this was particularly so in the upland areas. Table
1.5 shows how the corn crop acreage fell drastically from the 1870s.

TABLE 1.5   Changes in the arable acreage 1870-2 to 1912-14
(1000 acres)

Crops	1870-2	% of total arable	1912-14	% of total arable	% fall of crop acreage
Corn and pulse	601.9	49.9	349.2	47.0	42.0
Green crops and roots	150.3	12.5	107.1	14.4	28.7
Bare fallow	42.4		6.4		
Rotation grass	409.4	34.0	277.0	37.3	32.3
Others	0.2		2.8		
Total arable	1,204.1		742.4		

The total acreage under corn fell by 42 per cent and its share of
the total arable fell from 49.9 per cent to 47 per cent. Moreover a
fundamental upset in the 1801 cereal crop relationships took place
from the mid 1870s. Adverse economic factors meant that corn crops
from this time ceased to be grown for the market and the smaller
acreages on each farm were now given over entirely for animal feed.
This meant that oats were grown increasingly at the expense of wheat
and barley. Between 1870 and 1872 corn crops were composed of 25
per cent of wheat, 30.5 per cent of barley and 44.5 per cent of oats.
By 1912-14 the new relationship is seen by the fact that wheat occupied 12.9 per cent, barley 26.4 per cent and oats 60.7 per cent of
the total area under corn. (93)
   Turnips and rape were grown to but a small extent in Wales in
1801. The exceptions were south-east Monmouthshire, the Vale of
Glamorgan and Gower where these crops occasionally ranked third and
fourth in the overall crop acreage. Their culture here was to a
large extent owing to the accessibility of these areas to new ideas
and techniques practised in England. (94) The general paucity of
turnips and green crops is not surprising for, up until the mid century and beyond, the generality of Welsh farmers practised no systematic rotation of crops. However, by the 1840s it is clear that
turnip culture was on the increase. Rowlandson observed of north
Wales that between 1815 and 1856 turnip husbandry had 'made a permanent, though not extensive, footing on the best soils'. Fullarton
observed that both turnips and potatoes were being grown in Wales
more extensively by the early 1840s. In Pembrokeshire, turnips
began to take the place of bare fallows after 1840. (95) Over the
following years the spread of the four-course rotation system in
Wales saw the increased growth of turnips and their culture was particularly speeded up by the application of Peruvian guano as a
manure from the late 1840s. (96) Mangolds were grown in Glamorgan
and Montgomeryshire by mid century and became gradually adopted
throughout Wales over the next two decades. Progress was slow, however, for small farmers were reluctant before the 1870s to grow
green crops and roots because of the high costs involved both in
fencing and preparing the soil. (97) The acreage under green crops

and roots fell by 28.7 per cent between 1870-2 and 1912-14 but its
share of the arable increased from 12.5 per cent to 14.4 per cent.
Individual crop movements within this category showed wide variations in movements, each being dictated by the needs of the farm
economy. Green crops, notably peas and beans, declined in importance mainly because of the decreasingly subsistent character of
Welsh agriculture. (98) Acreages under turnips and swedes remained
fairly static down to 1900 but afterwards fell off rapidly. They
were used mainly as cleaning crops for had their chief purpose been
the supply of winter feed acreages would have moved upwards in response to the increasing numbers of livestock carried over these
years. Mangolds were the essential cattle-feed crop, their acreage
increasing absolutely and relatively to the total acreage. The introduction of superphosphates in the 1880s greatly facilitated their
growth. (99)
  The other important component within the arable sector was artificial grasses. At the beginning of the nineteenth century the most
popular of these was the common red clover which was used more as a
connecting link between courses of corn crops than as a lay-down
crop at the end of the course. Next came white or Dutch clover
which was used for laying down to pasture, and rye grass. Trefoil,
lucerne and sainfoin were also cultivated to a small extent. (100)
Widespread use of artificial grasses had to wait until the mid 1860s
when railways opened up the principality to new markets and better
seed varieties. (101) There was an overall drop of 32.3 per cent in
the acreage of rotation grasses between 1870-2 and 1912-14 but their
share of the arable rose from 34 per cent to 37.3 per cent. This
relative gain in temporary grasses occurred basically between 1890
and 1902 and was mainly at the expense, as earlier emphasised, of
corn.
  Over the period 1870-1914 there was an increase in grassland in
Wales - permanent pasture and temporary leys combined - of 499,000
acres. This growth, comprising the gains made from the switch from
tillage crops and also the increase in the cultivated area, represented a 25 per cent rise, but it must be emphasised that grassland
in these calculations excludes rough grazing, vital in Wales. This extension of grassland was reflected in the increase of livestock
carried on Welsh holdings although some of the growth in livestock
numbers was due to improvement in the pastures through the application of basic slag. Thus between 1870-2 and 1912-14 the cattle
population rose by 24.1 per cent, sheep by 26.7 per cent and horses
by 37.7 per cent respectively. (102) Measured collectively, the
number of stock units carried on Welsh farms rose by 24 per cent
between 1870 and 1914 but the important years of growth came in the
1870s, 1880s and early 1890s. (103) The slow down from the mid
1890s reflects the efforts made at a readjustment in the balance
between livestock and crops towards coming to terms with the problem
of animal feed. Extra food requirements were met to some extent by
the 25 per cent increase in grassland - permanent and temporary combined - over the years 1870-1914. But this increase in grassland
did not meet the problem of winter feed and improved yields in
arable crops could help to a certain extent only.
  Accompanying this increase in livestock carried on Welsh holdings
from the 1870s came a fall in the proportion, especially from the

1890s, of cattle of over two years of age and of sheep one year old and above. Physical factors, and to some extent the lack of enterprise of Welsh farmers, meant that railways did not bring about any fundamental change in the traditional rearing of store animals. But this trend in the livestock population towards younger and leaner animals, reflecting as it did the new consumer taste for succulent meat, implied a more rapid turnover of capital to the advantage of the Welsh farmer.

The fundamental characteristic of Welsh farming throughout the nineteenth century was its small margin of profitability. The poverty of Welsh agriculture is reflected in the low average yields per acre of the principal crops between 1886 and 1888 compared with those of England and Scotland (see table 1.6). Later discussion will show that an improvement nevertheless took place in Welsh farming practices, achieving a consequent increase in output in the second half of the century, particularly from the 1870s. From then onwards Welsh agriculture became more capital intensive. This is reflected in the greater use of machinery, especially in relation to the hay harvest, the carrying of more animals, the greater application of artificial manures, in particular the introduction of superphosphates in the 1880s and the widespread use of basic slag in the 1890s, and the increased use of purchased inputs like new seed varieties. The more intensive use of such seed varieties and of artificial manures effected a noticeable increase in crop yields on Welsh holdings between 1886-8 and 1912-14. Indeed the growth in yields of many crops was faster over these years than in England and in some cases Scotland so that the yields of 1912-14 were brought more closely together.

The question arises, how did this increased capital input come about in a time of falling prices? In the first place, by the late nineteenth century railways and better printed communications had eroded the traditionalism of the Welsh farmer and increased his susceptibility to new ideas and methods. Second the emphasis on lambs and younger store cattle producing a greater turnover of capital, the fall in labour costs, the fall in input costs - for example, in cheaper fertilisers - and the temporary abatements in rents, all meant greater efficiency. Greater efficiency went a long way towards preserving farmers' incomes. The maintenance of money income at a time of falling prices for consumer goods gave them a higher real income out of which savings could be made. Capital from this source and possibly increased borrowings from the bank under the pressure to maintain the level of income led to more investment. It is unlikely, however, that this state of affairs operated in the very low price years of the depression when farmers faced considerable hardship.

While recognising that Welsh agriculture became more capital intensive from the 1870s the fact still remains that throughout the century the great obstacle to agricultural development (besides the paramount physical and climatic factor) lay in its under-capitalisation. Landowners and tenants alike displayed for the most part a notable inability or reluctance to adventure capital. The reasons for this will be examined in the following chapters dealing with the human and institutional framework of Welsh agriculture.

TABLE 1.6 Yields per acre of the principal crops

Crop	Wales		England		Scotland	
	1886-8	1912-14	1886-8	1912-14	1886-8	1912-14
Wheat	22.20 bsls	27.32	29.10 bsls	30.83	33.72 bsls	40.68
Barley	26.46 "	30.66	32.23 "	31.98	34.25 "	37.06
Oats	30.99 "	34.19	38.85 "	38.03	34.30 "	39.01
Beans	27.47 "	27.35	26.01 "	28.73	26.90 "	37.00
Peas	18.71 "	23.18	25.40 "	23.98	21.32 "	25.91
Potatoes	5.59 tons	5.37	5.81 tons	5.96	5.68 tons	6.62
Turnips	12.44 "	14.87	11.74 "	12.23	15.00 "	16.14
Mangolds	14.93 "	17.50	17.78 "	18.22	15.85 "	19.73
Hay from clover	23.75 cwts	26.57	28.31 cwts	28.61	29.73 cwts	31.46
Hay from pasture	17.76 "	21.05	25.74 "	24.07	28.89 "	31.16

Source: The Agricultural Returns.

CHAPTER 2

THE STRUCTURE AND DISTRIBUTION OF LANDOWNERSHIP

The paucity of statistics relating to landownership in Wales in the period under study forbids any detailed discussion of its structure and distribution. The source which most readily provides information about the distribution of land is the 'Return of Owners of Land in 1873', commonly known as the New Domesday Survey. (1) Contemporaries were quick to point out the errors and shortcomings of this work, (2) but obvious defects in the figures were corrected to 1877 by John Bateman whose refinements bring us closest to the situation. (3) In so far as there was no radical upheaval in the balance of landownership until the opening decades of this century the position in the 1870s may be taken to apply in general terms to the nineteenth century as a whole.

The main categories of owners devised by Bateman have been adopted in the discussion which follows. (4) With the exclusion of waste, the land of Wales and Monmouthshire was divided between different owners as shown in table 2.1. These figures show that Wales

TABLE 2.1 Number of owners

Owners	Number	Area : 1000 acres	Number %	Area %
Peers	31	557.4	.053	13.52
Great landowners	148	1,263.1	.253	30.64
Squires	392	672.3	.673	16.30
Greater yeomen	1,224	612.0	2.098	14.84
Lesser yeomen	2,932	498.4	5.026	12.09
Small proprietors	17,289	431.8	29.639	10.47
Cottagers	35,592	7.3	61.010	0.17
Public bodies	723	79.7	1.239	1.93
Total	58,331	4,122.0	100	100*

* To the nearest figure.

was primarily a country of large estates in the possession of a
small number of landowners.   Estates of over 1000 acres occupied 60
per cent of the total area of the principality.   This concentration
of land was even more marked than in England where estates of over
1000 acres covered 53.5 per cent of the total area. (5)   Welsh
estates exceeding 1000 acres were in the hands of 571 owners which
constituted a mere 1 per cent of the total number.   Within this
category the squires' estates of between 1000 and 3000 acres covered
16 per cent of the total area, and those of the great landowners of
over 3000 acres, 44 per cent.   Smaller estates of between 100 and
1000 acres covered 27 per cent of the total area and were owned by a
class of yeomen who comprised 7 per cent of the landowners.   Owning
land from 1 to 100 acres was a numerous class of small proprietors
making up 29 per cent of the owners and holding 10 per cent of the
land.   Freeholdings of under an acre comprised only 0.17 per cent of
the land but their owners, the cottagers, made up 61 per cent of the
total proprietors.   Thus the small proprietors and cottagers between
them comprised over 75 per cent of the landowners and held only a
tenth of the land. Two per cent of the total area of land was owned
by public bodies, a group which constituted nearly 2 per cent of the
total number of owners.

The percentage of the total area (excluding waste) of each county
occupied by estates of over 3000 acres was as follows:

Caernarvon	67	Brecknock	42
Anglesey	61	Montgomery	40
Glamorgan	55	Pembroke	38
Merioneth	48	Radnor	37
Flint	45	Cardigan	36
Denbigh	43	Carmarthen	34
Monmouth	43	Average for all Wales	44

(Source: J. Bateman, 'The Great Landowners of Great Britain and
Ireland', London, 1883 ed.)

These estates were principally situated in the north-west and in
Glamorgan.   Their weakest concentration was in the south-west and in
Radnorshire.   Two-thirds of the north-Wales counties were above the
average proportion of 44 per cent while only a seventh (Glamorgan)
in the south exceeded this.   When this list of the estates of over
3000 acres is further sub-divided into those of 3000 to 10,000 acres
and those above 10,000 acres certain interesting features appear, as
shown below:

(a) Between 3000 and 10,000 acres		(b) Over 10,000 acres*		
Flint	45	Caernarvon	50	(10)
Anglesey	40	Merioneth	40	(12)
Brecknock	31	Montgomery	32	(13)
Glamorgan	30	Cardigan	26	(11)
Radnor	27	Glamorgan	25	(4)
Carmarthen	26	Monmouth	22	(9)
Pembroke	24	Anglesey	20	(2)
Denbigh	23	Denbigh	20	(8)
Monmouth	21	Pembroke	14	(7)
Caernarvon	17	Brecknock	11	(3)

Cardigan	10	Radnor	10	(5)
Merioneth	8	Carmarthen	8	(6)
Montgomery	8	Flint	0	(1)

* The rankings of each county in (a) appear in brackets in (b).
(Source: J. Bateman, 'The Great Landowners of Great Britain and Ireland', London, 1883 ed.)

Caernarvonshire and Merioneth were counties of very large properties, much of their coverage comprising vast sheep-walks. Half of the land of the former, excluding waste, was owned by six landlords whose estates between them averaged over 25,000 acres. Similarly, 40 per cent of Merioneth was in the hands of five owners whose estates between them averaged 24,000 acres. On the other hand, there was not a single estate of over 10,000 acres in Flintshire. Carmarthenshire, too, was singularly lacking in large territorial aggregations.

The distribution pattern of estates exceeding 3000 acres is largely reversed when the location of those estates between 1000 and 3000 acres is examined. Their distribution (in terms of the percentage of the total area, excluding waste, of each county) was as shown below:

Merioneth	22	Radnor	15
Cardigan	20	Glamorgan	14
Pembroke	20	Caernarvon	11
Brecknock	19	Flint	11
Montgomery	19	Monmouth	8
Denbigh	18	Anglesey	6
Carmarthen	17	Average for all Wales	16

(Source: J. Bateman, 'The Great Landowners of Great Britain and Ireland', London, 1883 ed.)

Anglesey, Caernarvonshire, Glamorgan and Flintshire, counties of extensive estates, were thinly covered by the estates of the squires. On the other hand, Cardiganshire, Pembrokeshire and Carmarthenshire, at the bottom of the league in coverage by estates of over 3000 acres, were counties of squires' estates. When the three categories are merged into the one group of estates of over 1000 acres, it is found that these estates were most concentrated in Caernarvonshire, Merioneth, Glamorgan and Anglesey and least so in Carmarthenshire, Monmouthshire, Radnorshire and Cardiganshire:

Caernarvon	78	Pembroke	58
Merioneth	70	Flint	56
Glamorgan	69	Cardigan	56
Anglesey	67	Radnor	52
Brecknock	61	Monmouth	51
Denbigh	61	Carmarthen	51
Montgomery	59	Average for all Wales	60

(Source: J. Bateman, 'The Great Landowners of Great Britain and Ireland', London, 1883 ed.)

The relative importance of each category of the smaller estates within their respective counties is shown in table 2.2. The estates

TABLE 2.2 Proportion of the total area (excluding waste) of each
county occupied by three categories of smaller estates and by the
overall category of 1-1000 acres in percentage of total area

County	300-1000 acres	100-300 acres	1-100 acres	1-1000 acres
Anglesey	9	9	13	31
Brecknock	16	13	8	37
Cardigan	14	13	16	43
Carmarthen	19	16	12	47
Caernarvon	7	5	8	20
Denbigh	15	12	9	36
Flint	15	13	11	39
Glamorgan	12	8	7	27
Merioneth	16	7	5	28
Monmouth	12	15	16	43
Montgomery	17	12	12	41
Pembroke	18	12	8	38
Radnor	16	16	14	46

with acreages of between 1 and 1000 were most concentrated in the
counties of Carmarthen, Cardigan, Radnor and Monmouth, all four
being poorly covered with estates of over 1000 acres. Similarly,
those counties with small aggregate areas of estates of this kind
were Caernarvon, Glamorgan, Merioneth and Anglesey - the counties of
the large estates. The percentage ratio of the total area occupied
by the greater yeomen, lesser yeomen and small proprietors - 14:12:10
- was followed closely by the corresponding groups in England -
14:12.5:12. (6) The ratio for Wales as a whole, however, was not
followed in all the individual counties. In Cardiganshire, Monmouthshire, Caernarvonshire and Anglesey, the small proprietors were
dominant over the other two groups. In Monmouthshire, too, the
lesser yeomen featured more prominently than the greater yeomen.
    It is beyond the scope of this study to inquire into the detailed
changes in Welsh landownership in the years between 1815 and 1914.
A general investigation suggests that the distribution of landownership in the 1870s was similar for the whole period under study. The
eighteenth century witnessed the extension and consolidation of
estates in England and Wales through marriage, inheritance and piecemeal purchase. This enlargement proceeded in Wales on a smaller
scale but the tendency towards large estate accumulation was, nevertheless, unmistakably present. (7) A large proportion of the landowning families and estates that were already established in the
early years of the century were also to be listed in the Returns of
1872-3. The long history of Welsh estates as economic entities and
owned by the same families was remarked upon by the Welsh Land Commission of 1896. (8)

    The operation of the law of strict settlement which regulated
family succession to gentry estates in the eighteenth and nineteenth
centuries kept estate aggregations largely intact. (9) In this way
only a limited supply of land came onto the market and hence it is
unlikely that the balance of estate ownership was much upset in the
period under study. The continuity of landed families and their
estates throughout the nineteenth century can be seen in the county
of Caernarvon, for instance, by the fact that of the twelve principal estates in the county in 1815 only two of them had been broken
up by the 1890s. The ascendancy of large estates in north Wales, a
marked feature in the 1870s, was commented on by Rowlandson in 1846.
In the years after 1870 outlying parts of the large estates in Wales
were being sold. The high agricultural prices of the early 1870s
created a favourable land market for the estate owners of England
and Wales whose political influence, after the extension of the
franchise in 1867, no longer solely depended on the ownership of
extensive estates. Outlying parts of the large estates were being
sold off, too, because these were the most costly to manage. Although this demand for land collapsed in England after 1878 with the
onset of agricultural depression, a favourable land market continued
in Wales throughout the 1880s and 1890s. The 'Estates Gazette'
recorded that in 1887 many Welsh estates were for the most part
being sold at the high price of 30 years' purchase and that in most
instances the tenants were the purchasers of their previous holdings. (10) This was partly caused by the relatively less serious
nature in the fall of agricultural prices in a basically pastoral
economy but, of greater importance, the land hunger kept up capital
values.
    This transfer of property, however, was not sufficiently great to
upset the traditional balance of landownership. The Land Commissioners of the early 1890s accepted Bateman's statistics as being applicable to Welsh landownership in the last decade of the century. The
significant break-up of Welsh estates was to come only after 1910.
The 'abnormal breaking up' of estates at this time in Denbighshire
and Merioneth, for instance, was commented upon in 1911. (11) Similar evidence exists for south-west Wales: 'It has become very
general to break up the large estates,' stated John Francis of Carmarthen in 1911. (12) Research into this particular area by Howard
Davies has revealed, however, that between 1911 and 1914 only a few
landowners sold their entire estates; most, still governed by the
instinct of self-preservation, sold outlying portions only. (13)
The Committee of 1911 inquiring into the position of tenant farmers
concluded that the increased sales were to some extent a consequence
of a feeling of apprehension among landowners as to the likely tendency of legislation and taxation in regard to land. (14) The
return of the Liberal Government in 1906 had brought to the landowners renewed fears of uncertainty. The Budget of 1909 aimed at
raising the extra revenue required for the implementation of poli-
cies of social reform by a big increase in death duties and by a
scheme of land taxes on further unearned increment of land values on
undeveloped land. Although the proposed land taxes were not implemented, it was clear that Lloyd George intended radical land reforms.
Thus landowners were induced to sell parts of their estates out of a
feeling of insecurity. Another and more important reason for such

sales was that landowners hitherto, for the sake of the social standing conferred by landownership, had been content to accept small
returns on their capital. But with the gradual erosion of the
social prestige attached to land this previous tendency now suc-
cumbed to financial realities. Of importance here was the improvement in agricultural fortunes by the second decade of this century
which created a better land market permitting vendors to pay off
mortgages and, also, to reinvest their capital in more remunerative
enterprises than land. (15)

Disintegration of estates reached a dramatic level only from the
close of the First World War. The war years had seen the cost of
living mounting rapidly and taxation had become severe. Thus many
owners were heavily in debt by the close of the war and were forced
to sell. There was also the desire to escape the mounting charges
for repairs and improvements which had been postponed or neglected
during the war years. Landowners in Wales could take advantage not
only of the high prices prevailing but also of their tenants' keen
desire to purchase their holdings. In 1919 the 'Montgomeryshire
Express' observed: 'Little short of an agrarian revolution is being
witnessed in central Wales, where large tracts of territory are continuously tumbling into the market.' (16)

The Welsh experience did not conform entirely to the English pattern of estate disintegration. In the first place Welsh landowners,
unlike their English counterparts, could, and to some extent did,
dispose of their estates from the 1870s. Second, as John Davies
points out, the break-up of Welsh estates was even more thorough
than in England. Welsh owners, socially and culturally divorced
from their tenants by language and religion, were more radically
stripped of local standing and influence after the rise of democracy
than were their English counterparts. The savage onslaughts of the
Welsh Nonconformist press engendered an all-pervading, ubiquitous
anti-landlord sentiment in Wales by the 1890s which landowners felt
keenly, and found difficult to comprehend. There were, then, more
compelling reasons for Welsh owners to sell. (17)

Other forces also helped to change the structure of Welsh landownership. First, there were the Crown lands in Wales. Welsh landowners from the 1820s bitterly contested the more rigorous current
management of Crown lands. They protested against the enforced payment of arrears of Crown rents and dues, and the holding of manorial
courts which had previously been allowed to lapse. (18) Part of
this hostility arose from a fear that the Crown might investigate
the titles to, and retake possession of, encroachments made on the
vast upland wastes, particularly in north Wales, within the previous
sixty years by the turning of these wastes into private sheep-walks.
This practice was referred to by the Crown agent in 1834:

In fact if things go on as they are in north Wales, the Crown
will soon have not one single acre of common-land left. It is
the practice of landed proprietors to turn the waste into what
they call sheep-walks; that is each man directing his farmer to
graze his sheep upon so much of the waste lands as are contiguous
to the respective farms. They take it one on one side and one on
the other, so that the whole waste is taken up. There is waste
of miles and miles attempted to be converted in this manner, and
the landed proprietors say the wastes are theirs and do not
belong to the Crown. (19)

Thus in a case heard before the Court of Exchequer in 1868-9 the
defendant stated categorically: 'We believe that wherever such a
custom has prevailed, the land, though unenclosed, has been private
property, and as well defined as if it had been enclosed land.' (20)
Petitions were made against the activities of Crown agents in Wales
and their claims to wastes and commons, in particular the one in
1838 when Mr Ormsby Gore severely criticised Crown agents in Wales.
(21) The Crown in response set up an inquiry into these objections
urged against its claims in Merioneth and Caernarvonshire, the
'Report' for Merioneth appearing in May 1840. (22) Disputes between
individual Welsh landowners and the Crown over payment of Crown
rents, in themselves small payments, and over boundaries separating
private from Crown manors were frequent throughout the nineteenth
century. The Wynns of Wynnstay, extensive landowners in north Wales,
were deeply involved in such quarrels. (23) Typical was the one in
the 1860s when a sharp difference of opinion arose over the boundary
separating Sir Watkin Williams Wynn's manor of Clâs Arwystli from
the Crown lordship of Perferdd. (24)

Besides adding to their estates by encroachments on the open
wastes of dubious legality, the private owners of Welsh estates also
purchased the vast acreages of Crown lands that came onto the market
in the nineteenth century. Between 1787 and 1894 an estimated
279,691 acres of Crown lands were sold in Wales and Monmouthshire.
About two-thirds of this area comprised land which had been allotted
to the Crown under the various Enclosure Acts. (25) Individual properties sold ranged from the very small to tracts covering thousands
of acres, the latter, needless to say, being bought by the large
landowners. The largest sale occurred in 1856 when the Crown sold
to Sir Watkin Williams Wynn of Wynnstay, Denbighshire, some 23,639
acres of mountain and moorland covering parts of Denbighshire and
Merioneth. The property went for a sum of £6,331. (26) By 1889
about 83,000 acres of unenclosed waste land still belonged to the
Crown as lord of the various manors. This property yielded manorial,
including sporting, rights, but not rights of pasturage. Actual
right of pasturage was limited to about 500 acres. In addition
there were 220,000 acres, originally common but enclosed by 1889,
where only the minerals belonged to the Crown. (27)

The structure of landownership was also modified to some extent
by the decline of the small owner-occupier with between 20 and 100
acres. (28) This category was still clearly in evidence in Wales in
the opening years of the nineteenth century, especially in the south-
western counties of Cardigan, Carmarthen and Pembroke. (29) The
fall in the prices of agricultural produce after 1814 spelt ruin for
many of them. It was claimed in 1833 that the number of small
landed proprietors in north-east Wales had declined. During the
prosperous war years the small owner-occupiers borrowed money either
to improve their property or to add to it by purchases at high
prices and in the difficult years after 1814 these sank increasingly
into debt and were finally forced to sell out to meet the demands of
their creditors. (30) These last circumstances apart, the fall in
prices seems to have been sufficient in itself to force many small
owner-occupiers with limited capital resources to mortgage their
properties and, finally, to sell out. Mr Thomas Frankland Lewis
testified in 1844 that the freeholder of 6 to 10 acres in Radnorshire

survived by making as much use as possible of the commons for grazing his stock during the spring and summer months. But what commonly occurred was that when the first difficulty arose - either by
family sickness or a bad season - they were driven to the necessity
of borrowing money from the solicitor of a neighbouring town. Soon
they were forced by failure of interest repayments to sell out.
Thus Lewis observed of the small freehold: 'It is very rarely that
it continues in the same family for many generations.' (31) Furthermore, the difficulties of this class arising from low prices were
accentuated by the fact that they were now denied the occasional
employment on large farms as labourers which was important to their
survival.

Other factors, too, operated towards the decline of the small
owner-occupier in the first half of the century. The growth of
alternate employment in the urban areas led some to sell their properties and to enter mercantile pursuits. For Wales there is some
evidence, too, that these freehold properties in certain instances
were divided among a man's children upon his decease, the resulting
constant morcellation ultimately rendering them uneconomic units.(32)

Finally, the problem remains as to the extent to which enclosure
of commons and vast tracts of upland wastes hastened the decline of
this class. In so far as allotments of the open commons were dis-
tributed in proportion to the incidence of the land tax on the respective claimants certain owner-occupiers might have found themselves debarred by the fact that they did not contribute to the land
tax. (33) Others may well have found the burden of the assessments
- levied on each recipient of an allotment to cover the costs of
enclosure - too much, and so sold their allotments. They may well
now have left farming altogether. (34) Indeed, even if the small
holder went through with enclosing it is debatable whether this was
sufficient to compensate for loss of common rights. For it has been
argued that 'in a pastoral country like Wales a small allotment, in
fee, of land requiring cultivation was no real equivalent for rights
of common over a large open tract which required no cultivation.'(35)
Thus the Welsh Land Commissioners of the 1890s considered this to be
an important factor in explaining the decline of the small owner-
occupier. There was some truth in this, especially in so far as the
larger freeholders were concerned, (36) but certain qualifications
have to be made. In the first place, by virtue of geographical circumstances, not all the freeholders possessed the right of common.
Second, the small freeholder in upland areas sometimes welcomed enclosure as, under the old system of exercising his right of common
upon the open waste, he was put to disadvantage by the over-stocking
and crowding out by his larger neighbour. This arose because of the
abuse of the customary practice of stint of common. (37)

For various reasons, therefore, but particularly the fall in
prices after 1814, the small owner-occupier was forced to sell out
in the first half of the century. His lands were for the most part
bought by neighbouring gentry, a factor which furthered the concentration of landownership. (38) In 1882 it was reported: 'Yet there
is no part of the Kingdom in which small properties have been more
extensively absorbed by the large landowners. The class of small
Welsh owners who were numerous enough 100 years ago is comparatively
limited now.' (39)

The disappearance of the hereditary occupying freeholders was
balanced to some extent, as we have seen, by a tendency in the years
after 1870 for tenant farmers to purchase their own holdings. Thus
the freeholders of the late nineteenth century were a race of new
men who had purchased their holdings after 1870. (40) The desire of
landowners at this time to sell outlying parts of their estates was
matched by the anxiety of the tenants to remain on the family holding even if this meant purchase at very high prices. One example of
a tenant desiring to hold on to his farm is seen in the case of
James Hancock, a tenant on the Llwyngwair estate in north Pembrokeshire. On 19 November 1870 he wrote to the owner, J.B. Bowen: 'I
may wish to become the purchaser of the Farm of Rhydyfran if it can
be sold separate from the rest of the Estate being the spot where I
was bred and born, my family have lived for so many generations.'(41)
Even greater importunity was manifested in a letter of 1 January
1892 from David Davies of Gwydre, Llangadock, Carmarthenshire, to
the Earl of Ashburnham concerning the intended sale of the Llanddeusant estate:

> I being your Lordship's present tenant at Gwydre, also my ances-
> tors have been here generation after generation for more than 300
> years naturally therefore as it has been the homestead of my rela-
> tions for so long a time that I should have the strongest attach-
> ment to the place, which feeling I know your lordship will not
> disregard. May I ask your Lordship to put off the sale of my
> farm ... if your Lordship should not grant me this I would most
> respectfully beg of your Lordship to have it put off for another
> 3 years when I will be prepared to buy it. (42)

This last request hints at the fact that some of the tenants at
least were reluctant to have to make the purchase and did so only as
the last means of remaining on their farms.

How were these tenant farmers, notoriously short of capital, able
to purchase their holdings at a time of continuing high land values
within the principality? The answer lies in their resort to borrowing a third or a quarter of the purchase money at a rate, according
to contemporaries, of 4 per cent. (43) During the depression those
freeholders with mortgages on their properties suffered, as in Britain generally, to a greater extent than did any other farming group.
(44) Whereas tenants at this time were helped to some extent by
abatements in rent the freeholder could not gain an abatement in
interest from the mortgagee. Thus men of this class were seriously
pinched in their circumstances and they were often able to survive
only by dispensing with all hired labour. (45) Years later, in
south Cardiganshire, none of the borrowed capital had been repaid.(46)

A small redistribution of ownership also came about with the disappearance of the class of squatters and cottagers following the
enclosure of commons and wastes in Wales. The rapid rise in population from the late eighteenth century brought immense pressures on
existing resources. The absence of alternative employment in the
countryside, and, in the pre-railway era, difficulty of access to
the emerging mining districts of south-east Wales from remote areas
of the Welsh hinterland, meant serious unemployment. One palliative
was encroachment onto the vast areas of open commons and wastes,
frequently upland tracts, of Crown and private manors. Such encroachment had taken place in the previous two centuries, but there

now occurred a marked increase. For example, the Leet proceedings
of the manor of Arwystli Uwchcoed, Montgomeryshire, between 1802 and
1819, were thronged with presentments brought against people for en-
croaching on the various commons. Many were fined 40s. for erecting
cottages and at the rate of 2s.6d. an acre for enclosing parcels of
land. (47)

The process of encroachment was facilitated by a Welsh custom
stretching back over two or three centuries whereby if a caban ûn
nos (literally a one-night cabin) was built on the waste in a single
night, and smoke should be seen rising from the chimney by dawn,
freehold rights to the cottage and a small parcel of land subsequently enclosed about it, were automatically established. The perimeter
of the enclosed property was allegedly determined by the squatter
throwing an axe in all directions from the doorway of his 'clod-hall'
or cabin. A nominal rent was usually charged by the Crown or private lord and this was readily given, the squatter interpreting this
payment as merely a chief or quit rent and so considering himself a
freeholder. (48) Such squatters or cottiers were drawn from people
of all conditions making up the lower orders, and included younger
sons of tenant farmers, farm labourers, artisans and workers in
quarries and mines. The process was still active in the early 1840s
but sharply declined about mid-century at the time of the Commons
Enclosure Act. (Nevertheless, squatters' settlements were still
being made in the 1880s in remote areas of Montgomeryshire.) (49)
There is evidence that the parish authorities connived at this tech-
nically illegal conduct. In a parish meeting held in 1807 the
labouring poor had been 'encouraged by the guardians of the parishes
of Llanwnda and Llandwrog, Caernarvonshire, to build a house for
themselves on the common as not to become chargeable to the rates'.
(50) Again in 1813 we hear how many 'cots' built on the mountain
slopes in the parishes of Llanllyfni and Garn, Caernarvonshire, had
been done with the 'consent of the Parish Vestries'. (51) Such encroachers, not legally entitled to their properties, suffered great
hardship in the early nineteenth century when their hard-won en-
deavours were threatened from several quarters.

One threat came from the enclosure of commons and wastes. The
Caernarvonshire petitioners of 1813 voiced their objections to enclosure. It would deprive them of their 'toil', which had incurred
extreme expense besides physical labour, and also of the Turbary
Ground, all-important to them at a time when 'coal is too dear' and
'cannot be had by us the Poor, in this Country'. They further
stated 'we are too numerous to have a Relief from the Parishes'.
These objections were typical of squatters elsewhere when facing enclosure and David Jones has claimed that they were 'possibly more
hostile "before" than after enclosure'. (52) Upon enclosure, those
squatters who had erected their small properties within the previous
20 years, or, in the case of Crown manors, within 60 years, to the
Enclosure Act concerned were either deprived of their homes or
forced to purchase them from the Enclosure Commissioners. Squatters'
encroachments on the wastes in Caernarvonshire were either sold to
cover the considerable expense of the enclosure, in which case they
were mostly purchased by the larger proprietors, or else they were
allotted to the respective freehold claimants of the commons. (53)
When the commons in Langwm parish, Denbighshire, were enclosed in

1863 squatters 'were sent away, and the property was sold to pay the
Enclosure Commissioners for the costs'. (54)

Enclosures, then, brought hardship and sometimes, no doubt,
tragedy to this wretched class. In 1806 one observer moralised on
the effects of enclosure on the squatters of the Rhoshirwaun commons
in Caernarvonshire: 'It is much to be regretted that what may be
called improvement for the common good cannot be executed without
injuring individuals.' (55) Those cottagers, too, who were not
squatters but, by virtue of ownership of some land, possessed common
rights, were injured by enclosure. The cost of fencing their small
allotments forced many to sell out to larger landowners. (56) Some
relief, it is true, was afforded squatters and cottagers in the way
of compensation for the losses they incurred but this was seemingly
inadequate. There is evidence in the Llandwrog Cottagers' Petition
of 1826 that squatters regarded the amounts granted as unsatisfac-
tory considering the labour expended in erecting the cottages and
cultivating the waste land. (57)

Squatters were threatened in other ways. Small freeholders and
tenants possessing legitimate rights of common were generally hostile to squatter encroachments which reduced the value of their
holdings. (58) It was claimed that squatters were prone to violence
and theft, especially sheep stealing. Consequently from time to
time commoners jointly smashed their small enclosures although there
is evidence that freeholders and tenants were often afraid to eject
squatters for fear of retaliation. (59)

Squatters were also challenged by the Crown and other private
lords of manors. Before the 1820s laxity of administration, and the
Crown's more favourable legal position as against that of private
lords of being able to evict the encroachers of within 60 years'
standing, had meant that small encroachments on Crown wastes had
gone on without any challenge or opposition. But, as remarked
earlier, from the third decade onwards the Crown became more vigi-
lant in the management of its property in Wales. Small encroachments were now offered for sale to the squatters at what the Crown
considered were favourable rates, but they normally lacked the means
of purchasing. (60) Some purchases did take place, however (many
through the squatters' fear of the threats of the Crown agents to
serve them with Exchequer processes), and the size of the properties
varied from the very small to the substantial. In the parish of
Llanfair Clydogau, Cardiganshire, for example, small encroachments
varying from thirteen acres down to less than a single acre were
sold between 1831 and 1833. The encroachments sold in the lordship
of Bromfield and Yale, Denbighshire, in 1834-5, were mostly under an
acre. (61) These sales of encroachments on Crown lands to squatters
continued throughout the century. (62) In Radnorshire, where the
Crown was lord of the manor of most of the waste, squatters suffered
worse than their counterparts on Crown lands elsewhere in Wales
because the offer of purchasing their small tenements was withheld.
Here the policy of the Crown was to sell whole manors to individuals,
including the Crown's rights over encroachments made within the previous 60 years. Trouble arose between the new owners and the squatters when the former began to assert their rights by demanding payment of rents for lands occupied. One commentator wrote of the
situation in Radnorshire in 1838:

The consequence has been a long and painful contest, and praedial agitation, and outrage, teaching the inhabitants of a peaceful district the last lesson a government ought to despise, the power of physical force; bad passions were roused on each side, the misery inflicted on the poor was repaid by their execration of the wealthy.(63)

Another means by which the Crown disturbed the squatters in the enjoyment of their properties was through charging them rents beyond the purely nominal ones they had initially agreed to pay. In this way the squatter was made to turn tenant. The rent was charged at a quarter of the annual value of the lands and buildings, and although this reduction was out of consideration for the fact that money had been laid out in erecting the building and enclosing the plot of land, squatters regarded such a rent with irritation. (64)

Encroachments by squatters were more frequent on the wastes of the Crown than on private manors. (65) But the owners of the latter, too, challenged the squatters in the course of the century. Thus on one of Lord Bute's manors between Cowbridge and Llantwit Major encroachments and buildings deemed to be illegal were sold as freehold lots in 1888, the squatters having first refusal at a below-market price. About half of them purchased their holdings. The objection, once again, was that Bute was behaving harshly in confiscating the capital and labour of the cottagers. (66) Raising of rent was another type of action which upset the squatters who believed, as we have seen, that the original nominal rents charged were quit or chief rents. Private landowners thought differently and at various times raised the rents to something like their annual value. This occurred, for example, on the waste in the manor of Ewloe, Flintshire, owned by a Mr Cooke, in 1872, and on the wastes in the parish of Llanbrynmair, Montgomeryshire, owned by Sir Watkin Williams Wynn. (67) It is instanced, again, on the Ashburnham estates in Brecknockshire. In 1883 Edward Driver reported:

I have however succeeded in several of these cases in making the Tenants /squatters/ attorn to the Rightful owner and also sign agreements to pay much higher rents and am proceeding to obtain the same desirable arrangement with the remainder, but as I doubt if all these persons will comply with my terms it may hereafter be considered whether any and what other measures should be taken to enforce the claim to them; as however the whole value is but very trifling, perhaps not exceeding £12 or £14 p.a. - yet I feel it my duty to use every means short of actual legal proceedings to endeavour to recover possession. (68)

Such an inflexible approach naturally provoked resentment and hostility among the squatters.

Some redistribution of property resulted from the process of estate consolidation. Marriage settlements often led to estates being widely scattered, a situation which was disliked by owners because of the managerial problems posed and because a fragmented property was 'aesthetically' unpleasing. (69) Consolidation of such properties was achieved by two main courses of action. First, owners could sell off the outlying parts and purchase instead land nearer home. For example, a survey in 1881 of the Welsh Ashburnham estates commented of the Llanddeusant estate in north-east Carmarthenshire:

The scattered nature of this estate and its distance from the
agent or any central office for looking after it suggests the
desirability of disposing of it and re-investing the money in
consolidating some other estate .... The cost of management must
necessarily be heavy, this would be saved and notwithstanding its
many drawbacks its a property that would sell well. (70)

The other course of action lay through exchange of properties between landowners. W.J.R. Powell, the owner of the Nanteos estate,
Cardiganshire, in writing to E. Evans of Llanddewi Brefi, Tregarron,
in 1863: 'Wishing to unite my property as much as possible by ex-
changing outskirts for land nearer home', was expressing a policy
shared by many landowners at this time. (71)

CHAPTER 3

LANDOWNERS AND AGRICULTURE

I

It is necessary at this stage to ascertain the extent to which agricultural land was occupied by its owners. The substantial estates, apart from their home farms, were let out to tenant farmers. This also applied to the smaller properties of under a thousand acres. These small owners in many instances found it more expedient to let their own lands while themselves becoming tenants of other farms on some neighbouring estate. (1) Others again of the small owner class lived the lives of small country gentlemen, letting their properties and retaining merely a small residence for their own use. They were distinguished by contemporaries from the large estate owners whose main source of income came from agricultural rents, by the term 'resident owners'. While they owned small properties, ranging from 200 to 1000 acres, their chief source of income was provided by a profession or a business. Typical of this class of small owners in Wales was the colliery owner, the lawyer, and the merchant in agricultural produce, who purchased their land for the social status it bestowed. They were naturally most numerous in the vicinity of towns, but some were to be found in the purely rural areas. Their numbers had risen from the early years of the century but the great increases only came after the 1870s when large estate owners began to sell outlying parts of their property. (2)

Although there were doubtless many in the upper ranks of these small owners whose life-style equalled or even surpassed that of the squires, they were not easily accepted in 'county' society. The squires clung to the traditional belief in the dignity of landowner-ship and its descent and regarded the newcomers from commerce as inferior in status. In 1853 Mr Davies of Castle Green, Cardigan, was described as 'a merchant there and largely interested in the shipping as well as a considerable landowner and J.P. for both Cardigan and Pembroke. Not particularly bright and looked down upon by the squirearchy as being in trade.' (3) This is yet one more reminder that the 'openness' of British landed society should not be overstressed.

The amount of owner-occupied land in Wales was, then, small throughout the century. Table 3.1 shows the situation from the 1880s.

TABLE 3.1   Owner-occupied land in Wales and Monmouthshire

Year	Area (1000 acres)	% proportion of total cultivated area
1887	338.5	11.1
1894	366.7	11.8
1905	313.3	10.3
1913	283.3	9.17

Source: 'The Agricultural Returns'.

From 1894 down to 1913 there was a steady decline in the area of
owner-occupied land. This is difficult to explain in so far as more
and more tenants were purchasing their holdings over these years.
Some of the decline was no doubt due to the fact that owners of
large estates were letting their home farms more frequently, while
small freeholds were often let on the retirement or death of the
former owner-occupier. (4)

The small owner-occupier was unfavourably regarded by contemporary writers. In 1870 James Loxdale, Esq., of Llanilar, Cardiganshire, commented on the freeholders of the county: 'These small
properties are farmed in the most wretched manner, the owners
possessing scarcely any capital.' (5) Around the same time Gibson
claimed that:

> Small freeholders are probably the worst farmers in the Princi-
> pality, and live from hand to mouth, a harder life than labourers.
> In no sense can their position be favourably compared with that
> of tenants on an estate where evictions are unknown and where in-
> creased rents are seldom heard of. (6)

They often took occasional employment as day labourers in order to
supplement the small incomes from their freeholds. (7) When prices
fell from the close of the 1870s their position, as stated earlier,
became critical. Their heavily mortgaged farms were in a desperate-
ly low state of cultivation. Cardiganshire was the stronghold of
the small freeholder, a situation that arose from the frequent sales
of Crown lands in this county. (8) Here, in 1888, their manner of
life was outwardly 'simple in the extreme'. They survived by dint
of cautious thrift, doing all the required labour themselves, and
paying attention to the small sources of income as the poultry and
the dairy. The abject poverty of this class was summed up in the
observation that 'the shadow of the mortgagee is over the land'. (9)

The three basic features of the gentry and greater landowning
classes were a family mansion or residence, however modest; a home
farm adjoining this residence and, finally, a landed estate, most of
which had to be let out to tenants. The landowners, therefore,
lived as a class of 'rentiers', most of them deriving their main
source of profit from their estates in the form of agricultural
rents. (10) Those landowners, however, who possessed manors and
freeholds containing valuable mineral deposits often drew the
greater part of their incomes from royalties paid by the lessees of
these minerals. For obvious reasons this was particularly the case

in Glamorgan and Monmouthshire. In March 1856 T.W. Williams of Tir-y-Cwm wrote to Mrs Williams of Aberpergwm, Glyn Neath:

> Glamorganshire is becoming one of the most affluent and important
> in the Kingdom - many families who were poor a few years back are
> becoming rich by developing the resources of their hitherto dor-
> mant properties - thanks to the railroads - and many more will be
> rich when there are more railroads. (11)

Besides income gained from mineral royalties, the sale of timber for
the south Wales industrial area was becoming an important item in
the economy of many of the south Wales estates from the 1850s. (12)
Again, landowners in this period of rapid industrial development
amassed vast profits from the leasing of building sites. A couple
of examples of these industrial estates must suffice. In the second
half of the century Lord Aberdare of Dyffryn, Glamorgan, owned
nearly 4000 acres of land. The high gross annual value of the
Dyffryn estate, just over £12,000, was due to the possession of
mineral royalties. At the same time the Marquis of Bute's Glamorgan
property, extending over more than 21,000 acres, returned a gross
yearly income of £100,000, a great part of it being derived from
mineral royalties and building leases. (13) Certain north Wales
estates were also enriched by mineral exploitation. Thus the profits yielded by the slate quarries on Lord Penrhyn's extensive property were approximately twice his revenue from farm rents. (14)

As most of their estates were let to tenants it followed that
Welsh landlords were unimportant as agricultural producers. Their
only direct farming activities took place on their home farms which
functioned primarily to provide food for the household and fodder
for the farm stock, stables and kennels. Only surplus stock and
crops were sold. In 1824, for instance, the Picton Castle home farm
raised £1,287 from sales of pigs, lambs, sheep, calves, horses,
barley, oats, potatoes, cheese and butter. This sum formed a mere
eighth of the income gained from agricultural rents. (15) Home
farms were often found uneconomic, for the experimentation with new
techniques was an expensive luxury. The steward of the Hawarden
estate, Flintshire, wrote in 1846: 'Home farms in the occupancy of
Landlords are seldom profitable concerns, often greatly the reverse.'
(16) The Picton Castle home farm was running at a loss in 1869 and
the family solicitors were advised that 'it would be far cheaper to
buy the articles drawn by the Castle from the Farm than to continue
the present system'. (17) Similar problems were faced in the 1860s
on the Golden Grove and Stackpole estates of Earl Cawdor. His agent
wrote to him in the summer of 1866:

> To advise your Lordship about the two home farms is very diffi-
> cult. If they could be strictly separated in every respect from
> the Demesnes - which I fear is impossible - they might be made to
> pay their way. It is the Demesnes that swamp the farms - and it
> is very easy for Bailiffs to charge the demesne that which would
> have to be borne by the farm, if there was but that one account.
> With the number of men employed here /Stackpole Court/ and at
> Golden Grove - at the present high rate of wages - the expense
> per annum must be very serious and the Demesnes make nothing
> towards it. (18)

Important from the point of view of agricultural development, if
a costly item in estate expenditure, were the experiments carried

out on the home farms with improved techniques. Walter Davies wrote
of south Wales in 1814 that every county contained landowners eager
to promote agricultural improvements and one means was by 'example
of improved culture'. (19)   In 1820 Cawdor's agent informed him that
a Lieutenant Brown was taking Merion Court (of 213 acres) 'and seems
fully impressed with the propriety of following the turnip system
particularly after seeing the result of that practice on your lordship's farm'. (20)   C.S. Read reported similarly of south Wales in
1849 that many gentlemen farmed on improved lines and expressed the
hope that some spirited tenants would follow their example. (21)
One such gentleman was C.R.M. Talbot of the Margam and Penrice
estate who in 1844 introduced turnip husbandry on his home farm at
Penrice Castle in Gower. This example of the alternative system of
cropping was publicised in pamphlet form by Talbot and circulated in
the Swansea district. (22)   The system was slowly adopted by the
tenant farmers so that in time the whole of Gower's farming was significantly improved. (23)   Another model home farm in Gower was
found on the estate of Sir Hussey Vivian. The latter's home farm,
Park-le-Breos, was noted for its shorthorns and the herd became
famous throughout the United Kingdom. In addition, the farm was
stocked with a select flock of Shropshire Down sheep, several good
Clydesdale horses and good classes of the Large and Middle white
breed of pigs. Leading to all the farm buildings was a permanent
tramway for conveying food to the stock and manure from the yards
and boxes to a covered depot specially made for its reception. (24)
Stock breeding, too, was enthusiastically pursued on the home farm
of Sir Charles Morgan of Tredegar in the 1840s. (25)   Similarly,
several gentlemen in north Wales during the early century introduced
Ayrshire and Galloway breeds onto their home farms. (26)   It will be
shown later how the Welsh gentry in the 1870s abandoned their former
preoccupation with the 'improved' breeds in favour of rescuing the
fast deteriorating breed of native Blacks.

   Landlords also encouraged improvements in husbandry by supporting
agricultural societies, ploughing societies, farmers' clubs, sheep
dog trials and the like. Thus in 1890 the owner of Wynnstay made
subscriptions to such societies totalling £84 8s. (27)   A number of
agricultural societies were founded by the gentry in the second half
of the eighteenth and first decade of the nineteenth centuries. In
the early years membership was restricted mainly to landowners but
from around 1810 it was increasingly extended to include substantial
tenant farmers. (28)   While no longer, therefore, the sole organi-
sers of the societies, the gentry continued in their support throughout the century. And if that support was not forthcoming societies
collapsed, as happened, for example, in the case of the north Cardiganshire Agricultural Society in 1885. (29)   A new impetus was given
to existing agricultural societies in the 1860s when landowners and
the more progressive farmers saw their value in improving the breeds
of Black cattle and other livestock at a time when prices were
moving upwards. Many new societies were founded at this time, a
feature observed by the 'Welshman' in 1874:

   The rapidity with which these exhibitions are multiplying in the
   country is a convincing proof of their popularity, and no doubt
   the fame of one society, or the knowledge of the good accomplished in one district, has led to the formation of other
   societies. (30)

Contemporary testimony ior the beneficial influence brought to
bear on farming by the agricultural societies is plentiful. In 1882,
for example, Mr Garnon Williams attributed the improvement in agriculture in Brecknockshire over the recent years to agricultural
shows. (31) Clearly the pronouncement of the owner of Cilgwyn, Cardiganshire, in 1872 that small local agricultural societies 'really
do no good and that it is a waste of money to encourage them' was
too sweeping. (32) But certain qualifications do have to be made
about the effectiveness of such societies. Tenants, it was claimed,
valued agricultural shows mainly for the prize-money which they
could win and failed to realise that the true object of a society
was to give landlords and tenants not money but good stock. On occasions they grumbled if the landlords won the best prizes, and prize
lists, therefore, came to be drawn up with primary consideration as
to the best means of financially rewarding the largest number of ex-
hibitors rather than as to the best way of improving the stock and
crops. (33) A solution to the problem was sought by the Merioneth
Agricultural Society in 1881 when it was decided to divide the Show-
yard into two parts, one for stock of tenants with incomes below
£300 a year and the other for landowners' stock. Money prizes were
awarded tenants while landowners received honorary rewards. The
same solution was adopted by the north Cardiganshire Agricultural
Society in the following year. (34) The fast growth in numbers of
these societies in the late century was also criticised. It was
claimed that such highly localised organisations were weak and that
it would be better to have a small number that would prove strong in
their resources and influence. (35)
    Certain of the larger landowners as Sir Watkin Williams Wynn of
Wynnstay in 1812, and Sir Charles Morgan of Tredegar between the
1820s and the 1850s, attempted to promote agriculture in their districts by instituting annual shows of stock. Prizes were awarded
for the best exhibits, and in the case of the Tredegar show bills of
the prizes to be won were printed on satin and sent to those ladies
who took an interest in the show. In 1851, Sir Charles, as the
sponsor, gave 16 silver cups, but cups were also donated by other
neighbouring gentry as William Style of Wentloog Castle, Thomas
Powell of The Gaer, Lady Hall of Llanover Court, and Joseph Bailey
of Glanusk Park. (36)
    Some landowners, too, attempted to promote agricultural improve-
ments amongst their immediate tenantry. Thus Oakley of Tanybwlch,
Cardiganshire, attempted during the 1880s to improve the herds of
his tenants by volunteering to sell at a reduced price newly born
bull-calves which had been carefully sired. (37) Similarly Corbett
of Ynysmaengwyn, Merioneth, purchased a shire horse for the use of
his tenants in 1891 while in south Wales during the same period Lord
Cawdor introduced superior horses for the use of his tenants at
nominal prices. (38) Efforts, too, were made to encourage the
growth of new crops. Thus Mrs Brigstocke of Blaenpant, Cardiganshire, promoted turnip culture amongst her tenants in the early
1870s by distributing prizes on rent day. (39)
    Welsh landowners made a further, if a more dubious, contribution
to the advancement of agriculture by enclosing commons and wastes
through Acts of Parliament. As far as the lowlands were concerned
enclosures had largely taken place before 1800, sometimes centuries

previously. There were still, nevertheless, some sizeable areas of
unenclosed coastal marsh and dune, some valley marshland used as
common grazing, and in a few areas as, for instance, coastal Cardiganshire, western Pembrokeshire, and the eastern vales and plateaux
of Montgomeryshire, a number of open arable fields. (40) The main
body of enclosures in the nineteenth century, then, occurred in the
wide upland tracts. Such enclosures became commonplace at a later
date than those in certain areas of England and their taking in of
moorland stretches meant that the movement had 'a different emphasis
from that in England'. (41)

Before 1797 Enclosure Acts had been passed in only five out of
the 13 Welsh counties and these were all areas of English influence.
Between 1797 and 1817 some 75 Enclosure Bills were passed relating
to Wales and Monmouthshire authorising the enclosure of over 134,622
acres. The movement slowed down considerably after 1817. In the
1820s three Acts were passed enclosing a mere 360 acres and, in the
late 1830s, seven, enclosing 3,587 acres. Acceleration occurred in
the 1840s when 14 Acts were passed covering 21,957 acres. In the
1850s some 47 Acts were passed authorising enclosure of 42,204 acres
and in the 1860s, 46, covering 63,967 acres. By the close of the
1860s the movement had spent its force. No Enclosure Acts were
passed for Wales in the following decade and in the years 1880-5
only five were procured enclosing 5,959 acres. (42)

Enclosures of the commons and wastes in the lowland areas were
frequently followed by agricultural improvements. It is highly significant that in many instances they took place in the high price
years of the French Wars when a number of landowners spent large
amounts of capital in the improvement of their properties. In doing
so they were influenced as much by their desire for higher rents as
by the current climate in which agriculture was becoming 'a fashionable study, as well as amusement'. (43) Following the enclosure of
the coastal marshlands in the parishes of Abergele, Rhuddlan,
Dysserth and Mehilen at the mouth of the Vale of Clwyd, Denbighshire
(the final Awards of the Enclosure Acts being made in the first two
instances before 1815 while the remaining Awards were completed by
1826), successful efforts were made towards improving the landscape.
A pattern of rectangular hedged fields took the place of the previously open marshland; new farms were created; the land was
successfully drained and the improved soil was placed under wheat
and barley crops. The work of enclosure and improvement here owed
much to the encouragement and financial support of such landlords as
Sir John Williams, Sir Edward Pryce Lloyd, Sir Roger Mostyn, Lord
Plymouth and Thomas Hughes. (44) During the French Wars the enclosure of Penmorva Marsh in Caernarvonshire and of Traeth Mawr sands
between Caernarvonshire and Merioneth, in both cases by W.A. Mad-
docks, led to improved cultivation. Similarly the enclosure (after
the Award in 1836) of the coastal waste and marshes of Morfa Dyffryn,
between Barmouth and Harlech, Merioneth, was accompanied by an improved system of agriculture. (45) Again the enclosure of commons
in the neighbourhood of Rhayader by the river Wye gave rise to more
scientific husbandry. Enclosures, too, in the vales and plateaux of
eastern Montgomeryshire - in the parishes of Manafon, Bettws and
Berriew - led to the creation and reorganisation of farm units and
an increase in arable land. (46)

What were the motives of landowners in undertaking costly enclosures of moorland commons? During the boom years of the French Wars
extension of the cultivated area may well have been a prime consideration. Certainly, marginal lands were now ploughed up for corn culture as never before. Similarly, high livestock prices before 1814
led to the enclosure of some upland commons for hay, cabbages and
turnips for the rearing of stock. It was held, too, that the growth
of timber for the Navy on enclosed tracts would help to win the war.
(47) The fall in prices during the post-war years led to a situation of lower profitability, and in some instances such land ceased
to be cultivated. (48)

Enclosure of the moorland commons continued, however, throughout
the century and it is clear that landowners were not generally concerned with extending the margin of cultivation. The rugged nature
of the terrain and the thinness of the soil dictated that such lands
were suitable only for sheep and pony grazing. The problem of the
open commons in Wales had always been the uncertainty of individual
rights. In the early nineteenth century, as earlier, the freeholders and tenants of a particular township possessed by virtue of
their holdings the right to depasture in the summer months as much
stock upon the open common as their holdings would carry in the
winter. One difficulty that arose from this practice was that certain parties abused this right of 'stint' by overstocking the commons. Another problem arose from the right of the different parties
to use any part of the common. Acquisition of the choicest grazing
areas inevitably produced bitter and protracted wrangles. In many
instances, it is true, agreements had been reached between parties
possessing common rights as to the respective tracts each was to
graze. Such tracts were known as 'sheep-walks' and each man's walk
usually bordered on the holding concerned. Imaginary boundaries
were established such as a road, a dingle or a watershed. Very
often, however, these boundaries were blatantly ignored. Large
stockholders encroached on the rights of their smaller neighbours
and 'coursing' of sheep back and forth across the common at the dead
of night by shepherds and their dogs led to great brutality and violence, even the destruction of sheep. Such a situation saw constant
litigation though many confrontations never reached the courts as
witnesses in this brutalised society were afraid of revenge. (49)

Large owners took advantage of the facilities afforded by the
Enclosure Acts to determine the precise area under their legal ownership and to define their exact rights. They were anxiously assisted
in doing so by solicitors and surveyors who stood to do very well
out of the business. (50) Individual rights on the open commons
were frequently most violently abused by small encroachers, and
landowners in making enclosures were often motivated primarily by
their desire to end such encroachments. The reason for Sir Watkin
Williams Wynn's decision in 1856 to enclose land in the parish of
Llangurig, Montgomeryshire, was stated as follows:

> The fact is that the parish of Llangurig is an immense district
> consisting of very large exclusive sheep walks. And very small
> portions of land, comparatively speaking, available for cultiva-
> tion. The Boundaries of these sheep walks are well known. And
> the parties owning the Herbage would gain nothing by an Inclosure
> in the great bulk of the district. And consequently they would

not consent to one if it were at a serious sacrifice .... Sir
Watkin does not care about the game .... He is therefore quite
willing to give this up, but the inconvenience he experiences is
that parties are continually making small inclosures or encroach-
ing in one way or another and he is thrown into disagreeable
collision with them. The minerals of the district are very valuable. And these little Encroachments by continuously biting off
marginal bits reduce the ambit of his territory. If an inclosure
were to take place all these bickerings would be extinguished.(51)

Similarly, Lord Cawdor's agent was thinking about these little
encroachments and the precise rights of the 'commoners' when he
wrote to him in 1865:

In your reply to the Penboyr petitioners I think you may say that
you wish to put a stop to much of that which they pray to have
continued viz. the wholesale stealing and burning of the turf and
soil from the Commons by which they are very fast becoming quite
worthless for any purpose. To prevent an increase of pauper population in the neighbourhood. To give employment in enclosing and
cultivating or planting any portions of the Commons that are
worth the outlay. To prevent abuse of the Commons from pasturage
or otherwise - by those who have no right therein,and to make
those who are interested to know their own, and to do as they
like with it. (52)

Enclosure Awards allotted lands to individual owners and sometimes they were physically enclosed by earth balks or dry stone
walls. Only on the larger estates was this accompanied by desirable
improvements like drainage and planting, a considerable outlay of
capital being necessary. (53) One such improver of upland wastes on
the Hiraethog Moors was Henry Sandbach, a wealthy Liverpool merchant
who had purchased the Hafodunos estate of 5000 acres in 1833. (54)
Fenced land, even when unimproved, resulted in a higher standard of
upland farming. The very fact that sheep were now contained within
a fixed area and undisturbed by other flocks was bound to lead to
some improvement in the breed of sheep over the long term. The
agent of Sir Charles Morgan of Tredegar had this in mind when he
wrote of the mountainous Palleg estate in 1842:

No good can be effected on Palleg whilst 20 different parties
graze in common .... I am therefore after much experience and
observation satisfied that the county /Brecknockshire/ cannot be
improved until the mountains are inclosed and every man's stock
undisturbed by themselves. (55)

Thus a limited amount of agricultural improvement followed enclosure
by fences although, as Thomas rightly indicates, little was done to
improve the quality of the grass. (56) Often, however, Enclosure
Awards were not followed by actual fencing. Nevertheless, some
improvement occurred even here for allotments prevented violent disputes and midnight coursing on the commons.

By the close of the century wide tracts of upland waste still
remained unenclosed. In 1894 the 'cultivated' land in Wales (we
have seen already) amounted to 59.8 per cent of the total area of
the country while in England it was 76.4 per cent and in Scotland
25.1 per cent. (57) The main factor retarding enclosure was the expense involved and this was relatively higher than usual, given the
marginal type of land. The situation was aggravated by the lack of

capital in Welsh agriculture. Thus proprietors were sometimes prevented from enclosing the commons because their tenants, poor and
unenterprising, were unwilling to contribute to the costs by paying
higher rents representing, perhaps, 4 per cent on the capital outlay.
(58) At other times landowners merely let the allotments to the
tenants who were themselves expected to make outlays on fencing and
building. Both large and small owners often charged unrealistic
rents in this process. The agent of the Wynnstay estate, for example, argued that the allotments made on Waun Bryncoch in the
parishes of Llanuwchllyn and Llanycil, Merioneth, were let at too
high rents (averaging 10s. an acre), and that tenants expended considerable sums in fencing and building. In the Wynnstay Rentals for
1824 and 1825 he noted that both these factors meant that great
losses had been sustained and called upon W.W. Wynn to make allowances towards these expenses.
    In the case of many tenant farmers and freeholders, too, enclo-
sures were opposed because it was generally held that the right to
graze livestock on the open commons made all the difference between
survival and failure. The turning out of horses, sheep and cattle
to graze on the mountains in the summer enabled farmers to save more
fields for hay and so keep many more sheep and cattle throughout the
year than could be done if the stock had to be maintained on the enclosed lands of the farm during the summer. (59)
    A crucial development of these years was the coming of the rail-
ways. How did Welsh landowners respond to the opportunities they
would obviously present in the opening up of the countryside? Many
of the large owners were enthusiastic and became directors. (60) In
their construction of the South Wales railway between Swansea and
Carmarthen the company concerned were facilitated in their proceedings by several of the landowners of the district allowing them to
take possession of their land and agreeing to postpone the payment
of the purchase money. (61) Glamorgan landowners like John Nicholl
Carne of Dimlands Castle, Mr Homfray of Penllin, Rowland Fothergill
of Merthyr and Nicholl Carne of St Donats Castle were promoters of
the Cowbridge to Merthyr railway 'not upon the instigation of any
Railway Company but from their desire to have it in their district'.
(62) In west Wales one notable railway enthusiast was E.C.L. Fitzwilliams of Cilgwyn, Cardiganshire, who saw rail facilities as vital
for the conveyance of lime into the county. (63) Similarly John
Jones, High Sheriff for Carmarthenshire and a landowner near Llandovery, supported the Towy Vale railway project because of its
crucial importance for lime carriage. In north Wales, likewise,
Lord Mostyn, a Merioneth landowner, strongly advocated the Aberystwyth and Welsh Coast railway for its value in conveying lime which
had hitherto been brought to Merioneth from Ireland and Anglesey.
Support for this line also came from W.W.E. Wynne of Peniarth, MP
for Merioneth. The shareholders of the Llanidloes and Newtown railway project in 1853 were 'principally landowners and residents in
the district'. Nearly ten years later a strong supporter of the
Bala to Dolgelly line was Richard Meredith Richards who owned
property in the parish of Dolgelly. (64)
    Some of the larger owners and most of the small ones were, how-
ever, apathetic to rail development. Fitzwilliams of Cilgwyn
reported in 1853 that the Carmarthen and Cardigan railway was

progressing satisfactorily 'but the squirearchy are very lukewarm
about it'. (65) In 1879 the directors of the Whitland and Cardigan
railway expressed their regret at the lack of support from landowners. (66) One obvious objection was to the nuisance caused by
the lines crossing their lands, a vexation shared by landowners and
tenants alike. In 1845, for instance, Sir Richard Bulkeley Philipps
of Picton Castle opposed the South Wales railway project because it
was scheduled to pass through four miles of his property. The owner
of the nearby Slebech estate stated that the line might cross his
lands providing that he had the right to halt the train 'on the spot
in question on a given signal being given'. Mrs Owen of Glansevern,
Montgomeryshire, objected to a railroad passing too closely to her
lodge on the estate. Fitzwilliams of Cilgwyn pointed to a more
general reason underlying gentry apathy to rail development - their
reluctance 'to mix themselves up in anything at all mercantile' together with their want of ready cash, 'no very hopeful commodities
to mould into directors even if you can get them to be named as
such'. (67)

II

The peculiar situation in Wales where landlords and their tenants
were divided not only on a social level but by the language barrier,
religious persuasion and, increasingly from mid century, by political affiliation, led the contemporary Nonconformist press and other
political Radicals to depict landlords as totally out of sympathy
with their tenants and harsh in their dealings towards them. In the
'Baner' of 24 November 1886, for instance, Welsh landlords were
castigated as 'devourers of the marrow of their /the tenants'/
bones'. (68) For the remainder of this chapter, and in the ensuing
ones on the tenant farmer, the attitude of the landlords to their
estates and tenants will be examined in order to test the validity
or otherwise of this contemporary criticism, for upon such an attitude much of the fortunes of agricultural progress depended.
     The employment of agents and, sometimes, other minor officials,
to manage the landed estates allowed the owners to give a great deal
of their time to political and social pursuits and to live the
leisurely lives of country gentlemen. (69) On very rare occasions
only did the landlord manage his estate himself. There were, too,
according to a Cardiganshire landowner in the 1830s, strong financial inducements for a landlord to place the running of his estate
in the hands of an agent. The landowner's personal management of
his estate rendered it unlikely that the rental would be sufficiently professional to constitute supporting evidence in matters of dis-
pute over certain agreements or arrangements made with the tenants.
Again, an agent would act decisively in collecting the rents when
the owner might hesitate to make himself unpopular by so doing. (70)
But it would be erroneous to see landlords as leaving the management
of their estates entirely to agents, content to spend the yearly
incomes derived from their properties. There is abundant evidence
from the letters exchanged between agents and their landlords that
the latter were in touch, while absent from their estates, with the
everyday running of estate affairs - the repairs being carried out,

arrears of rent, the suitability of prospective tenants to vacant holdings, and the like. (71)

The amount of active participation in estate affairs varied from landlord to landlord and it is impossible to assess the degree of independence allowed agents in decision making on important matters of business policy. In certain instances, letters of landlords to their agents reveal that the formulation of estate policy remained in their hands. C.R.M. Talbot of Margam wrote to his agent in 1833: 'I object "in general" to grant any leases, and will only make exceptions where it is clearly my interest to do so.' Indeed, Talbot interfered with the style of management of his agent. In June 1834 he wrote to Llewellyn: 'More than half your trouble arising from the management is attributable to the want of general rules, and the consequent uncertainty as to whether tenant or landlord is liable.' (72) Generally, when exceptional action had to be taken outside the normal routine agents wrote to their employers for instructions. In the difficult farming year of 1850, for instance, Charles Bishop, agent for the Ashburnham properties in Carmarthenshire, wrote to Lord Ashburnham: 'I shall be about beginning my audits in the first week of August and I must again ask your lordship whether I may make any and what allowances to the tenants.' (73) While agents left the final decision in these difficult situations to the landlord there is, nevertheless, plentiful evidence that they were prepared to question the advisability, even justice, of certain lines of action. This emerges clearly in a letter of John Harvey to his employer, Lord Kensington, about the treatment of tenants in 1831:

> Permit me to request your Lordship to cast your eye over them
> /the arrears/ once more and to instruct me whether I am to put
> the officer of the law upon the Phillips' of Harrolds Inn and
> Welman of Velum Hill. If so, I shall do my duty, but I must not
> conceal from your lordship that it would be the utter ruin of the
> parties .... I trust your lordship will not misunderstand my
> language, but this is really not the time to call on farmers to
> make any extraordinary exertions. (74)

Agents, moreover, offered strong advice about the necessity for a certain course of action to be taken. In 1843, for example, we find Lord Bute's agent writing: 'I also consider it my duty to say that if your Lordship wishes to let your farms as they become vacant to a better class of farmers the houses and buildings will require being put into decent repair.' (75) Essentially, then, as F.M.L. Thompson has pointed out, estate management was 'very much a co-operative enterprise' between landlords and their agents and other estate officials as bailiffs, woodwards, gamekeepers and park keepers. (76)

A wide range of duties was enjoined on the agents in the day-to-day running of estates. They had to select the tenants, decide the conditions of tenure, settle and receive the rents, superintend the necessary estate repairs, keep an eye on the cultivation of the farms, instruct the tenants in agricultural improvements, arrange for the sale of bark and timber, and see that the conditions of tenancy were not infringed. Agents, too, were important in managing the political affairs of the owner. To mention but one example, in 1869 Cawdor's agent wrote to him: 'I have been hunting up additional voters on the Estates in this county - and by making joint tenancies etc I hope we shall add 70 names to the Register.' (77) They

were also expected to attend and represent their employers' interests at any Vestry or other local meetings. (78) The choice of
agent was obviously, then, of great importance for it was upon his
character, training and conduct that good or bad relations between
landlord and tenant often depended. And further, as Bute was informed in 1842: 'Much of the success of agricultural improvements
depended upon the skill, exertion and practical knowledge of the
Agent in the details of actual management.' (79) In the following
year it was reported that the 'present backward state of Agriculture'
on Sir Stephen Glynne's Hawarden estate in Flintshire lay in 'the
management'. There was no lack of expenditure for more than half of
the rental in 1842 had been laid out for improvements. The Report
concluded: 'If Sir Stephen intends to execute any considerable improvements on his estate he will require to do so in a better arranged and more economical manner than hitherto, otherwise the whole
rental will go little way in the matter.' (80)

In 1887 Fitzwilliams of Cilgwyn, Cardiganshire, observed that
'nowadays the management of landed estates is rapidly walking out of
lawyers' offices into regular land agents' establishments', and advanced as the reason for this: 'No lawyer agent that ever I came
across likes his clients as he calls them to interfere in any way.'
(81) Yet, as far as Wales was concerned, constant complaints were
made to the Land Commissioners at the close of the century that
agents were often bank clerks, auctioneers, retired army officers
and especially solicitors. (82) That such men had no experience of
farming was a proper complaint but many witnesses were unrealistic
in calling for agents to have had practical experience as tenant
farmers. This latter claim was basically the reaction of the tenantry to the landlords' appointing as agents members of their own
class. If landowners chose for agents local solicitors, auctioneers
and retired army officers - men without farming experience or knowledge of estate management to meet the standard required to deal
with the increasing complexity in the agricultural economy - they
could, nevertheless, be relied upon for honesty in the numerous
financial transactions involved in their work. Moreover, in the
case of auctioneers a knowledge of the value of land and its poten-
tial for development was certainly not irrelevant, and indeed served
as an asset. (83)

Welsh land agents were frequently accused by contemporaries of
being harsh towards the tenantry, concerned only with extracting
from them the last penny. (84) But the Welsh Land Commissioners
concluded in a different vein: 'Nor can the land agents of Wales as
a body be described as harsh, unscrupulous, arbitrary or cruel.' (85)
This last impression is conveyed, too, by agents' letters to their
employers, particularly those written in difficult farming years.
In 1817 William Jones, agent of the Glansevern estate, wrote to his
employer 'it was very much my wish to avoid selling under distress',
and advised that the tenants should be given abatements and other
forms of help. The agent of the Kensington estate, Pembrokeshire,
asked his employer in 1822 to appoint someone to replace him as he
was reluctant to proceed against tenants in arrears. The Wynnstay
agent, likewise, showed a realistic appreciation of tenants' difficulties. He wrote in the 1826 rental, for instance, of Owen Edwards,
a tenant in the parish of Llanuwchllyn, Merioneth: 'An industrious,

deserving man and worthy of indulgence and encouragement.'   John
Hughes, agent for various properties in Cardiganshire, wrote to one
landowner in 1832:   'Your tenants here I am inclined to think presume too much of my dread of distraining as I can only get promises
from them.'   Agents, too, were sympathetic towards the general position of their tenants outside years of crisis.   Lord Cawdor's agent
wrote to him in 1867:

> I attribute in great measure the good receipts lately to an
> impression amongst the Tenantry that we intend to treat them
> fairly as to houses and buildings - and it will be useless to
> expect the present rents to be paid, unless we do give better
> accommodation both to the Tenants and their Stock. (86)

But there were, if a minority, the unsympathetic and unscrupulous
agents.   The manager of the Glynllech estate, Brecknockshire, in the
1840s was referred to as 'a drunken vagabond'. (87)   Apparently the
worst kind of agent in upsetting relations between landowner and
tenant was not the chief but the sub-agent.   C.R.M. Talbot of Margam
wrote to his chief agent on this matter in 1840, observing that a
sub-agent was 'a kind of being to which I have always had a very
great objection, because he always in the end obtains an undue power
over both tenants and employer'. (88)

In the remoter predominantly Welsh-speaking areas, agents, no
matter how well-intentioned, were often out of tune with the feelings of the tenantry through ignorance of the language.   This was a
real grievance of many of the tenants.   For example, on the Wynne
Finch estate in Denbighshire, where nearly all the tenants were
Welsh, the agent at the end of the century, a Mr Trethwy, while
agreeable and fair in all respects, could not speak Welsh.   The
owner, Colonel Wynne Finch, admitted that it would be an 'immense
advantage' if the agent could speak the language. (89)   E.C.L. Fitzwilliams of Cilgwyn was seemingly exceptional in acting to remedy
the situation.   In the 1860s he made it a rule that his under-agent
should speak the Welsh language. (90)

The charge made by contemporaries that Welsh landowners were
largely absent from their estates during the nineteenth century was
ill-founded.   The 'Baner' for 25 April 1888 claimed (in translation):

> The majority of them /i.e. landlords/ live in England, and the
> poor Welsh, through the sweat of their brows, are collecting
> every half penny in the neighbourhood for them to have the
> pleasure of spending them in England or on the Continent.   Remem-
> ber the above are facts and not groundless dreams. (91)

The Welsh Land Commissioners acquitted them of this charge.   They
properly distinguished between the practically continuous residence
of the small Welsh squire, too poor to support a London residence,
and the partial absenteeism of an owner who had a residence in his
county, and who brought his family there for a considerable portion
of the year. (92)   Such partial absenteeism came in for criticism by
an Eisteddfod prize essayist in 1850 on the grounds that it denied
close contact and co-operation with the farming community. (93)
There was obviously some truth in this, but it overstated the problem in so far as absentee owners kept in close contact with their
estates through regular correspondence.   It is likely, too, that
absenteeism grew less as the century advanced.   In particular, railways more readily disposed Welsh owners towards residing on their

estates. (94) Thus the evils attendant upon the complete absenteeism of many Irish landlords, with uncontrolled authority in the
hands of agents,were not a feature of the Welsh situation

Landlords were of necessity involved in the business of agriculture through their sinking of fixed capital in their property in the
form of buildings, fences, roads and drainage. The division of responsibility between landlord and tenant as to improvements (this
term is meant to include repairs) changed as the century advanced
and varied from district to district. Under the system of leases
for lives or for years in the counties of south Wales, which came to
an end only gradually in the first half of the nineteenth century,
the responsibility for repairs lay with the tenants. By mid century
yearly agreements had become the basic form of land tenure in Wales,
and under these the landlord was made responsible for improvements.
A common practice in Wales under these yearly agreements was for the
landowner to provide materials, and to pay for the mason and joiner
in the case of buildings, and for the tenant to provide the haulage
and unskilled labour.

It is here necessary to refute contemporary allegations that it
was the tenants who in practice bore the whole burden of agricultural improvements. Samuel Roberts blamed the landlords for failing to
improve their estates, while later it was claimed by Welsh Radicals
in the House of Commons and in print that agricultural improvements
were, as a rule, financed and carried out by the tenants. (95) On
16 March 1892 T.E. Ellis, Liberal MP for Merioneth, claimed in the
House of Commons:

> But I venture to say that, with regard to the vast mass of perma-
> nent improvements on the agricultural land in Wales, including
> drainage, fencing, and those long and dismal lines of stone walls
> to be seen in many parts of Wales, the reclamation of waste and
> marsh, manuring, chalking the land, I say the mass - the over-
> whelming mass - of such improvements is effected by the tenants
> of Wales. (96)

This was a gross distortion and bore no resemblance to the realities
of the situation. Estate rentals and correspondence, together with
the valuable statistical evidence brought before the Land Commission
of the 1890s, show that most landowners devoted some part of their
annual incomes to the improvements of their estates. The amounts
invested by the larger owners were indeed considerable, and only
small returns were yielded in increased rents on their outlays. Improvements were made for reasons other than the sole desire for
profit. Indeed, the Land Commissioners reported that landlords believed property-owning had its duties as well as its rights; they
also felt some compunction at the squalid lives of their tenants in
dilapidated farmhouses; and they found satisfaction in giving to
their estates an orderly, neat appearance. (97)

Welsh landowners were undertaking an increasing share of the
repairs and improvements on their estates from the 1820s. The
eighteenth-century policy of enjoining repairs on the tenants under
long leases had worked out disastrously in practice. Tenants had
simply allowed their buildings to fall into ruins. (98) Such was
the prevalence of dilapidated holdings that even when lives leases
survived, landowners increasingly undertook improvements themselves.
The necessity for extensive repairs owing to previous neglect was a

common theme in estate correspondence of the 1820s, 1830s and 1840s, as, for example, of the Bute, Chirk Castle, Ashburnham and Glyn- llivon estates. (99) In 1826-7 Lord Newborough of Glynllivon was carrying out massive repairs to his Denbighshire property. Substan- tial repairs were being undertaken on the Ashburnham properties in south Wales between 1830 and 1832, and on the Bute property in the early 1840s. Extensive rebuilding was commenced on the Edwinsford estate, Carmarthenshire, on the accession of Sir James Williams in 1829 and large sums were laid out over the next 32 years before he died. Buildings were erected and draining was done by a head drain- er, assisted by three or four labourers, all the costs being borne by the landlord. (100) In 1833 James Price of Glynllech wrote to Sir Charles Morgan of Tredegar concerning the lettings of the Palleg estate: 'The state and condition of the Houses, farms etc. are far superior to what they have been seen in memory.' (101) By 1848 David Davies of Froodvale, Cardiganshire, could write of south-west Wales:

> The improvement in farm buildings in this part of the country is astonishing within the last twenty years. The miserable mud hovels of former days are now giving way to neat farm houses all slated with good sized windows and the inside finished off so that it is impossible to satisfy the tenants unless some little is done for them. (102)

We have some evidence, too, that landowners and agents realised that outlays on repairs were all the more necessary because of the difficulties facing farmers in the years after 1814. Thus in a letter of 1817 written by William Jones, agent to the Glansevern estate, to his employer, it was urged that repairs should be done 'to enable tenants to go on and pay their way'. (103) Another means of keeping tenants in business during the difficult early years of the century, and so helping to guarantee landlord incomes, was by granting lime allowances. Such allowances were given in the 1830s, for instance, on the Cardiganshire property of A.T.J. Gwynne, Esq., and on the Nanteos estate of W.E. Powell. (104)

Details of the sums expended by landowners in the first half of the century are available for certain of the larger estates. On the vast Wynnstay estate the percentage ratios of the gross rents spent on improvements are summarised in table 3.2. Outlays on drainage were operative only from the 1840s. Most went on buildings and re- pairs and the percentage ratio of gross rent spent on buildings and repairs over these years averaged out at 8.91 per cent. On the Rug estate, Merioneth, buildings and repairs between 1834 and 1838 aver- aged 11.6 per cent. It seems that the amount spent by the large owners on buildings and repairs fell out at around 10 per cent in these years up to mid century. C.R.M. Talbot of the Margam and Pen- rice estate was exceptional among Welsh landlords in forcing his tenants, farming under yearly agreements, to undertake the necessary repairs and on this basis he reduced the rent (significantly) by 10 per cent each year. His reasons for this course of action are interesting:

> The man who lives constantly in a house and knows that repairs are upon him, and will be enforced, will naturally do a stitch in time to save nine, whereas if he has a hope that his landlord will repair for him, he will not be such a fool as to spend one

TABLE 3.2   Percentage ratio of gross rents of Wynnstay estate
spent on improvements

Year	% ratio on buildings	% ratio on fencing and drainage
1820	9.37	0
1821	-	-
1822	11.39	0
1823	9.85	0.68
1824	8.16	0.43
1825	10.69	0.23
1826	11.11	0.05
1827	6.65	0.12
1828	9.93	0.11
1829	15.24	0.45
1830	7.49	0.27
1831	6.78	0.07
1832	-	-
1833	9.63	0.01
1834	13.15	0.21
1835	9.90	0.19
1836	6.97	0.30
1837	5.98	0.07
1838	6.89	1.36
1839	9.43	1.03
1840	11.71	2.19
1841	6.86	2.26
1842	9.66	1.68
1843	6.97	3.89
1844	7.49	1.20
1845	9.90	1.36
1846	8.66	1.14
1847	8.03	2.21
1848	6.46	1.41
1849	6.52	1.31
1850	8.16	1.75
1851	6.95	1.52
1852	10.62	1.60
1853	7.55	1.22
1854	8.05	1.24
1855	9.19	1.14
1860	10.78	2.86

Source: Wynnstay Rentals.

shilling to save the landlord twenty, and as the latter will not
be called on till an extreme case can be made out, a much greater
outlay will be necessary than would have originally sufficed.
This did not work out in practice on the Margam portion of the
estate where tenants in receipt of the 10 per cent reduction still
asked Talbot to pay for repairs. (105)

Many landowners, however, neglected to make repairs and improvements to their estates in the early century. The steward of the
Cilgwyn estate argued in 1825 that the expense would absorb a large
proportion of the rent and that it was desirable 'not to increase
but to diminish the ranks of small holdings'. (106) Owners of the
smaller Welsh estates could not afford any extraordinary outlay.
Although estate accounts of the lesser owners, the gentry, are few
and fragmentary, it is clear from contemporary comment that many
small properties at this time were encumbered. E.C.L. Fitzwilliams
of Cilgwyn acutely observed of their owners in 1853: 'Each Welsh
gentleman is a petty prince possessing a little mind and not able to
see further than his nose with at the same time an unbounded opinion
of his own consequence and a vast amount of jealousy of his neighbours and but in general a very small amount of ready cash.' (107)
Samuel Roberts' strictures were thus largely justified with regard
to the small owners. Their poverty prevented them from adequately
discharging their duties.

The rising prices, particularly of livestock products, after 1853,
and the opening up of the remoter areas to the growing industrial
markets with the coming of the railways, presented Welsh landowners
and farmers with an opportunity for increasing their profits. Certain landowners realised that higher rents could be legitimately
charged only if they substantially improved their tenants' holdings.
Furthermore, in many instances, even on the substantial properties
where some progress had been made earlier, repairs were found to be
all the more weighty because of the neglect of former years, whether
owing to landlord or, as under long leases, tenant apathy. In 1866
Cawdor's agent wrote to him that '10 per cent should keep these
estates in repair - but 10 per cent per annum will not put them in
repair after the neglect of past years'. (108) Again, a report on
the Gregynog estate, Montgomeryshire, in 1877 showed the farms to be
badly in need of repair and the owner consequently embarked upon a
heavy programme of expenditure 'in order to prevent the farms from
being thrown up'. (109)

Increased landlord investment occurred basically on the large
estates and on those with incomes from mineral and urban property in
addition to farm rents. The owners of these had the necessary capital. As in the early century many of the smaller owners were poverty stricken. (110) In 1870 it was argued that there were three
great obstacles to agricultural improvement in Carmarthenshire: 'A
very wet climate, "heavily burdened estates" and small holdings.'(111)
This same poverty was alluded to by the 1870 commissioners in their
discussion on Welsh cottages: 'The great cottage difficulty is the
poverty of the landowning class, the possessors of heavily burdened
estates.' (112) Such encumbered estates, arising from the system of
family settlements, were not peculiar to Wales and until legislation
was passed in 1882 facilitating the transfer of land, landowners

were hampered in making improvements to their properties. (113)
Small Welsh owners had to meet the burden of settlement charges and
a rising cost of living throughout the century from estates whose
often infertile terrains meant that incomes were restricted by relatively low rents per acre, even though they were fixed at a competitive level. It is likely that the poverty of many small owners was
aggravated by poor management and careless accounting. Thus 'Old
Squire' Lloyd, owner of the thousand or so acre estate of Rhagatt,
near Corwen, Merioneth, which yielded a rental in 1872 of £792,
wrote to his son and successor around mid century: 'Know exactly
the state of your affairs and keep regular and intelligible accounts',
and added ruefully 'would that I had done so'. (114) Small owners
were thus too poor and ill-organised to invest in the development of
their estates.

The fact that Welsh tenants were particularly anxious to continue
on the 'family' holding may have allowed many of the smaller owners
to neglect repairs on their estates. Had new tenants (particularly
those with capital) taken these farms owners would have been obliged
to make greater outlays on repairs. This factor was explicitly mentioned in a letter written by the agent of the Plas Llanstephan
estate, Carmarthenshire, to his employer, in 1862:

Rees of Hendy called. I told him you would not let it under £150.
The family have occupied the farm for 97 years and you will be
invariably no richer in giving them a trial - the question of
repairs will be got rid of as they will be satisfied no doubt
with the present buildings which I am told are in fair repair -
they are, however, very old and all the roofs thatched .... If
a new tenant comes in I fear there will be great difficulty in
satisfying him. (115)

What proportion of their gross rents were Welsh owners spending
on the improvements of their estates in the second half of the century? Estate accounts show that the large owners were in many instances investing as much as 20 to 25 per cent of their gross incomes in improvement. The level of investment on the Wynnstay
estate, covering some 142,000 acres in five north Wales counties, is
shown in table 3.3. The capital input showed a marked upturn in the
early 1870s and, after falling off in the mid 1880s, reached a
record level from 1889, reflecting one aspect of the landowner's
attempt to come to his tenants' rescue in difficult times. Just
over 20 per cent of the gross rental for 32 years was spent, on
average, each year. The Land Commissioners commented: 'Nothing can
be plainer that in this estate of Wynnstay the landlord is to all
intents and purposes a partner with each of his tenants in an agricultural business.' (116)

Many other large estate owners similarly invested large sums of
money in their properties, for instance on the estate of Lord Powys
covering 45,000 acres (mainly in Montgomeryshire) quite considerable
percentages of the gross decennial rentals were spent on improvements over successive decades, as shown below:

10 years ending 1849:	13.39	10 years ending 1879:	27.88
10 years ending 1859:	19.92	10 years ending 1889:	28.36
10 years ending 1869:	23.67		

(Source: Figures calculated from statistics provided in P.P., XXXIV
(1896), p.270.)

TABLE 3.3 Percentage of gross rental
expended on estate improvements

Year	%	Year	%
1862	11.76	1878	26.07
1863	11.45	1879	19.04
1864	15.48	1880	21.08
1865	10.50	1881	22.80
1866	12.35	1882	19.40
1867	12.07	1883	18.41
1868	16.33	1884	18.99
1869	15.55	1885	18.45
1870	16.73	1886	17.58
1871	18.29	1887	17.42
1872	19.72	1888	25.18
1873	18.80	1889	32.21
1874	24.84	1890	35.15
1875	23.99	1891	27.72
1876	26.12	1892	34.71
1877	25.48	1893	24.61

Source: Calculations from figures
provided in P.P., XXXIV (1896), p.266.

Once again the increasing amounts spent from the 1870s are noticeable. The total amount spent on buildings and permanent improvements from 1840-91 averaged out at just under 25 per cent a year.
The Earl of Dunraven, who owned an estate of 24,000 acres in
Glamorgan, spent 27½ per cent of his gross rental on average each
year on improvements between 1872 and 1893. On Lord Penrhyn's
estate, covering 41,348 acres in Caernarvonshire and 2,625 acres in
Denbighshire, nearly a third of the gross rental on average each
year was spent on repairs and improvements. Between 1868 and 1893
an annual average of nearly 20 per cent of the gross rental was
spent on Lord Lisburne's Cardiganshire estate. Again, on the Gwydir
estate in north Wales just under a third of the gross rental was
spent on average each year on improvements between 1872 and 1893.
Exceptional sums were sometimes spent on carrying out improvements
on those estates which had been permitted to fall into a chronic
state of disrepair. For example, between 1886 and 1890 50 per cent
a year of the gross rental was spent on improvements to the dilapidated Garthmeilo estate of Colonel Lynes in Denbighshire and Merioneth. (117) Clearly, owners of the large estates carried out substantial improvements. It cannot be claimed of these substantial
properties, then, that the tenants were the improvers and that the
landlords confiscated the fruits of their labours.

It has been shown how on the smaller estates poverty hindered improvements. The poverty of most lesser Welsh owners and of most of their tenants meant that the two interests were 'almost always at clashing point'. (118) Thus small owners were prepared to take as much as they could from the land, while giving back as little as possible. Indeed, tenants of certain small owners were compelled in the last two decades of the century to carry out their own improvements subject to provisions made for compensation by Parliament.(119) But tenants, too, on small estates can be blamed for their unwillingness to pay an increased rent following improvements carried out by their landlords. Gibson observed in 1879 that 'tenants are not willing to pay landlords 5 per cent for draining' and increased rents for improvements in general. (120)

Estate improvements were made also from loans from the Government and public companies which became available from around mid century. Interest rates on these loans were low compared with the market and ample time was allowed for repayment. Welsh landowners took advantage of these loans, although the detailed information required about the 'whole' homestead on which certain improvements were intended meant that no less an owner than Lord Cawdor found it impossible to comply with such demands when he was in negotiation with the Lands Improvement Company in 1865. (121) The total amount borrowed by Welsh landowners from public sources between 1847 and 1892 was just over £618,000. (122) On an area ratio the amount of Welsh indebtedness should have been a tenth that of England and Scotland combined, but in fact it amounted to a mere twenty-fifth. If we consider drainage alone, under the Public Money Drainage Acts £4,000,000 were placed at the disposal of landowners in Great Britain. In England there were 1000 applicants who took £1,780,000; in Scotland 900 applicants who took £2,200,000 and in Wales (excluding Monmouthshire) 50 applicants who took £100,000. Thus Welsh indebtedness was a fortieth of that of England and Scotland combined. (123) Here, then, we have one more indication of the lack of capital in Welsh agriculture.

Once again, landowners were not solely to blame for this low investment. Tenants often refused to pay any interest and allegedly sometimes failed to keep the mouths of the drains open. (124) An example of this is provided by the conduct of tenants on the Ashburnham estate in south Wales. In 1887 a certain Arthur Read wrote from London to the agent:

Referring to what Mr. Pugh Davies says in his letter to you of 14 May as to the collection of the drainage money I cannot understand why there should be any demur on the part of the Earl's tenants to paying the interest. The money was borrowed by his lordship on the advice of his sub-agent and with the distinct understanding that the tenants would pay the interest and therefore I am at a loss to understand why they should accept the benefit and refuse to pay for it. (125)

Like their English counterparts, many of the large Welsh owners who carried out substantial improvements received only a small return in the nature of a rent increase on their outlay. (126) The agent of the Wynnstay estate claimed of the rent increases on that estate: 'the rent is only a moderate interest upon the amount of the owner's money that has been expended on the land and its

maintenance'. (127) Often no specific rent-charge was levied following these improvements, for rents were generally fixed on the large
estates on the assumption that landlords would keep up the farm
buildings. Thus Cawdor's agent wrote to him in 1866: 'Our building
expenses are very heavy and must be for some years I'm sorry to say,
if we are to maintain the advance of rents.' (128) In those few
cases in Wales where landlords by themselves undertook the drainage
schemes they charged their tenants a percentage on the expenditure
incurred. Thus on the Wynnstay home estate in the 1850s a large
amount of drainage was done for the tenants, and 5 per cent of the
sum expended was then added to the rents. But the general practice
in drainage was for the work to be carried out jointly by landlord
and tenant, the usual procedure being for the landlord to supply the
pipes and the tenant the haulage and labour. In such cases no interest was charged by the landlords for their outlay on pipes.
While tenants played their part in improvement schemes through providing the labour, it still remains true that large owners were investing large sums in their properties for small returns. Large
owners were distinctly uncommercial in their attitudes towards the
agricultural sectors of their estates. (129)

   The large owners whose estates covered the rich mineral deposits
in south-east Wales require special mention in this respect. As far
as the leasing of mineral royalties was concerned, they exacted the
highest possible payment. But these same owners treated their farm
tenants with an extraordinary degree of generosity and kindness.(130)
Such a situation was to be found on the Bute estate in Glamorgan.
Its historian has written:

   The enormous non-agricultural income of the estate made it possible to subsidise agriculture; rents were kept at a low level,
   expenditure on improvements continued throughout the agricultural
   depression of the late nineteenth century and, when attacks upon
   the Bute estate gathered momentum in the 1880s, no mention was
   made of the agricultural estate. (131)

It was estimated in the 1880s that the returns from the Bute agricultural lands were not sufficient to pay 5 per cent on the money
expended in farm-buildings and improvements. (132) John Davies
asserts that 'Over the nineteenth century as a whole ... the estate's return on investment through increased rents must have been
negligible.' (133) Similarly, Lord Windsor treated his farm tenants
with the utmost liberality. These landlords, possessing rich mineral
property, could of course afford to be generous in this way to
their tenants.

   Contemporary estate surveys commented on the improvements that
were being made on Welsh farmsteads late in the century, particularly from the 1870s. The Welsh Land Commissioners in the 1890s paid
tribute to the landowners who had borne the main expense of improving many Welsh farmhouses in the previous fifty years or so. Much
improvement was also effected in the last quarter of the century in
farm outbuildings, especially in the erection of Dutch barns. Slate
roofs had nearly everywhere replaced the old thatched roofs. (134)
At the same time, estate surveys and newspaper columns emphasised
how relative all this improvement was, for by the end of the century
the majority of farmsteads were still inadequate for tenants' requirements. This was particularly so with regards to the appalling

lack of drainage. (135)   Under-capitalisation was especially a feature of the many small estates.   By the closing decades of the century the cumulative impact of neglect over many generations of
owners was clearly visible.   Gibson claimed in the late 1870s that
there were 'scores of estates in Wales that require the entire
rental expended upon them for many years merely to bring them back
again into fair cultivation'. (136)

Landowners also showed sympathy towards their tenants during the
difficult years.   One way in which they cushioned their tenants was
by allowing them to run up high arrears.   Agents frequently informed
their employers that to distrain would result in the immediate ruin
of the tenants concerned.   Bute's agent wrote on 27 July 1822:   'I
am making application everywhere but the scarcity of money is such,
that the general answer is that they will pay as soon as possible
and if they are now distrained on utter ruin will be the consequence.'
(137)   To some extent owners had no choice but to allow arrears for
Welsh farmers were small and notoriously short of capital. (138)
Besides, it was often clear that to distrain or take other harsh
measures would achieve nothing.   In a letter of 24 February 1833
John Hughes, estate steward of Nanteos, wrote to the owner: 'If I
distrain no one will purchase for want of money to pay.' (139)   Furthermore, the effects so distrained often raised by sale less than
the sum of the arrears outstanding.   Thus when certain distresses
were made on the Glanllyn section of the Wynnstay estate in 1824
irrecoverable arrears resulted, as, for example, when the effects
distrained of Hugh Lloyd of Llawrybettws raised a mere £30 16s.8d.,
leaving an irrecoverable arrear of £113 3s.4d.   Indeed, in certain
instances on this estate there was no stock or property of any kind
upon a number of the farms, the tenants living by selling the hay,
subletting the land and taking cattle to ley.   One way of overcoming
the problem of recovering arrears on the Wynnstay estate was for the
tenant in arrears to be removed to a smaller holding and contracted
to pay the outstanding arrears over a period of time.   In other instances tenants were moved to smaller holdings and the arrears left
unsettled.   Thus Robert Roberts' widow of Lôn in the parish of Llanuwchllyn had 'six small children in great distress' and on Lady Day
1824 she was removed to a smaller place and allowed to take two cows
and her furniture.   £62 12s.6d. were left as irrecoverable arrears.
(140)   Thus many Welsh landowners, partly out of sympathy for their
tenants, and partly because they had no choice in the matter, allowed arrears to accumulate in times of difficulty.   Some, as indicated, were never recovered.   They realised at the same time that
such arrears constituted a deadweight on the shoulders of the
tenants. (141)

Besides permitting arrears, landowners similarly sustained their
tenants in hard times by allowing them to pay their half year rents
irregularly and at their own convenience.   Thus rent day would find
agents granting tenants an extension in the settling of their rents
until a certain local fair had been held.   The owner of the Slebech
estate, Pembrokeshire, wrote to his London banker in 1852 that both
great and small tenants 'think it is a great thing to have the
"Privilege" of trying the different Fairs, and so paying in driblets'.
In another letter he commented that (in Pembrokeshire) 'we take what
we can get, and when we can get it, and are much obliged'. (142)

Like their counterparts elsewhere Welsh landowners granted allowances in the difficult years. Thus abatements were given in the
intermittent crisis years between 1814 and mid century. Rent allowances were made on an unusually well-organised basis on the Edwinsford and Court Derllys estates in Carmarthenshire in 1822 whereby
tenants were divided into different classes. Edwinsford tenants
were divided as follows: first class (allowances from 10 to 15 per
cent); second class (19 per cent); third class (24 per cent); and
fourth class (25 to 30 per cent). (143) Abatements were made over
the two years from 1822-3 on the Wynnstay estate, and, in 1824, permanent reductions (often larger than the previous abatements) were
granted which were continued until 1842. In that year a general
revaluation was made and rents were once more restored to around
their pre-1822 levels. Reductions between 1824 to 1842 ranged between 10 per cent and 40 per cent, averaging between 20 and 25 per
cent. (144) A 'considerable abatement' was made on the Cilgwyn
rents in 1822, and in the following year Lord Kensington made allowances of nearly 10 per cent on his Pembrokeshire property. (145)
These allowances were understandably more generous on the large than
on the small estates. Small owners found it difficult to accept a
fall in income. Their position was typified by Mrs Paynter, owner
of a small estate in Carmarthenshire, who in 1844 wrote to her agent:
'I suppose I must agree to what my neighbours have done. Though
they having large estates or commerce to fall back on can much
better afford to lose it than I whose means are already so small.'
(146)
Large as well as small owners, however, failed to make adequate
adjustments in their rents during the crisis years of the early
1840s. J. Lloyd Davies of Alltyrodyn, Cardiganshire, urged his
fellow magistrates in 1841 that they should all lower their rents.
(147) Two years later John Harvey, the land agent, was advising
Lord Cawdor that a revision of rents was certainly demanded in south
Wales by the continued depression. (148) Part of the problem was
that landowners granted allowances as temporary abatements only,
which by their very nature could not wholly satisfy the needs of the
farmers. The valuer of the Nanteos estate wrote in 1843:
   I beg strongly to advise that the farms be at once let to the
   several tenants at the reduced rents I have named and not made to
   them as an annual allowance. This would give them confidence and
   induce them to cultivate their land with a greater spirit. (149)
Two factors, as we have seen, operated against widespread and substantial reductions. First, competition for farms induced landlords
to keep up rents and, second, the frequency of encumbered estates
and the unwillingness of the 'fundlords' to grant abatements on
interest meant that landowners simply could not afford to make
realistic rent reductions. (150)
Allowances were also given during the depression later in the
century. Their amounts varied from estate to estate and from year
to year according to local circumstances and the severity of the
times. A 10 per cent allowance was granted tenants on the Nanteos
estate in 1880-2. It then lapsed until 1885 when once again it was
renewed until 1888. The same allowance was re-introduced in 1892
and continued until 1896. In 1897 5 per cent only was allowed and
this was discontinued from the following year onwards. (151) This

estate was fairly constant in the level of its abatements but on some, like the Gregynog estate, far more variation occurred between different periods of the depression years. A noticeable factor was the raising of the general level of abatements on many estates in the second half of 1892, a time of very low livestock prices. The general extent of abatements ranged between 5 and 20 per cent, 10 per cent being perhaps the most representative figure for the whole of Wales. Permanent reductions, however, were a feature only of the arable districts of Flintshire, Denbighshire and Glamorgan. They did not generally exceed 10 to 15 per cent. (152)

Certain owners preferred to aid their tenants by giving them bones and manure, and expending sums in drainage, rather than by granting abatements. Such help in kind was often calculated to represent around a 10 per cent abatement. (153) Others granted this form of aid alongside abatements. A good example of the latter is provided by Lord Powys, on whose large estate of 45,000 acres, mainly. in Montgomeryshire, between 1886 and 1894, £9,491 was expended on drainage and £2,642 on bones and permanent grass seeds. (154)

Abatements were widespread among large and small owners, but there were those who refused to grant them. Charles Fitzwilliams of Cilgwyn thought that if he were to appear 'squeezable' to his tenants he would be inviting 'trouble all round'. (155) Again, Lord Stanley, owner of 5,600 acres in Anglesey, disapproved of abatements on principle, but this is hardly surprising given that his rental had not been revised over the whole century. (156)

Those owners of between 100 and 1000 acres who had bought lands in the sales occurring from the 1870s were the least sympathetic in these years. Many had come from business, had bought at inflated prices, and afterwards squeezed the rents to get a return on their purchase. Relations with their tenants were based far more on commercial lines. (157) Welsh landowners as a body, however, were criticised by the contemporary Nonconformist Radical press for their failure to make adequate allowances during the depression. It is now apparent that much of this criticism was ill-founded.

Even the substantial landowners of the principality suffered financial hardship in the 'Great Depression', owing to the decrease in the rental value of land. According to Schedule A of the Income Tax assessments there was a decrease of 23.7 per cent in the gross annual value of lands in England between 1879-80 and 1893-4 compared with 6.1 per cent for Wales. But the Welsh fall was higher than this because these assessments did not take into account temporary abatements in rent, very common on Welsh estates, and, furthermore, the assessments in Wales in former years were not approximated as closely to the rentals as in England with the result that the fall was not apparently so pronounced. (158) On the other hand, the Welsh decrease was understandably much smaller than England's, for the arable culture of many areas of the latter required far more substantial and permanent allowances than those needed in an area of small pastoral holdings like Wales. Besides the decrease in the rental value of their properties, certain landowners also incurred losses from the gifts of feeding stuffs and manures and from cumulative arrears in rent, some of the latter having to be finally written off. Also larger owners were increasing their outlays on improvements in the difficult years. Thus the net income of the

landowner fell off to a greater extent than is shown by a comparison
of the gross rental of the 1890s with that of the early 1870s.

The crucial factors determining the relative pecuniary position
of an owner in these depression years were two fold: first, whether
or not he possessed other resources of income or of capital beyond
the agricultural, and, second, whether or not there were charges
upon the estate, either as mortgage or family charges.   Howard
Davies indicates the stress imposed on the landowners of south-west
Wales at this time by mortgage payments.   The situation, for example,
of Baron Rudolph de Rutzen of Slebech, Pembrokeshire, was desperate
in the early 1890s when falling rents were not matched by a fall in
the rate of interest on mortgages.   Mortgage repayments at this time,
according to John Francis, the Carmarthen land agent, were crippling
the landlords of the area. (159)   If landowners depended solely on
their farm rents, while, at the same time being faced with mortgage
repayments, their position could be critical and often, indeed, more
serious than that of their tenants.

CHAPTER 4

LAND OCCUPANCY AND
SIZE OF HOLDINGS

I LAND OCCUPANCY

It is now clear that a high proportion of the agricultural land of
Wales in this period was occupied by tenant farmers as distinct from
owners. In 1887, of the total extent of cultivated land in Wales
and Monmouthshire, 88.9 per cent was occupied by tenant farmers as
against 11.1 per cent by owners. (1) The situation was similar in
England and Scotland. The percentage proportion of tenanted to
owner-occupied land in the former was 89.4 to 10.6 and in the latter
87.4 to 12.6. This high proportion of tenanted land in Wales continued with small variations until the years immediately following the
First World War, when, in both England and Wales, as shown earlier,
'a wild buying spree' led to a considerable increase in owner-
occupation. (2) Thus, for Wales, the returns show an increase of 36
per cent in the area farmed by owner-occupiers between 1919 and
1922. (3)
    During the nineteenth century tenant farmers in both England and
Wales held their land either by leases of varying terms or by yearly
agreements. In the eighteenth century the most common leases were
for terms of lives, especially three lives, and, to a lesser extent,
for terms of years. But by the close of that century leases for
lives in England were declining in favour of tenancies from year to
year. This general development was due to the fact that landlords
were reluctant to adhere to the long-lease system of fixed rents
during a period of fast rising prices. A more fundamental decline
in long leases in favour of yearly tenure occurred in the post
Napoleonic War period, especially in the crisis years of the early
1820s. Landowners now found themselves obliged to make temporary
abatements in the rents even of those who held under leases, while
the latter, in turn, were unwilling to risk the uncertainties of the
future at a time when prices were falling so drastically. (4)
    The change over from long leases to yearly tenure in north Wales
was in harmony with this wider movement. It was observed in 1810
that there were in Merioneth and Caernarvonshire still a few estates
which granted leases for lives whereas in Denbighshire, Flintshire and
Montgomeryshire leases had given place entirely to yearly tenures.
Anglesey, however, continued to favour long leases until about 1830.

The counties which first went across wholly to yearly tenures were, significantly, those in closest contact with English farming systems. (5)
    In south Wales this change in length of tenure was far less rapid. Comparing south with north Wales in 1814 Walter Davies wrote: 'Leases are much more numerous and much more in credit in this district, than that in north Wales.' Leases for lives were, nevertheless, giving way to those for terms of years, especially twenty-one years. (6) It was observed in 1828 that yearly tenure already prevailed in Monmouthshire, while in Carmarthenshire and Glamorgan leases were most commonly granted for terms of fourteen years. (7) In the west-ernmost county (Pembroke) at this date, leases for three lives were still predominant. (8) As late as 1849, however, Clare Sewell Read was still able to report that in south Wales leases were generally for lives. But he drew a distinction between the south-west and the south-east. Whereas the leases in the western counties were often granted for three lives, leases for the life of the tenant only and for a term of years were more common in the east. (9) Many land-lords had abandoned the practice of granting leases and let their farms from year to year. The situation was complex but the progres-sion was from long leases for lives to leases for terms of years and, finally, to tenancies from year to year.
    The fact that leases for lives fell in at different times through-out the nineteenth century meant that even on a single estate no clear-cut abandonment of leases in favour of yearly tenures could occur in a short space of time. Albeit, by the late 1850s yearly tenancies were the most common throughout the whole of Wales. The absence of leases in north Wales was commented upon in the 'Baner' on 7 October 1857. In the first edition of Dixon's 'Law of the Farm', published in 1858, it was stated that in north Wales yearly tenancy generally prevailed. Leases for one or two lives and for seven, fourteen and twenty-one years were not uncommon in Cardigan-shire and Pembrokeshire. But in these counties leases for lives were not so general as they had been formerly and the usual tenancy was from year to year. In south and east Glamorgan leases for seven or fourteen years were still common, but in the west of the county leases were the exception. Leases had become uncommon in Carmarthen-shire, were exceptional in Monmouthshire, and were not mentioned in Radnorshire and Brecknockshire. (10) By the late nineteenth century leases were extremely rare.
    The substitution of yearly agreements for leases met with little opposition from the tenant farmers. When yearly agreements had become the norm by the late nineteenth century tenants rarely asked for leases. Landlords, for their part, were generally willing to grant leases to any tenants who desired them. (11) In 1880 Garnon Williams, a Brecknockshire landowner, stated: 'Farms are not generally let on lease in this neighbourhood. I have made it known that I would grant leases if desired, but I find that my tenants as a rule prefer yearly takings.' (12) On the other hand, the fact that landlords saw fit to adopt and to continue with yearly tenan-cies points to their predilection for this system. It is necessary at this stage to determine the reasons for this preference for yearly tenure. In so doing some of the advantages and disadvantages of the old leasehold system will emerge.

Tenants were generally reluctant at times of uncertainty and price fluctuations to tie themselves to the payment of a fixed long-term rent. The long, if broken, period of depressed prices for farm produce from 1814 to mid century impressed upon tenants the futility of binding themselves to long-term leases. This was a grievance of certain farmers in south-west Wales at the time of Rebecca: 'Some of the renters of land who have been before the Commissioners have stated that they held leases upon three lives which were taken when prices were very high.' (13) In the last decade of the century the agent for the Wynnstay estate claimed that in such a time of uncer-tainty it was unlikely that tenants would agree to take their farms under long leases. (14) Again, and connected with this first objec-tion, tenants disliked the general rule whereby reductions and abate-ments of rent at times of crisis were far less frequent under leases than under yearly agreements. (15) Tenants were also averse to the general practice of being charged an increased rent as a kind of premium for a lease. The underlying psychology here was examined by Gibson in 1879:

> He will admit perhaps (under yearly tenure) that his rent will be raised 2 or 3 times probably in the course of the next twenty years, but that does not seem to him a good reason for not avoid-ing the increase as long as possible. (16)

Another unattractive feature of leases from the tenants' point of view was their covenanting the lessee to do the necessary repairs. By the 1870s, also, much of the land of Wales had been so worked out that a large injection of capital would have been necessary to re-store it to fertility, and tenants realised that the longest type of lease then available, that for twenty-one years, gave insufficient time to recover the outlay. (17)

Landlords, for their part, saw certain disadvantages in leases. Some of them sentimentally objected that leases introduced commer-cial principles, and that they questioned the landlord's honour which, once given, should be accepted as the best of all securities. 'The word of Sir Watkin is as good as law, there is no need for any leases on my estates' was allegedly a frequent saying of one of the Wynns of Wynnstay. (18) By the end of the eighteenth century, also, landlords were fast realising that leases tended to produce careless and wasteful tenants who, secure in their holdings, neglected to cultivate their lands to the best advantage. The frequent uneconom-ic rents charged under long leases was another factor hindering enterprise. Clare Sewell Read remarked of south Wales in 1849: 'cheap leases made the Welsh tenant indolent and careless and that an increase of rent has bettered his condition by making him a more active and industrious tenant'. Furthermore, in times of depression the landowner could do very little about the leaseholder. Lewis Pryse Jones, owner of the Glanranell estate in north Carmarthenshire, wrote to his agent in March 1825:

> I have never known an instance when the benefit has not been altogether on the side of the Tenant, and to the disadvantage of the landlord. The Lease is binding on the latter 'only' in effect. In good times all is well perhaps; but when the markets are low and land is neglected, or the farm thrown up. And what remedy has the landlord? None, for in all probability he has a bankrupt to deal with, and if he holds on to the end of his term,

the farm is generally given up in a state of exhaustion, dilapi-
dation and waste. (19)

Political motives, too, may have influenced landlords in their substitution of yearly tenures for leases. Leases for lives had been
popular before 1832 because the lessee, in the eyes of the law a
freeholder, possessed greater electoral privileges than a yearly
tenant, or even than a lessee for a term of years. (20) But after
the widening of the suffrage in 1832 it was politically in the landowners' interest to substitute for these long leases yearly agreements which would enable them to exercise greater power over their
tenants at election times. (21)

Under the system of yearly tenure the landlord and tenant signed
an agreement which was binding for a year only. Written agreements
were found on most estates towards the end of the nineteenth century,
but they were less common in earlier years. In the absence of written agreements verbal ones were the rule and were to be found in the
1890s, for instance, on the Cawdor and Edwinsford estates in Carmarthenshire, throughout the whole of Brecknockshire, and in the adjacent districts of the Swansea Valley and the Vale of Neath. (22)
The lack of written agreements met with criticism at the time, but
the virtual practice of hereditary succession on many estates and
the continuance of the same rent amongst a particular family as an
old standing arrangement meant that there was no urgent necessity
for putting well-known conventions into writing. Sir J.R. Bailey,
owner of the Glanusk estate, Brecknockshire, referring to the absence of written agreements in his county, asserted: 'The tenants
do not like them. They have always had an agreement under what they
consider a well-known custom. They know they will be fairly treated
and do not wish for agreements.' (23) Significantly, there was a
tendency to adopt a written instead of a parole agreement when a
change of tenancy occurred other than one of hereditary succession.
(24) Nor can the accusation made at the time that tenants suffered
injustice by not being given copies of their written agreements be
wholly accepted, for many owners and agents, in reply, stated that
copies were both given and explained, where necessary. There were
numerous instances, too, where a tenant, having been offered an
agreement, declined to accept it, preferring to go on in the old
style. (25) The fact, however, that on a handful of estates only
were written agreements printed in Welsh undoubtedly created difficulties for a sizeable group of monoglot Welsh tenants. (26)

Tenancy from year to year did not result in holdings frequently
changing hands. It is a remarkable feature of Welsh land tenure
throughout the century that families remained tenants on the same
farms from generation to generation. G.K. Moore, steward of the
Ashburnham Carmarthenshire estate, wrote to his employer in 1851
concerning compensation to be paid tenants by railway companies: 'I
have said to Mr. Jones that I hoped the company would treat the tenants liberally, for although they were tenants at will experience
had proved they might be tenants for life.' (27) At the close of
the century it was stated of the Wynnstay estates in north Wales:

> The custom of continuous family succession in tenancy has always
> been a predominant feature of this estate .... When there is a
> member of the family eligible to succeed, the preference is given
> to him or her ungrudgingly, and I cannot record any case where

the widow was not allowed to succeed her deceased husband if she
so wished, or, failing her, the son or other near relative. (28)
The same tendency prevailed on most other large estates in Wales and
it was frequently at work on smaller estates as well. Furthermore,
through intermarriage of families, some Welsh estates were virtually
in the occupation of one family. Gibson observed in 1879: 'these
intermarriages go on from generation to generation and owners of
estates in Wales, rather than rudely break up these clans, put up
with the losses and inconveniences of a low state of cultivation.'(29)

If families did not always remain from generation to generation
on the same farm it nevertheless often happened that they remained
tenants on the same estate. Jenkins, in his analysis of one Welsh
farming community, demonstrates that the movement of a family between farms of different sizes was a vital way in which the change in
composition and requirements of the family over time (mainly induced
through marriage of farm children) were accommodated to the needs of
the farm. The farmer was identified in the community above all as
belonging to a certain kin group, and an essential function of kinship was that it facilitated such family movements between farms of
different size. (30) This was dependent, of course, on the co-operation of the landlord. Furthermore, it will be recalled that the
owner of Wynnstay (and probably others) allowed tenants in severe
difficulties to move to smaller holdings.

Such pronounced tendencies towards hereditary family succession
was primarily a consequence of the Welsh people's passionate sentimental attachment to the family homestead. Thus cases arose on the
Wynnstay estate in the late century where tenants doggedly refused
to quit dilapidated homesteads in order to move to new buildings
nearby. (31) It also stemmed to some extent from sentimental ties
between tenants and gentry families of old Welsh stock. Even after
the uncompromising rejection of gentry political and social leadership in the 1880s and 1890s their personal popularity often continued intact. Llywelyn Williams, a Welsh Radical witness before the
Land Commission of the 1890s, conceded: 'The tenants have certainly
never shown any lack of respect, loyalty, and even affection for
their landlords.' (32) It has been shown that the old families, for
their part, indulged tenants' fretful longing to continue in the
family homestead.

Changes of tenancy became more frequent from the 1870s than had
hitherto been the case. The situation continued stable on the consolidated nuclei of the large estates, but on the smaller and more
scattered properties certain factors now came into operation to
force an increasing number of tenants off their holdings. Many
owners of properties of under a thousand acres or so failed for one
reason or another to grant suitable rent abatements in the periodic
difficult years after 1878. Tenants were forced, therefore, to
leave their farms voluntarily or after receiving notice to quit. (33)
Such evictions naturally produced feelings of insecurity, well-
founded or otherwise, among neighbouring farmers. More important in
causing increased changes of tenure and consequent feelings of insecurity in the tenant community at large were the growing number of
sales from the 1870s of outlying parts of the large estates and of
entire small properties. Freeholds of up to 1000 acres, it has been
shown, fetched high prices in Wales in the last decades of the

century and impoverished owners were tempted into the market. Farmers were occasionally given the first refusal of their holdings by
private negotiation, but property was generally sold by public auction. Although tenants were not usually displaced directly in consequence of such sales it frequently happened that the rents of
their holdings were raised so as to obtain a satisfactory return on
the capital represented by the purchase money. Changes of tenancy
arose from farmers leaving on account of such rent increases. (34)

The Welshman's passionate attachment to the family holding, together with the intimate ties of the local community - ties of kinship, the Nonconformist chapels and the language - partly accounted
for the raging land hunger of the period. At the same time it is
likely that attachment to family holdings by producing a high degree
of hereditary succession further contributed to land hunger because
far fewer holdings became available to 'outsiders' than would have
happened otherwise. In addition, possession of a farm bestowed rank
and status, and this was particularly so in Wales where the gentry
and squires had opted out of their 'natural' position as leaders of
the community. While residing for most of the time in their respective localities, they lived apart from the rest of the inhabitants,
expending much of their energies in shooting, hunting, fishing and
coursing and in attending petty sessions and vestry meetings (they
were usually more diligent administrators at a local than county
level). In this situation the farmers came to regard themselves -
and were acknowledged as such by their neighbours - as the 'aristocracy' of the community. (35) Finally, farm size played a vital
part in promoting land hunger for the small Welsh holdings meant
that even farm labourers could realistically aim at becoming farmers.
What pushed this propensity towards land hunger to a dangerously
neurotic level was the phenomenal rise in population.

Only one member of the family - usually the youngest or the one
who remained longest unmarried - could hope to succeed to the family
'patrimony'. The rest had to seek farms in competition with other
farm children and often agricultural labourers. (This frequently
entailed a long wait, the period sometimes being spent on the family
holding which consequently became overcrowded with married children
and their families.) (36) Such was the craving for land that appli-
cations for vacant holdings were often made with indecent haste upon
the demise, or, worse, even likely demise, of the former occupant.
In 1866 Henry Davies wrote to the owner of the Llwyngwair estate in
north Pembrokeshire that the tenant of Travelmych had died that
afternoon at about 2 o'clock. The lease of the farm was out after
his death, and Davies reflected: 'I should not wonder that there
will be several for it before he will be buried.' (37) It also
meant that farmers within their close-knit, intimate neighbourhoods
reluctantly stooped to dissimulation in order to obtain holdings.

The fact that yearly tenants were kept on for life on many
estates does not necessarily mean that at the time they felt secure
in the face of land hunger. It is fairly clear that tenants on the
large estates did not feel insecure, and did not live in dread of
eviction. They knew that their landlords were too good-natured and
honourable to turn them off their holdings, and consequently they
shared a general sense of fixity in the occupation of. their farms.
(38) This satisfactory state of affairs was probably absent among

tenants on lesser estates. Although small owners often allowed families to remain on the same holdings over long periods, nevertheless
many of their tenants very likely felt insecure, fearing that pressure for farms would push up their rents.

Farmers in these years did not generally live in dread of capricious eviction resulting from the political antipathy between themselves and their landlords. They could be threatened with eviction,
and sometimes were evicted, for voting against their landlords in
the years before the secret Ballot Act of 1872. But in the first
half of the century Welsh tenants were content to support their
landlords at elections, and actual evictions were rare. However,
the situation changed in the 1850s and 1860s, when the Welsh Nonconformist press and pulpit and, in particular, the efforts of the
Liberation Society, channelled traditional Nonconformist grievances
into a radical and distinctly Welsh political programme. (39) Conflict between tenants and their English-speaking, Tory, Anglican
landlords became unavoidable. The landowners' indignation at this
novel and ominous threat was reflected in a letter from E.C.L. Fitzwilliams of Cilgwyn to Lord Emlyn in 1852 concerning the parliamentary election for the Cardigan Boroughs:

> Mr. Richard Jenkins writes me that the preaching influence was
> exerted to the utmost at every place. If all Landlords do not
> unite as one man to repel the invasion in these Counties, by
> making their displeasure felt in the unmistakeable way of putting
> a termination to the connexion of landlord and tenant ..., and
> dealing only with (i.e. supporting) those tradesmen who will sup-
> port the landlords and their interest, they will be acting with
> great folly from a present feeling as to what is the natural
> course of proceeding for self preservation. (40)

Watkin Williams Wynn, owner of Wynnstay, wrote impatiently to his
son, Hugh, in 1858: 'What am I to do about Methodist Parsons?' (41)
The independence shown by tenants at the Merioneth election in 1859,
and in various Welsh counties in the elections of 1868, unleashed
the most vicious display of political landlordism witnessed before
or since in the principality, when offending tenants were evicted
from their holdings. K.O. Morgan rightly points to the portentous
significance of such evictions in providing the Welsh Liberal cause
with its first martyrs. (42) However, the number of such evictions
was grossly exaggerated at the time. Thus T. Mousley informed his
employer, Lord Cawdor, in 1869:

> There are some wonderful reports in circulation as to the number
> of Notices that we have issued - one is that I have served bet-
> ween 200 and 300. I believe we have served fewer than usual!
> 18 for the County /Carmarthenshire7 and 4 in Pembrokeshire. (43)

Moreover, it is important to recall that many notices to quit which
were served on tenants after the 1868 election were subsequently
withdrawn, one landlord instructing his tenant 'not to make a fuss
about the matter, as the notice was only given just to show who the
master was'. (44) Landowners and their agents defended their coer-
cive measures and threats as a legitimate counter to the 'chapel
screw'. Cawdor's agent wrote to him on 21 May 1869:

> It ought to be represented to the World that at the last election
> there was not more interference by the Conservative than by the
> Radical Landlords - with the freedom of voting by their tenants -

and certainly nothing to be compared with the systematic intimi-
dation of the Dissenting Preachers. (45)
Such considerations suggest that there may be some truth in Davies'
remarkable claim that the Radicals were 'constructing their myth /of
oppression7 before the election of 1868, for some of their speeches
and pamphlets display an almost masochistic desire for persecution'.
(46)

After the passing of the Ballot Act landlords rarely interfered
with the way their tenants voted. Besides the protection afforded
by the Act, strength of public opinion obviously deterred them from
taking intimidatory measures. Nevertheless, in one or two isolated
instances, owners continued to exert pressure. For example, coercion was brought to bear on tenants of the Picton Castle estate
during the unsuccessful election struggles in the 1880s of its owner,
C.E.G. Philipps, against the Liberal candidate, William Davies of
Haverfordwest. A sinister note was struck in a letter written to
Philipps in April 1880 by 'a friend': 'I beg to inform you that one
of your tenants by the name of John Evans of Little Temperness, has
voted against his landlord. I trust you will allow no time to slip
before Evans has notice to quit Temperness.' A few months later
Thomas Rowlands wrote to Philipps from Fishguard: 'At the last contest I was offered £3 to go to Solva to be out of the way - this I
refused - and am turned out of my farm at Penrhiew, parish of Llanwnda, and am at present without any employment.' (47) The few evictions that took place in the 1870s and 1880s were generally confined
to the smaller estates, however. One blatant instance occurred on
the Alltyrodyn estate, Llandysul, Cardiganshire, where the landlord
evicted not only tenants but also the preacher and congregation from
the local chapel. (48) To repeat, political evictions were rare
after 1868. Although T.E. Ellis, Liberal MP for Merioneth, constantly asserted that tenants continued to be evicted capriciously, and
so were afraid to appear on political platforms, such politically
motivated claims were based on extremely slender evidence. (49)

Nor did tenants live in fear of eviction as a result of their
religious persuasion. The Radical allegation that landowners joined
with the clergy to persecute Nonconformist tenants was largely ill-
founded. Even during the Anti-Tithe campaign of the late 1880s
there were at most only four cases where prominent farmers in the
movement were actually evicted. One such farmer was W. Watkin of
the Moat in the parish of Manafon, Montgomeryshire, and it is significant that the landowner probably gave notice to quit as a consequence of a visit from the vicar of the parish. (50) As Nonconformist tenant farmers were encouraged, sometimes pushed, into outright
opposition to their landlords by the Dissenting ministers with their
vendetta-stricken mentality so, too, were landlords occasionally
driven into open conflict with their tenants at the prompting of the
clergy.

It has been argued that pressure for farms probably played some
part in creating feelings of insecurity amongst tenants on the
smaller estates. Excessive land hunger also explains a number of
other features of Welsh agriculture. It meant, for instance, that
there were few holdings unoccupied even at times of agricultural
distress. This situation equally pertained to the many mountain
farms whose occupants, according to one land agent, 'even in good

times were able to exist with infinite difficulty, eking out a miserable and laborious life'. (51)   Thus the correspondent to 'The Times'
wrote of mountainous Caernarvonshire in the difficult years of the
late 1880s: 'There is not, and never has been, the smallest difficulty in obtaining abundant applicants for a vacant farm.' (52)   It
is significant, also, that in bad years farmers strongly opposed any
estate policy of taking farms into hand.   The agent for the Dunraven
estate, Glamorgan, where such a plan had been adopted, wrote about
tenant opposition to this in 1882: 'they wish in all possible way
to sicken a Landlord from keeping Lands in hand'. (53)   Similarly,
land hunger bred opposition to multiple holdings.   Resolutions were
passed during the Rebecca ferment that no man was to hold more than
one farm, and any transgressor was threatened with incendiarism.

Craving for land also explains why tenants so often took farms
without sufficient capital.   So acute was the shortage that it
became the usual practice to give three to six months' credit at all
sales by auction of farming stock. (54)   Throughout the century this
want of capital was singled out as a major cause for the low state
of farming.   In 1834 C.R.M. Talbot, owner of the Margam and Penrice
estate, wrote to his agent: 'Welsh tenants are not like English
farmers who bring a money capital with them on their farms.' (55)
Later, in 1843, John Harvey, an experienced south Wales land agent,
pointed to lack of capital as one of 'the real grievances of Wales'.
(56)   John Smith, Inspector-General in Bankruptcy, highlighted the
problem when explaining the agricultural failures in Wales in the
1880s and 1890s.   He stated:

  The most frequent cause I think is admitted both by the debtors
  themselves and the official receivers, to be the want of capital.
  I have taken out instances in the Carmarthenshire court.   One
  farmer failed with liabilities of £423, who was insolvent when he
  took the farm.   Another, who started without capital, failed for
  £695 liabilities.   Another who started with £100 capital, and
  whose annual rent amounted to £360, failed for £953. (57)

Other witnesses before the Land Commissioners stated that many
tenants took farms far beyond their means and were forced to make up
the deficiency by borrowing, the interest on the borrowed capital
becoming in effect a second rent.   The smallness of the holdings,
indeed, often tempted labourers to take a farm too soon.

Want of capital, then, was a fundamental cause of lack of success
in farming, and this was so despite the fact that less capital was
required in Wales than in many English areas.   Pastoral land was
less expensive to work than arable, and costs were further reduced
by the prepondernace of family labour.   Also, the general absence of
a tenant-right claim of outgoing tenants - an exception was the area
covered by the custom of Glamorgan - meant that little money passed
from the incoming to the outgoing tenant in respect of any claim for
tillage.   It was only the bare working capital, then, and that on a
reduced scale, that was required on Welsh holdings.   Major Sandbach,
agent of the Hafodunos estate, maintained that £5 an acre was sufficient on Welsh farms, while a farmer in Pembrokeshire believed that
on the poorer soils as little as £2 10s. was ample. (58)   This fell
far short of the English standard of £10 an acre.   Even so, Welsh
farmers still lacked capital.   The owner of the Cilgwyn estate wrote
to his agent in 1861: 'I suppose £2 /an acre/ is above the average

capital for a Welsh tenant.' (59)   Later, in 1882, Doyle observed:
'it is notorious that these small farmers will enter upon occupation
of land without as much as 40s. an acre to stock and work it'. (60)
    Landowners and agents endeavoured to secure tenants with adequate
capital. Agents of the large estates, when informing their employers about an applicant, invariably commented upon his or her capital.
On 20 April 1821, Cawdor's Stackpole agent wrote to him: 'Mr.
Powell of Trewent has offered himself as tenant for Bangeston Farm.
He is a man of sufficient capital and one who I have no doubt will
be very regular in the payment of his rent.' (61) Similarly, in
1863, the steward of the Ashburnham properties in south Wales issued
the following instructions concerning an applicant for the tenancy
of Blanly Farm: 'If he is a respectable person with sufficient
capital you had better see him at once.' (62) However, owners and
agents often realised that they had very little choice in the matter.
At the close of the century W.O. Brigstocke, a Carmarthenshire landowner, submitted that landlords in order to fill vacancies had no
alternative but to accept men with inadequate capital. (63) One
observer (Doyle) claimed that this was partly a consequence of the
'Welshness' of the rural inhabitants who harboured resentment towards strangers and so restricted competition from outsiders with
capital. Substantial owners accepted that their best course in letting small farms was to pay close attention to the character, thrift
and industry of the applicant. These large owners looked for capital (albeit often in vain), industry and integrity in selecting a
tenant rather than the amount of competitive rent he was prepared to
pay.
    Furthermore, allegations that landowners laid great store by the
political and religious persuasions of applicants were generally
untrue. A preference for Churchmen existed only on very few estates.
A notorious example is afforded by the Picton Castle estate, Pembrokeshire, where applicants to vacant holdings in the 1880s were
carefully screened. Sackville Owen, the estate agent, wrote to the
owner, C.E.G. Philipps, in 1886 concerning the vacancy about to
occur on Broadfield Farm, Saundersfoot: 'Morgan of Brains is a
Radical but who swears he voted for you - is the first applicant.
Howells of Jefferston, another Radical and local preacher, 2nd. and
Hughes of the Hill last.' In the following year a letter to Philipps marked 'private' read: 'Every person that I know have applied
for Norton, parish of Llanstadwell, are liberals and under Mr.
Davies, M.P.' (64) Such obvious partiality was possible only in an
untypical area like south Pembrokeshire where English was spoken,
and where a significant number of farmers worshipped in the parish
church. No doubt it was the overwhelming majority of Nonconformists
among the population that persuaded landlords to accept the fact of
a Nonconformist tenantry as unavoidable. It is to their credit that
they came to treat Nonconformity with remarkable tolerance, allowing
chapels to be built on their properties, for instance, under highly
favourable terms.

II SIZE OF HOLDINGS

Frequent reference in this study has been made to the small size of

Welsh farms. Sir Thomas Phillips exactly portrayed the Welsh situation when he wrote in the late 1840s:

> The Welsh farmer presents, however, a stronger contrast than even
> the Welsh labourer to the same class in England. He occupies a
> small farm, employs an inconsiderable amount of capital, and is
> but little removed, either in his mode of life, his laborious
> occupation, his dwelling or his habits, from the day-labourers by
> whom he is surrounded. (65)

The first body of statistics relating to farm sizes in Britain came
with the 1851 Census Returns. The figures show that 68 per cent of
the farms of south Wales were under 100 acres, 22 per cent between
100 and 200 acres, and only 10 per cent above 200 acres. In north
Wales 75 per cent of the holdings were under 100 acres, 16 per cent
between 100 and 200 acres and the remaining 10 per cent over 200
acres. These figures require careful handling for they were the
acreage returns of 'farmers and graziers' of the amount of land they
farmed. In this way the farmer, not the holding, was the basis of
measurement. It is likely, therefore, that a number of holders of
small plots did not make returns because they did not consider themselves 'farmers'. Had holdings been enumerated, no doubt the percentage figure for farms of less than 100 acres would have been
bigger and that for holdings of over 100 acres correspondingly
smaller.

Reliable returns are available from 1875. The mean size of Welsh
holdings in 1875 was 47 acres, and this remained remarkably stable
over the next thirty years. A comparison with England and Scotland
brings out both the smallness of farms in the principality and the
stationary average size between 1875 and 1905 (see table 4.1). The

TABLE 4.1   Mean size of holdings (acres)

Year	Wales	England	Scotland
1875	47	58	57
1885	47	60	60
1895	48	66	61
1905	48	66	62

difference between Wales and the rest of Britain would have been
even greater but for the large number of small holdings of under
five acres in England, and to a lesser extent also in Scotland.
Doyle observed in 1882 that gardens and small plots of land were a
common feature in the suburban districts of England but were notably
absent in Wales. There were only 596 market gardens recorded for
the whole of Wales in 1876 and 312 of these were, significantly, in
Glamorgan. (66) Furthermore, the proportional number per cent of
small holdings of between 5 and 100 acres in 1885 was appreciably
greater in Wales than in either England or Scotland: 65 per cent in
Wales as against 52 per cent in England and 53 per cent in Scotland.
The percentage of holdings above 100 acres was, conversely, less in
Wales than elsewhere in Britain: 14 per cent in Wales compared with

18 per cent in England and 19 per cent in Scotland. Finally, there was very little change in the balance of the size of Welsh holdings between 1885 and 1913.

It was estimated in the third quarter of the century that a farmer needed at least 40 acres in Wales to make a living from his farming. (67) Tenants of holdings of below 40 acres or thereabouts depended upon some form of supplementary income; indeed, frequently other jobs furnished the main income. A particular feature of Caernarvonshire and Merioneth was the large number of small holdings of between three and twenty acres whose occupants depended chiefly upon work in the slate quarries for their livelihood. They looked after their holdings in their spare time. Wages at the quarries paid the rent while the produce of the holdings - with the exception of occasional sales of calves and young stock - went to clothe and feed the family. (68) The greater concentration of the mining industries in south-east Wales within a confined area worked against the existence of a similar system of small holdings. Colliers and coal-carriers in the anthracite district of south Pembrokeshire, however, frequently farmed small holdings. Thus some thirteen men residing in the parish of Williamston, who were principally occupied as miners, were also returned in the 1851 Census as 'farmers' of holdings varying between five and fourteen acres. (69)

In the purely rural areas this same phenomenon of a dual economy was widespread in relation to holdings of five to fifteen acres or so, thereby permitting these otherwise uneconomic units to survive. In mid nineteenth century Montgomeryshire and south Cardiganshire, for example, men who derived their main livelihoods from occupations as weavers, blacksmiths, wheelwrights, butchers, fullers, flannel manufacturers, tailors, masons and carpenters, also farmed little holdings. (70) A.H. John has shown that from the 1830s the occupiers of these small holdings in south-west Wales also sometimes migrated in the winter months to Merthyr, and paid the rents with money earned in the 'works'. (71) An example of this is provided in the Cilgwyn rental for 1846 where the steward remarked of the tenement of Cwmdu in the parish of Llandyfriog: 'His wife promised to clear arrears when he returned from Merthyr.' (72)

One further consideration has to be borne in mind with regard to the size of farms in Wales, namely, that the official figures do not include mountain and heath land used for grazing. As shown, many upland enclosed holdings had attached to them extensive sheep-walks. On the vast upland reaches of the Wynnstay estate, for example, the total acreage held at the close of the century by T. Vaughan of Sychtyn, in the parish of Llanerfyl, was 1100 acres, of which 300 acres were enclosed and the rest sheep-walk. These sheep-walks were let at very low rents. On the Wynnstay estate in 1875, for instance, Edward Hughes rented 136 acres of Graiglwyd sheep-walk at £3 a year. (73) Holdings on these upland slopes stretched upwards from the valley floors to the mountain land above, and the farm unit was commonly divided into three: the improved land about the homestead comprising both arable and meadow land; poorer pasture fields flanking the steep slopes of the main and tributary valleys and providing the winter grazing when the moorland higher up was not available; and the moorland grazings, either as open common or exclusive sheep-walk. In a very real sense it is misleading to think in terms of

size when discussing upland farms. For such holdings with their
sheep-walks were not measured by the farming community in terms of
acres, but rather by the number of cattle or sheep they were considered able to maintain. (74)

One reason for the small average size of Welsh farms lay in the
system of gavelkind in the Welsh areas until Tudor times, whereby a
holding was equally divided among the sons upon the death of the .
father. For this reason farms were generally larger in the English-
speaking areas than in the Welsh districts. Equally important in
determining the small units in Wales, as in the north and north-
western counties of Britain in general, were the physical conditions
of the country. The infertile nature of the terrain and remoteness
from large markets made for the persistence of small farms and a
semi-subsistence agriculture. The more favourable farming conditions of the lowlands, together with the historical situation of the
'Englishry' influence there, promoted larger holdings than were generally found in the upland districts. The Vale of Glamorgan and
south Pembrokeshire were, in particular, two areas where the interaction of history and the physical environment made for larger farms.
Thus farms in the Vale at the close of the century averaged from 160
to 180 acres, while in south Pembrokeshire holdings were generally
larger than in any other part of Wales. To cite but one example, in
Castlemartin parish in 1870 of the total number of holdings there
were thirteen under 100 acres and nine above 100 acres. (75)

Land hunger naturally led to the farming community's viewing with
hostility multiple holdings and consolidation of farms. Multiple
holdings meant, of course, that the size of holdings did not necessarily dictate the scale of the farmer's business. Sometimes this
situation arose when a farmer held a second farm for a second son,
or a mountain farm as a bye-take for the sake of the sheep-walk.
While they were a rare phenomenon in the remoter Welsh areas they
were seemingly not uncommon in areas of English influence. Certainly this difference was the pattern which Griffiths found to be emerging in various Glamorgan parishes by mid century. In the industrial areas, particularly, multiple holdings were sought after in
order to exploit mining rights. Thus in the parishes of Llansamlet,
Llangyfelach, Llancarfan and Merthyr Tydfil the number of multiple
holdings approached 50 per cent of the total number of farms. (76)

Agricultural writers and estate agents throughout these years advocated the consolidation of farms. In 1810 Walter Davies emphasised that

> Were the uplands thrown into large farms, they would be taken by
> men of large capitals who only could afford to bestow on them
> that improved system of husbandry, which in their present neglec-
> ted state they stand so much in need of.

He stated that the common plea of the majority of surveyors of counties was 'accumulate them still in a quintuple ratio'. (77) In 1823
Jacob Nockolds advised Sir Stephen Glynne, owner of the Hawarden
estate in Flintshire, to marry adjacent small holdings so that 'one
set of buildings would be saved'. (78) Two years later the steward
of the Cilgwyn estate, Cardiganshire, was writing to his employer:
'it is desirable not to increase but to diminish the ranks of small
holdings'. (79) Cawdor's agent, T.T. Mousley, forcibly expressed
his dislike of small farms:

Some of the formidable hindrances to an improved state of agriculture in Wales, are the want of capital and agricultural education and enterprise. The great proportion of farms are small and
occupied by men who really belong to the labouring class, and who
too frequently have to struggle harder for existence than the
cottager who has his weekly wage to depend upon.

The remedy, he urged, lay in consolidation:

Landlords ought, by degrees, to merge their small holdings to
save themselves the perpetual expense of restoring so many homesteads, which would enable them to give better accommodation for
larger holdings, and thus making them more attractive to men of
capital and enterprise; if they do not, the country must remain
as at present, very little advanced from a state of nature as
regards farming. (80)

Some consolidation of holdings occurred before the 1870s in both
upland and lowland areas as landowners strove to reduce the costs of
upkeep of farm buildings and to introduce a more efficient system of
farming. The extent of the movement must not be exaggerated, however. It was reported of Anglesey, Caernarvonshire, Denbighshire
and Flintshire in 1870 that 'the consolidation of small farms is not
going on so rapidly as appears to be the case in England'. The same
commentator observed what has already been noted of Welsh tenancies,
namely, that, as a general rule, on the death of a tenant, no matter
how small the farm, the landlord permitted another member of the
family of the deceased tenant (should the family contain a suitable
person) to continue in occupation of the farm. (81)

The chorus of protest against the marriage of holdings was based
on the claim that those brought up on the land had a moral right to
remain on it for life. The Glynllivon estate steward wrote to his
employer, Lord Newborough, in 1827 about the proposed consolidation
of his Denbighshire property:

But if such thing was to be done there the dispossession of any
of the old families would create such lamentations and woe as
would be very likely more than what your lordship's feelings and
philanthropy could stand. Such doing is looked upon with a
degree of horror by the country people in general. (82)

The 'Baner' newspaper denounced it in 1857 as an 'evil on the increase at present'. Doubtless, the process caused much hardship for
dispossessed families and young married couples anxious for a holding; they either fell on the parish or left the countryside for
industrial areas. Some emigrated, chiefly to the USA. Consolidation was, nevertheless, sometimes done in the best interests of the
tenants. In the upland districts of Montgomeryshire, where the
grievance against consolidation was particularly felt, landowners
like Sir Watkin Williams Wynn amalgamated farms in the closing
decades of the century because they realised the impossibility of
living off such small holdings. Up to the 1860s tenants were accustomed to supporting themselves very much on what they earned elsewhere. In the years that followed, mechanisation changed the system
of harvesting in England; weaving, a mainstay of every farm family
in this district, as in so many other areas of Wales, had come to an
end with the reorganisation of woollen manufacture; and, finally,
threshing machines replaced the age-old use of the flail, which had
brought regular work in the winter months. (83)

Consolidation as deliberate estate policy slackened off from the late 1870s. Indeed, from then onwards large farms were in some instances sub-divided. Landowners realised that a policy of consolidation in depressed times was against their interests: it would result in decreased rents, for tenants with sufficient capital to take large farms were scarce. (84)

CHAPTER 5

TENURIAL RELATIONS

I CONDITIONS OF TENURE

The foregoing discussion was concerned with the general circumstances under which tenants held their land. This chapter examines
the more precise 'conditions' of this occupation as defined in the
contract of tenancy between landlord and tenant - by a lease or a
yearly agreement - and in the various local customs. Down until the
last quarter of the century there was an entire absence of 'statutory'
control of the relations between landlord and tenant.

It was maintained in the early nineteenth century that a period
of twenty years was sufficient to establish the validity of a custom
in any particular district. (1) Customs had grown up in the various
localities of England and Wales from the eighteenth century to provide compensation to outgoing tenants for unexhausted tillages and
farmyard manures. In some (though by no means all) areas of England
these local customs were extended during the first three-quarters of
the nineteenth century to afford increasing security for tenants'
improvements. Thus a report on customs published by the Central
Chamber of Agriculture in 1875 drew particular attention to the
marked difference between customs prevailing at that time and those
in operation in 1848 when Pusey's Select Committee issued its report.
(2) Customs, then, in some districts had 'moved with the times'.
Clearly, where new, more capital-intensive and market-centred farming techniques began to be employed the 'customs' were extended to
provide the necessary confidence and support to tenants to continue
in such a course.

The only area in Wales where a well-defined custom existed which
entitled tenants to compensation for unexhausted improvements was in
central and east Glamorgan. The custom advanced and adapted itself
in the early nineteenth century to the necessities and growth of the
agriculture of the district, and farmers were thereby given a strong
incentive to adopt the new techniques. (3) Elsewhere there was
hardly any custom at all, except as to the date of entry and a few
minor matters of a similar kind. (4) They were very varied and in-
definite, and failed to provide compensation for unexhausted manures
or feeding stuffs, outlay on buildings, or other permanent improvements. Many contemporaries attributed the backward state of Welsh

73

agriculture partly to the absence of such compensation. How much credence can be given such a view will be discussed later.

The Agricultural Holdings /England/ Act of 1875 was the first statutory provision giving tenants legal security for their improvements. Its fatal defect was that it was permissive, and landlords throughout England and Wales contracted out of its provisions. However, a few of the larger Welsh owners such as Lord Penrhyn, Sir Watkin Williams Wynn and Lord Lisburne, while excluding the Act from operation on their estates, introduced liberal clauses into their agreements for the purpose of compensating tenants for their improvements. (5) In response to the demands of the Farmers' Alliance, the effective remedy was provided by the Agricultural Holdings Act of 1883 which was basically a re-enactment of the earlier one, except that now compensation for tenants' improvements was made compulsory.

Everywhere in Britain the tenants' claims to compensation were frustrated after 1883 by the provisions in leases controlling cropping and the sale of certain produce. The Agricultural Holdings Act of 1906 removed this hindrance, for the tenant was in future to be at liberty to follow any system of cropping he pleased, and to dispose of the produce of his holding. An Act of 1908 consolidated the law relating to agricultural holdings and so saved cross reference to the various statutes passed since 1883. A Committee of 1912 was satisfied that by the Act of 1908 'full compensation was already secured to the tenant' in English counties. However, Wales was singled out for special attention, and certain additional items were recommended to be added to Part III of the 1908 Act. (6) These amendments were advocated chiefly on the grounds that 'the customs as to repairs and improvements' differed from the practice followed in England. It has been shown how Welsh tenants shared in the work of improvements by doing the unskilled labour and the haulage. The disadvantage this brought the tenant in qualifying for compensation was indicated by R. Edwards, a Merioneth tenant farmer:

I have done a good deal of draining, the landlord supplying the pipes and giving half the labour, and I providing the other half of the labour with the cartage. That at once debars me from claiming under the Agricultural Holdings Act, even if I leave in 12 months' time. Of course, if I left under five years I should be a serious loser. Again, a great deal is done with regard to building, and in that connection cartage is a very serious item.(7)

Cumbersome modes of procedure, loss of time involved, and a prejudice on the part of tenants, in some areas, towards the old customs, meant that the implementation of the 'statutory' provisions for compensation was far from being widespread in England. (8) In Wales the Act of 1883 was even less widely adopted. Tenants in Glamorgan were quite content to continue under the old custom, and the same held for tenants in west Monmouthshire who farmed on estates where a liberal custom prevailed. Elsewhere many landowners of the large estates framed agreements affording compensation in substitution for that provided by the 1883 Act, and tenants expressed themselves satisfied with such an arrangement. The Land Commissioners nevertheless criticised such 'substituted compensation' as circumscribing and limiting the advantages of the Act. (9) It is also clear that in many instances tenants were passive and indifferent towards the Act and made few claims under it. The Land Commissioners were

'struck with the fact that many tenant farmers appeared wholly igno-
rant of its existence and of its provisions', and attributed this to
the fact that there was no Welsh version. (10) A more likely explanation of their lukewarmness was the fact that many tenants were
notoriously short of capital and were characteristically slow improvers, farming in the tradition of the small family farm with
limited expectations of what they could or, indeed, should yield.
The cumbersome and expensive machinery of the Act was, again, unlikely to appeal to this type of tenant farmer.

In the absence of a well-developed body of custom, the relationship between owner and tenant was for the most part regulated by
contract. Down to the beginning of the nineteenth century there
were virtually no restrictions either on cropping or on the sale of
produce in most Welsh leases. Their main clauses were primarily
concerned with defining the respective responsibilities of the landlord and tenant with regard to such matters as repairs, and with
making sure that the lessee did not abuse the property. In the absence of such restrictions, tenants exhausted the soil and impoverished themselves by taking from five to seven or even eight corn
crops in succession from the same land. (11) The tendency was aggravated by the stimulus given to grain production by the Napoleonic
wars. Landowners, therefore, at different times in the early nineteenth century (the occasion often depending upon the expiration of
a long lease as far as south Wales was concerned) introduced into
their conditions of tenancy certain restrictive clauses binding the
tenant to a particular rotation of crops.

The introduction of a crop rotation onto the large Stackpole
estate of Lord Cawdor, covering some of the most fertile corn growing land in Wales, came in 1821. Cawdor's agent wrote to him:

It gives me great pleasure that I have been able to let the farm
of Longstone (parish of Warren) under an agreement for the tenant
(being a native of the county) to farm the lands in a regular
four-course system of husbandry which is the first instance that
has taken place upon the Estate. However I have no doubt Mr.
Young's neighbours will soon perceive the advantages he will
derive from pursuing a system so far superior to that generally
practised in the Country that they will be induced to adopt it,
and more particularly as he is a native of the country. I have
therefore no doubt in a few years by your Lordship's supporting
the Agricultural Society and by a strict attention on the part of
your Lordship's Agent in exacting upon the Tenants whenever the
opportunity offers such a system as is best adapted for the soil
that this district will become as well cultivated as any
country. (12)

The importance of the good example for others to follow is again
underlined in the agent's letter from Stackpole on 11 May 1820:

He /Mr Brown/ is very willing to enter into a lease for a term of
years and to be restricted from taking two straw crops in succession and seems fully impressed with the propriety of following
the turnip system particularly after seeing the result of that
practice on your lordship's farm and Mr. Dudgeon's and I have no
doubt his capital is equal to the undertaking. (13)

In this rich corn-growing area of Castlemartin a progressive system
of farming was being encouraged by example, and enjoined on the
tenants in their contracts.

Generally, however, the soil and humid climate of Wales meant
that the strict application of the celebrated system of eastern England was impracticable. In many parts of Britain there was a need
to accommodate the new system to the physical characteristics of the
area concerned. This was not given sufficient consideration by
Welsh owners in drawing up their contracts. The Welsh Land Commissioners claimed that clauses regulating cultivation in Welsh agreements were 'framed for the most part to suit a system of arable
farming, and many of them have no doubt been imported direct and
with but little change from England'. (14) Thus in most agreements
tenants were directed to follow the four-course system. An example
of this lack of modification emerges in the agreement given to the
tenant of Derwydd farm on the Derwydd estate, Carmarthenshire,
around mid century. In 1855 a report on this particular farm stated
that 'the arable land, in the hands of a good tenant, is capable of
being farmed on the four course. The present tenant has approached
this system but has not fully carried it into effect.' (15) In
April 1856 the tenant concerned wrote to the London solicitor acting
for the estate:

> With all respect to your opinion the four-course system will not
> suit either the landlord or the tenant in this instance or per-
> haps in any case in this neighbourhood .... I shall have to
> trust to the opinion and the discretion of my landlord as to
> whether he will enforce it .... Still I am willing to insert in
> lieu of this hard condition that I shall farm the land according
> to the most improved system of husbandry in this country. (16)

Similarly, in 1845 the tenant of Rhydypennau on the Bute estate in
Glamorgan forcibly expressed his dislike of 'covenants which are
usual in England where the highest cultivation is carried on by
tenants'. (17)

There were many other stipulations as to tillage: tenants were
forbidden to plough up permanent pasture and meadow land, and to
breast-plough, pare or burn any of the lands; two crops of hay were
never to be taken in a single year; no more than a specified amount
of grassland was to be mown in the same year; nettles, thistles,
ragweed and docks were to be mown in July and August of each year;
not less than a quarter of the fold-yard manure was to be placed on
the meadow and pasture land yearly; excessive application of lime
was proscribed; and all hay, straw, fodder, turnips, mangolds and
green crops were to be consumed on the premises and were not to be
sold, the idea being that in this way farms would be adequately
manured. Heavy penalties could be imposed for breaking any of these
clauses. (18) However, it was a general estate policy for many of
these provisions to be relaxed and overlooked from the late 1870s in
order to give the tenant a better chance to adapt to the changing
conditions of agriculture. (19)

They were undoubtedly arbitrary and oppressive on paper, and it
was claimed at the time that they stifled tenant initiative. (20)
However, landowners and agents saw the educational necessity for
them amongst a backward tenantry. Thus the second Marquess of Bute
wrote to his agent in 1845:

> As a general rule where tenants are less acquainted with what
> they ought to do, more stringent covenants are required than in
> an improved country, and the tenants should be bound to do cer-
> tain things in return for outlays by the landlord. (21)

Perhaps more compelling, owners regarded such restrictions as protection against careless and lazy tenants. The Baron de Rutzen of Slebech in Pembrokeshire wrote to his solicitor in this vein in 1832: 'How necessary it is to have something in black and white I have had a proof of a few days ago - when one of our tenants broke up a very fine meadow and that besides his due proportion!' (22) Owners rightly contended that these covenants were never enforced in respect of enterprising and diligent tenants. The clamour against them was nevertheless fierce, and can be explained only in the wider context of the Welsh Land Question in which all aspects of landownership came under attack from the Nonconformist Radicals.

Leases and agreements contained other important clauses like those relating to repairs (already discussed) and to game. The latter reserved for the landlord the exclusive right of shooting game of every description on his property. (The Game Laws allowed the landlord to make what conditions he pleased.) However, the Ground Game Act of 1880 limited this previous monopoly by granting tenants the right to destroy rabbits and hares on their holdings notwithstanding any provision to the contrary in their agreements. They were nevertheless understandably afraid to exercise their rights if their landlord was openly hostile to this legislation. Despite the Act, the Game Laws were weighted heavily in the landlords' interest throughout the century and inspired a deep loathing amongst the rural community. (23) This is not to state that Welsh squires enforced the Game Laws with drastic severity. The available evidence points to the contrary. Records of the Petty Sessional Courts show that in the Troedyraur, Cemmaes and Cilgerran divisions of south Cardiganshire and north Pembrokeshire there was an average of between one and two poaching convictions a year between 1880 and 1893; in the Rhayader division of Radnorshire there was one conviction a year on average between 1877 and 1894, and, in the ten divisions of Carmarthenshire there was an average of $3\frac{1}{2}$ convictions a year between around 1875 and 1894. (24) Matters were made worse by the harsh, insensitive attitudes of the gamekeepers, who, according to the Chairman of the Carmarthenshire County Council in 1894, caused 'more mischief between landlord and tenant than all the other causes combined'. (25)

Relations often deteriorated to the point of breakdown when landlords in the third quarter of the century increasingly took to breeding of game for the purpose of battue shooting. Game breeding in order to produce an artificial glut for mere sport did away with the former physical effort involved in hunting and shooting. It was rightly condemned by H.M. Vaughan as 'artificial, selfish and decadent'. (26) Increasing numbers of tame pheasants now destroyed crops, and the tenant was powerless to prevent it. Further harm resulted from landlords at the same time leasing some of their property to sporting tenants, who covered the ground with insufficient regard for farmers' fences and crops. Fitzwilliams of Cilgwyn recognised this when he wrote in 1872: 'You can tell him a Mr. Molesworth that my son Jack and himself will be the only ones I shall give leave to, but will not "let" the shooting to anyone as it is "when let" a barrier to getting "good" farming tenants to take the land.' (27) Evidence of the farmers' abhorrence of sporting tenants is plentiful. The general sentiment was encapsulated in the words of a tenant of a 300 acres farm in the neighbourhood of Llanbedr, Merioneth, who considered the sporting tenant 'the greatest hardship and the greatest oppression in the country'. (28)

Damage done to crops by game was a constant complaint before the 1880s, lowland farmers complaining loudly about rabbits and upland ones about grouse and mountain hares. Such complaints were wholly justified. Thus, in 1844 the agent of the Nanteos estate in Cardiganshire noted of Bwlch farm in the parish of Llanbadarn Fawr: 'The damage done this tenant's crops in 1844 by rabbits was very great and which I have estimated at £24 0s.0d.' The annual rent of this holding was £34 0s.0d. Again, it was remarked of Penyquarrel in the same parish: 'Very serious damage was done to this tenant's crops in 1844 by rabbits and I have calculated the loss at £90 0s.0d.' The yearly rent was £50 5s.0d. (29) Dissatisfaction with rabbits was partly dispelled by the Act of 1880, although friction continued on lands adjoining the home covers and (perhaps) also on the many estates whose landlords were allegedly hostile to tenants taking ground game. Furthermore, complaints of damage done to crops by pheasants and partridges continued down to the close of the century and beyond. (30)

Some landlords had come to recognise the problem of damage to crops well before the Ground Game Act. In the first place, compensation was paid to tenants although it is impossible to determine the adequacy or otherwise of such provision. (31) Second, a few owners like Lord Ashburnham in 1869 and Earl Cawdor in 1871 allowed their tenants to kill hares and rabbits on their farms. (32) However, in the interest of winged game they were forbidden to use a gun or dog. Such timely measures were exceptional and did little to ease the widespread tension over the Game Laws. The reactionary spirit of the landowning classes was echoed in the advice given Earl Cawdor by his agent in 1869: 'The propriety of giving tenant farmers the game on their holdings depends, I think, upon the Class of Tenant - and to grant the privilege to 9/10 of your Lordship's tenants would, I fear, encourage poaching and cause great annoyance to Gentlemen and bona-fide sportsmen.' (33)

Poaching was prevalent throughout the century and was usually done by labourers, cottagers and rural craftsmen. However, farmers sometimes defied the law, and this was especially the case with regards to salmon poaching along the banks of the Wye and its tributaries. The formation of the Wye Preservation Society at Builth in 1856 introduced a far more rigid application of the salmon laws, and those local inhabitants who had previously taken salmon from the Wye and its tributaries in the winter months without challenge were henceforth restrained from doing so. The determination of the community about Rhayader to resist what they considered to be a violation of their rights led to the re-appearance of 'Rebecca and her daughters'. They realised that only by operating in large gangs would they be able to intimidate the watchers along the river banks. Thus, in December 1856 a large gang of men, eighty strong, with blackened faces and dressed in women's clothing, marched around the market place in Rhayader firing guns, before proceeding to poach for salmon in a local section of the Wye. There they were joined by an additional forty or fifty men. When the steward of the local landowner, T. Prickard of Darw, attempted to interfere, shots were fired,

one entering his elbow. (34) The gang met again in 1858 after which
the area was peaceful until the mid 1860s. Then, in 1866 a midnight
affray occurred on the banks of the Ithon, a tributary of the Wye,
between poachers and water-bailiffs. In 1867-8 armed gangs 'burned'
the rivers Eddw, Irfon and Cammarch. A quiet period again followed
which lasted down to the late 1870s. (35) The renewed conflict between 1877-82 reached an unprecedented pitch, for now gangs of Rebeccaites operating in the areas of Llandrindod, Llanddewy, Llanbister,
Penybont, Llananno, Newbridge and Rhayader increased their membership in response to a still more determined effort on the part of
the authorities to stamp out salmon poaching. (36)

Here, on the Wye and its tributaries, resistance in large gangs
was as formidable as that experienced on Irish rivers. Gentlemen
with fishing rights were afraid to testify for fear of their cattle
being destroyed and their stacks burned. (37) These gangs were comprised largely of farmers, their sons and servants. While the farmers who poached the Cammarch in the 1850s were of the category who
had one labourer and a boy, some of those involved at Rhayader in
the same decade were the 'head farmers about the place' and, similarly, the poachers who clashed with the water-bailiffs on the banks of
the Ithon in 1866 were 'well-to-do farmers'. (38) Farmers elsewhere,
as in the area of the upper Towy and its tributaries in north Carmarthenshire, poached salmon in defiance of the authorities, though
with far less organised resistance and proneness to violence. (39)

Poaching of ground game, involving gangs with blackened faces
operating under the cover of darkness, was on the increase in Merioneth and probably elsewhere from the 1860s. Farmers' sons and
labourers were active participants. If the farmers themselves (in
most areas a noticeably 'respectable and respected section of the
community') seemingly refrained from poaching ground game, they increasingly came to give it their tacit support from the 1860s in the
face of the new and irksome 'sporting' system. (40)

Common to all contracts was the covenant binding the tenant to
the payment of rent. The history of rent movements was examined in
chapter 1. Attention was drawn to the crucial importance of railways in accounting for rent rises on most Welsh estates from mid
century to the early 1880s. The greater rises occurring on estates
in west Wales must be explained not in terms of the less sympathetic
Welsh landlords of that area compared with the more generous English
type further eastwards (an explanation favoured by Gladstone), (41)
but rather in 'catching up' terms, now that this remote area was
served by railways. Another important factor promoting rent increases was the charging of interest on permanent improvements effected by landowners. The problem that must now be examined concerns
the validity or otherwise of contemporary accusations that, first,
landlords raised rents following on tenants' improvements, and,
second, that they screwed up rents in response to land hunger.

The first criticism was made by many Radicals, including Samuel
Roberts in the 1850s, and T.J. Hughes (Adfyfr) and T.E. Ellis later
in the century. What needs emphasising first of all is that on
large estates it was the custom for landlords to help provide the
bulk of permanent improvements. Thus Ellis and others were inaccu-
rate in depicting a general situation in which tenants effected the
mass of improvements, which were thereupon confiscated by increased

rents. Second, although the system of yearly tenure presented landlords with the opportunity to raise rents on tenants' improvements,
this did not generally happen in practice. Despite Samuel Roberts'
claim that many tenants had been 'long relentlessly robbed of the
just fruit of their toil', (42) it was a certain number of small
owners only who confiscated improvements in this way. O.O. Roberts,
a prominent social reformer and Radical in the early century, struck
a likely balance when he wrote in 1850:

> Instances frequently occur where impoverished tenants have had
> their farms revalued, and the rents increased, in consequence of
> an improved value produced by skill and an extra outlay of their
> own capital. Such dishonest proceedings, it must be owned, would
> not knowingly be sanctioned by the generality of landed proprie-
> tors; but still such a course has been pursued by a less
> scrupulous section of landed proprietors. (43)

Where instances of this deliberate raising of rents were alleged
before the Land Commissioners in the 1890s, the majority were proved
ill-founded: in some instances witnesses were shown to be inaccu-
rate in their figures, while in others it was proved there were
special and sufficient grounds for such rent increases. Throughout,
the Radical indictment took no account of railways and the growth of
new markets in raising land values.

Nevertheless, tenants had some grounds for dissatisfaction at a
system of valuation which often did not take into account the value
of their improvements, but rather what the holding was worth to a
new tenant. Although the main factors promoting an increase in the
value of holdings in the third quarter of the century were better
marketing opportunities and landowners' improvements, there was,
nevertheless, an element of tenant investment which in this way was
unfairly ignored. (44) However, a number of large owners recognised
this, and fixed their rents below the level recommended by the
valuer. This happened, for example, on the Cawdor estate in 1863
when rents were reduced to 17 per cent below the revaluation price
calculated in the previous year. The agent explained:

> I had a great many things to take into consideration by Lord
> Cawdor's instructions - where there had been what could be called
> permanent improvements by the tenants, not exhausted, and when
> they had an undoubted claim, his lordship advised me, 'I think it
> quite right that we should acknowledge and make some allowances
> in our relettings'. (45)

The initial suggestion came from the agent himself, who had written
to Cawdor on 30 July 1863:

> Some of Mr. Hall's values in that district I find cannot be en-
> forced - without driving away a number of hard-working tenants.
> In many cases we shall have to deduct a percentage for recent
> outlay by the Tenants upon their houses and buildings. (46)

A similar reduction below the valuation price took place on Lord
Dynevor's estate in Carmarthenshire in 1874. Likewise, it was the
practice on the Wynnstay estate after the revaluation had been made
for the tenants to submit a claim for improvements to the landlord
'to be threshed out and settled'. Tenants' improvements were again
the grounds for ignoring a valuation of the Penrhos estate, Anglesey,
in the 1860s. Moreover, on the estates of Lord Penrhyn in Caernarvonshire the agent took into account tenants' improvements when

valuing the holdings. (47) Once again, then, on several of the
large estates the alleged confiscation of tenants' improvements in
the very process of revaluation was simply not true. Furthermore,
there were many estates which were not revalued. On these rents
were increased on separate holdings, such increases usually occurring when a new tenant came into the property. As far as the large
estates were concerned, rents were never raised on individual holdings for the sitting tenant or his family. Here, again, it is clear
that tenants' improvements were not followed by rapacious increases
in rent. Embarrassed owners of small estates, on the other hand,
were readier to accept implicitly the result of a valuation which
disregarded tenants' improvements.

      Although rents were not generally raised on tenants' improvements
as a matter of policy, rises of this nature frequently occurred once
lands had been sold. Much hardship ensued, and such suffering increased dramatically from the 1870s when growing quantities of land
came onto the market. When property changed hands by purchase the
land was often valued as it existed without any reference as to how,
or by whom, that value was produced. The purchaser proceeded to fix
the rents in order to obtain a satisfactory return on the purchase
price, and in this way the tenant's rent was raised regardless of
his improvements. (48) Some landowners recognised the unfairness of
this, and called for legislative action to secure compensation to
the tenant. P.P. Pennant, owner of the Nantllys estate, Flintshire,
urged an addition to the 1883 Act for this purpose. He claimed that
'This would obviate what has sometimes proved a source of misunder-
standing between the new landlord and the tenant. In fact, I believe that three-fourths of the grievances that you hear of from
tenants have arisen in this kind of way.' (49)

      The second charge against landowners was that they exploited the
land hunger by charging competitive rents. Owners of large estates
magnanimously did not exploit the feverish competition for holdings.
Indeed, on the substantial properties farms generally came onto the
open market only when no relatives of the previous tenants stepped
forward. Moreover, such a relative often paid exactly the same rent
as hitherto, which in most cases was far lower than its market price.
The owner of the Margam and Penrice estate, deeming this practice
harmful to agriculture, instructed his steward in 1829: 'I am
decidedly against that species of favouritism of letting a farm at
a lower rate because the new tenant is a relation to the last.' (50)
It has been shown that when a holding on a large estate became
vacant the agent made careful inquiries about the capital, integrity
and industry of the applicants. Colonel Cornwallis-West, agent for
the Penrhyn estate, insisted before the Land Commissioners in 1894:

      It has been repeatedly stated that rents have been 'screwed up'
      by competition. I believe that statements of this sort cannot be
      substantiated, but that on the contrary the oftener the facts
      connected with large estates are examined the more it will be
      discovered that tenants are selected from character and ability
      to farm well rather than from mere considerations of rent. (51)
Similarly, C.E. Morgan-Richardson, a land agent for various properties in south-west Wales, testified that on large estates a farm was
never let to a man simply because he was the highest bidder. (52)
      This did not necessarily mean, of course, that competition had no

effect on the level of rents charged on large estates. In some instances large owners or their agents deliberately refused offers
which they considered beyond the true value of the land. D.W. Drum-
mond, agent for the Cawdor, Edwinsford and Derllys estates, Carmarthenshire, claimed in 1894 that he had turned down such offers because acceptance would have harmed both parties. (53) On the other
hand, pressure for farms undoubtedly pushed up rents on some large
properties. Charles Bishop, agent for certain estates in south-west
Wales, claimed that the high offers resulting from competition led
some landowners to think that lands were of greater value than they
actually were. (54) The chief agent for the Wynnstay estate similarly admitted that in the years before the depression of the last
quarter of the century 'land went above its value' because of demand.
(55) The point needs stressing, however, that owners of large estates where rents were pushed up by competition did not exploit the
situation by bidding-up applicants, nor did they make the level of
rent their prime consideration. T.T. Mousley, agent for Lord
Cawdor's Pembrokeshire property from 1863 to 1893, in answer to the
question 'do you know of any farm let to the highest bidder?' rep-
lied: 'No. I daresay it very often is, if the highest bidder hap-
pens to be the best man, it is very natural that he should be the
accepted tenant; it does not follow that because he is the highest
bidder he should be accepted.' (56) In certain instances, then,
rents on large estates were fair, even lenient when holdings stayed
within the same family and were not revalued as part of a general
estate reassessment. In others, they were admittedly affected by
competition. But no evidence has been found that large estate
owners deliberately forced up rents in the face of competition for
holdings.

Land hunger had a positively harmful effect on the level of rents
charged on the frequently encumbered smaller estates of under 1000
acres or so. Their impoverished, needy owners were all too ready to
avail themselves of offers of increased rents. Here, the level of
rent was the first consideration, and farms went to the highest bid-
ders. (57) Nevertheless, it is doubtful if these small, impoverished owners ruthlessly manipulated the desperate struggle for holdings. The 'Cambrian News', the farmers' weekly in mid and west
Wales, reflected in 1892:

Landowners in Wales have been so long accustomed to competition
for their farms that they are somewhat astonished they have not
been less moderate. They feel that they might have imposed still
harder conditions and have demanded much higher rents. They know
that they have abstained from extorting all that they might have
extorted and they feel that they are not therefore the rapacious
monsters they are sometimes represented to be. We have never
represented Welsh landlords as exceptionally tyrannical, or
exacting or cruel. (58)

The worst type of small landlord was not the hereditary Welsh
kind whose only real sin, apart from pride, was, as Howard Davies
suggests, poverty, (59) but rather the newcomer owning small properties of between 100 and 1000 acres. Unlike hereditary owners, such
people regarded land as a purely commercial investment. The situation in Wales was aggravated because capital values were kept up by
land hunger. The fourth Lord Sudeley, the Liberal Unionist owner of

Gregynog, wrote to the secretary of the Welsh Landowners' Defence
Association in 1892 that it was on estates belonging to this category of owner that cases of tenant hardship were likely to turn up
in the course of the Land Commission's inquiry. (60) His hunch was
sound. An experienced south Pembrokeshire valuer, Rule Owen, thus
informed the Commissioners that the highest rents in his district
were on the estates whose owners had made their money in other busi-
nesses 'and have been accustomed to good percentages'. (61)

In addition to money rents there were other duties and services
in kind, survivals of an earlier non-monetary economy. By the nineteenth century they had become vexatious to tenants as symbolising a
certain degree of servility. (62) These payments were divisible
into two broad categories of food rents and service rents. The
former, including pullets, hens, geese or capons, had to be presented to the landlord at certain times of the year, and survived in
south-west Wales down to the close of the century. Elsewhere, they
were gradually commuted to money payments. Service rents mainly
involved team-work for haulage, and these survived on most estates
until the close of the century. Another duty commonly enjoined down
the early 1880s was that tenants should send their corn to be ground
at the lord's mill. Again, there were duties or services connected
with hunting and game preservation. The commonest of these was that
of rearing a dog for the landlord, or of walking a hound puppy for
him. O.O. Roberts claimed in 1850 that the annual cost of rearing
and keeping a fox-hound was at least equivalent to the sum required
for rearing and fattening two pigs, each of twenty score weight.(63)

Finally, tenant farmers had to pay tithes, local taxes and rates.
At the opening of the century tithes were either raised in kind or
commuted to money payments. Agricultural writers were urging commutation as a way of removing an obstacle to improvement. (64) With
the coming of widespread commutation, however, it was found that the
tenant would often prefer to pay in kind, as this afforded some
opportunity to bargain with the collector. Furthermore, the peasant
economy which prevailed at this time involved only a limited use of
money on the part of the tenantry. The Tithe Commutation Act of
1836 increased the payment by 7 per cent in south Wales. But considering the previous low level of tithes in this area, and the fact
that parochial rates were now included in the tithe payment, the
legislation of 1836 did not impose, as was then claimed, an unfair
financial increase on the tenant community. (65) The misfortune was
that the demand for money payments came at a time of agricultural
depression and consequent acute shortage of circulating coinage.
Sir James Graham made another important observation concerning the
resentment towards tithes in south Wales:

> The complaint may probably be traced to the payment of the Rent
> charge by the occupier in South Wales, whereas in many districts
> of England this burthen is now borne by the landlord, who, by
> undertaking it, renders the collection easy and is enabled to let
> his land free from tithe. (66)

Perhaps most important of all, opposition to tithes was becoming
increasingly based on religious principle. Nonconformist farmers
resented paying tithes to support the Anglican Church. And, as K.O.
Morgan observes, the 'chagrin of paying tithe to the Church of an
acknowledged minority of the population infused religious protest
with national sentiment'. (67)

Payment of tithes was one of the chief grievances of Rebecca's
followers. Indeed, an acute observer of south-west Wales, Edward
Lloyd Hall, wrote to Sir James Graham in 1843: 'I find the tithes
excite the greatest dislike, then poor rates (church rates they
hardly know anything about) and then the high amount of the rents.'
(68) Opposition to the system grew steadily with the greater poli-
ticisation of the community in the second half of the century. The
tithe disturbances later in the century significantly coincided with
the acute fall - by at least a third - in price of stock in 1885 and
1886. The farmers were aggrieved that although the tithe rent
charge had fallen, it had not dropped sufficiently because of the
operation of the seven years' average. (69) The first agitation towards procuring a reduction occurred in January 1886 in Denbighshire,
and especially at Llandyrnog. The farmers' requests were refused,
and the first distraints were made later in the year on 17 August at
the village of Llanarmon. As a consequence of this the Anti-Tithe
League came into being at a farmers' meeting at Ruthin in early September. (70) The League's original aims were claimed to be economic,
to support the farmers in their efforts at gaining tithe rebates.(71)
But a spokesman for the League maintained that events soon led to a
change in its overriding objective whereby the initial agitation for
a rebate developed into opposition to tithe on principle. (72) He
declared that 'there is a great difference in the views of the
people now to what there was when the League was formed. Now a
great many people would resist the tithes in principle that it goes
to an alien church.' (73) Farmers and others admitted before the
Tithe Inquiry that they desired the tithe should be devoted to
national objects like the maintenance of the poor and education.

The League attributed the cause for this switch in objectives to
the refusal of the clergy to listen to appeals for reductions and to
the irregularity of the proceedings of the Ecclesiastical Commissioners in making distress sales. There can be no doubt that the resistance of the clergy and the subsequent conduct of the Ecclesiastical
Commissioners in distraining under police and sometimes military
protection, proved highly provocative and an incitement to mob riots.
But this explanation for the move to principle from the original
sole economic aim is open to doubt in so far as the leadership was
concerned. It is likely that the latter aimed at resisting payment
of tithe on principle from the outset. Of great importance in encouraging the farmers actively to oppose tithes on principle were
the Nonconformist preachers, and it is no accident that the first
protest and the subsequent Anti-Tithe League came into being in the
locality of the most powerful and influential of Welsh Calvinistic
leaders, the Rev. Thomas Gee. His hatred of payment of tithe to an
alien Church was intense. He exerted a powerful influence over the
Anti-Tithe League - his son, Howell, was its secretary - and it is
therefore likely that from the beginning the officers of the League
aimed at disestablishment and disendowment. The Nonconformist
leadership of the League seized upon the distressed economic situation as an opportunity for advancing sectarian and political ends.
Farmers who all along resented tithes on religious grounds were now
particularly malleable.

Despite Gee's widespread prestige, Dunbabin may well be right in
claiming that the troubles which took place outside Denbighshire -

in Flintshire, Anglesey, Caernarvonshire, Merioneth, Cardiganshire,
and to a lesser extent, in Carmarthenshire and north Pembrokeshire -
were locally inspired. He demonstrates that the central League did
not fully dominate local branches. (74) But in all areas the role
of local Nonconformist preachers was a crucial factor. Their preaching against payment of tithes to an alien Church was a highly attractive message to a Nonconformist farming community feeling the pinch
of agricultural depression. The activities of the preachers in
south-west Wales were feelingly referred to in a letter written by
Lord Dynevor in 1886:

> Our tenants here are well affected towards their Landlords and
> would not join the Farmers' Alliance some years ago. The Tithe
> Question, however, is very dangerous. All our tenants are Dis-
> senters. The attack on the Tithe and the Church is most taking
> with them and advocated from all the Dissenting Pulpits. (75)

Thus the Welsh 'Tithe War' grew out of a mix of economic and
religious grievances. Of the two it was the religious which was the
more important. Dunbabin shows that south-east England was more
heavily tithed than Wales, and agricultural depression was more
keenly felt there. Yet the amount of opposition to tithes in England at this time was far less than in Wales. (76) Religion was
therefore the controlling factor, and here the role of the Welsh
Nonconformist leaders was vital. After the passing of the Tithe
Rent Charge in 1891 most of the unrest ceased, although disturbances
continued in south Cardiganshire, particularly in the parish of Pen-
bryn, until 1895. (77) Tithes were now recognised as the responsibility of the landlord. However, the situation remained virtually
unchanged for henceforth the tithe charge was included in the rent.

There was considerable variation in practice from area to area as
to the payment of taxes and rates. A common arrangement seems to
have been for the tenant to pay the land tax and all the local rates,
and the landlord the income tax. Complaints were made by the tenant
farmers throughout these years of the burdensome nature of these
taxes. In the early nineteenth century the rise in poor rates and
other parochial taxes weighed heavily upon the tenant community. (78)
One observer writing of south Wales in 1846 referred to 'the difficulty of finding wherewithal to meet the continual demand of local
taxation'. (79) This mounting taxation understandably formed a
major grievance of the farmers of south-west Wales when they struck
out in 1842-3.

II THE LAND QUESTION

> The Welsh aspect of the Land problem cannot be dallied and
> trifled with without danger: it is about the most urgent ques-
> tion of the day, and, unless it is equitably settled, it will
> also speedily become the one question of the 'night'.

Thus wrote T.J. Hughes (Adfyfr), one of the redoubtable champions
of the Welsh land reform movement of the last two decades of the
nineteenth century. He subjected 'Landlordism' in Wales to a sear-
ing attack from a burning conviction that it 'dwarfs and blights
everywhere our national growth'. (80) Equally harsh in its criticism of Welsh landlords was the Welsh Nonconformist vernacular press,

notably the 'Baner' newspaper whose editor was Rev. Thomas Gee.
From November 1886 a ceaseless tirade against the evils of Welsh
Landlordism poured from this widely circulated weekly journal. Thus
on 24 November 1886 Welsh landlords were scathingly castigated as
'the devourers of the marrow of their /the tenants'/ bones', while,
later, on 2 November 1887 it pronounced: 'The landowners of our
country are, in general, cruel, unreasonable, unfeeling, and unpity-
ing men.' The attack was also taken up with vigour by the Liberal
leaders. Gladstone made a celebrated speech near Beddgelert at the
foot of Snowdon in early September 1892, strongly criticising Welsh
landlords for their inadequate, ungenerous behaviour to their
tenants during the depression years from the late 1870s. (81) His
remarks were heavily dependent upon a parliamentary speech made a
few months earlier by the Merioneth MP, T.E. Ellis, who had portrayed Welsh landlords as unscrupulous rack-renters and evicters of
tenants for political and religious reasons. (82)

The party of agitation thus drew attention to a Welsh Land Question. A number of specific allegations were made within the agrarian indictment. Welsh landowners were blamed for charging exorbi-
tant rents and for failing to meet the depression by adequate abatements or reductions. Strong criticism was made of the system of
tenurial relations which made for insecurity of tenure. Thus farmers dared not improve lest they should receive notices to quit, or
their rents should be raised upon their own improvements, or circumstances should bring about a sale of the entire (or part of) the
estate where their holdings were situated. Allegations were made
that landowners showed a preference for Churchmen and Conservatives
as against Nonconformists and Radicals when farms became vacant, and
that they made capricious ejections for political reasons. Landlords were also criticised for forcing on their tenants excessively
strict forms of agreement. Finally, landowners were strongly
attacked for their cruel operation of the Game Laws. The evils of
the Welsh situation had arisen, it was argued, because with the
division between owners and tenants in language, creed and politics
'there did not exist that community of feeling between landlords and
tenants in Wales which alone could make agriculture successful'. (83)
It was pointed out that this divide did not feature in England, and
it was urged that such was the difference between the two classes
that separate legislation for Wales was essential. The Welsh Land
Question, contended its champions, could be solved only by legislation along the same lines as had been achieved for Ireland - by the
implementation of a Land Court to provide 'fair rents', fixity of
tenure and free sale.

It is clear that the agitation was to a considerable extent the
product of sectarian and political grievances. The Liberal Unionist
landowner, the fourth Lord Sudeley of Gregynog Hall, Montgomeryshire,
wrote in 1892 of the 'Land cry which they /the Gladstonian Liberals/
are now making such good use of for party purposes'. (84) Until the
anti-tithe agitation became a burning issue little was heard of a
Welsh Land Question. The 'Baner' newspaper of 13 August 1887 warned:
'The landlords are fools enough to shield the clergy. The effect of
this will be to change, or rather to extend the battlefield.' The
association of the landowners with the Church's cause in the mid
1880s thus led to the agitation on the Welsh Land Question in the

vernacular press. Welsh farmers were now subjected to brilliant and
emotional propaganda dwelling on the evils of Welsh Landlordism
which was sectarian and political in its aims. Throughout, religious prejudice was used as the major weapon against the landowners.
Furthermore, the depression in farming was blamed on the landowners
who were accused of failing to make timely abatements and reductions
of rent. Lord Dynevor of Dynevor Castle, Llandeilo, Carmarthenshire,
wrote: 'The landlords have done their part, but the worst of it is,
the Radicals and Revolutionary Party are trying to make capital out
of the Farmers' losses and the depression of trade.' (85)
      There is no mistaking the deterioration in landlord-tenant rela-
tions from the 1880s as a direct consequence of the agitation in the
press and from the pulpit. The storm over the Land Question raged
most fiercely in north Wales, precisely where the 'Baner', 'Genedl'
and 'Celt' newspapers were most influential, and where Calvinistic
Methodism was dominant. Here in particular the old ties between
landlord and tenant were weakened. A similar (though less acute)
erosion of the previous identity of interests was evident in other
Welsh-speaking areas of the principality. Significantly, agitation
was virtually non-existent in the Border counties, where Welsh was
rapidly giving place to English and where the vernacular press was
thus limited in its influence. (86) Everywhere, however, there was
far less support for the programme of land reform among the farmers
than Gee and others had anticipated. It was not so much that
tenants were afraid to come forward as the fact that the party of
agitation had overestimated the extent to which traditional landlord-
tenant relationships had dissolved.
      The reformers were unrealistic in endeavouring to draw parallels
between the Welsh and Irish situations. The circumstances on which
the doctrine of dual ownership and the practice of tenant right
were held to be founded in Ireland (namely, the expenditure by the
occupier alone of the whole, or almost the whole, amount required
for the maintenance of holdings and their development by improvements) was not the normal practice in Wales. It could not justly be
claimed that the agricultural improvements within the principality
were, as a rule, the fruit of the labour and the expenditure of the
tenant, nor that landlords as a body confiscated the fruits of their
labour. Furthermore, the evils of complete absenteeism prevalent in
the Irish situation did not apply to Wales, nor were Welsh landlords
of alien stock. They were overwhelmingly of Welsh descent. Finally,
the landlord's control in Wales almost entirely prevented that sub-
division of holdings which led to the congestion of a rural population upon holdings too small to maintain the occupiers, the system
which prevailed in Ireland and the crofter districts of Scotland.(87)
      At the heart of the Welsh land question lay the allegation that
Welsh tenants suffered from feelings of insecurity and were simply
too afraid to improve their farming under these daunting circumstances. We have seen that much of this was a gross exaggeration.
Thus, apart from the 1860s, it was extremely rare for tenants to be
evicted from their holdings for capricious and political reasons.
Furthermore, when holdings became vacant landowners seldom took into
consideration the religious persuasions of the applicants. It was
superficially convincing to argue that tenants' improvements would
be followed by an increase in their rents. The land hunger, it was

stressed, meant that tenants were in a particularly vulnerable position, for any improvements they might carry out would automatically
invite eager applicants for the holdings concerned. Furthermore,
for most of Wales there was not even a well-developed local custom
which would afford some degree of security. We have seen that these
allegations were totally unjustified in so far as the large estates
were concerned. Rents were on the whole fair, indeed, often lenient,
and yearly tenants in fact became tenants for life. Their refusal
to take long leases testifies to their firm belief that yearly
tenure was an equally effective form of security. Much of the improvement was performed by the landlords, but what the tenants themselves accomplished was not confiscated automatically in higher
rents. Even though revaluations (occurring only at long intervals
of thirty years or more on the large estates) generally ignored
tenants' improvements, many substantial owners reduced the proposed
new levels to take account of such improvements.

   Some doubt remains, however, as to whether lack of custom in
Wales, besides absence of statutory compensation until the 1880s,
hindered larger tenants from investing capital. Thus Lord Cawdor's
agent, T. Mousley, offended his employer in 1868 over his suggestion
to the Carmarthenshire Chamber of Agriculture that some form of
tenant right be established

   that would protect the Landlord's property, and give an improving
   tenant a fair security for the Capital expended in the improvement of his farm, in case he had to leave it otherwise than by
   his own free will., I believe that such an Agreement would be
   more applicable to this country than leases - and our Agricultural improvement will be very slow, unless some such additional
   confidence is established. (88)

Again, a north Wales farmer who wrote a well-balanced article in
1860 on Welsh farming contended that: 'Were the tenant to know that
if he does all he can to improve his farm, he should be reimbursed
were his farm sold, or were he to leave, the great obstacle to improvement would be removed.' (89) There may have been some truth in
this, but it was certainly not the basic constriction on improvement
in nineteenth-century Welsh agriculture. It was applicable only to
tenants with plentiful capital, and there were few of these: the
amounts required from the incoming tenant to compensate the outgoing
one would have been too burdensome for most Welsh tenants. The problem was the same everywhere. Thus a Nottinghamshire witness testified before the Parliamentary Commission on Tenant Right in 1847:
'An extensive tenant right would require more capital and would consequently shut out men of small means.' (90) Significantly, on the
Bute estate, the Glamorgan custom (where compensation usually did
not exceed two years' rent) was disliked by incoming tenants with
little capital. In 1829 the second Marquess of Bute himself compensated the outgoing tenant of Rhydypennau on the understanding the
new tenant would make no claim when he left. (91) As far as the
average Welsh tenant was concerned, all his money was required to
stock and work the farm. The owner of the Wygfair estate in Denbighshire and Flintshire stated that for this very reason he would not
allow any tenant to pay goodwill. (92) But local customs do not
seem to have been widely advocated before the sales from the late
1870s, even by the larger tenants. Perhaps this was simply because

tenants whose families had been in possession for many generations
on the large estates (where usually the larger holdings were located)
and who felt in no danger of being disturbed, were seldom faced with
the problem of compensation. Custom under these conditions was unlikely to have been a burning issue.

It was precisely when this sense of fixity of tenure gave way to
feelings of insecurity as a consequence of the growing number of
land sales from the late 1870s that lack of compensation became a
meaningful factor in retarding improvements, particularly in so far
as tenants with capital were concerned. We have seen how tenants
often had their improvements confiscated through changes of ownership. The Agricultural Holdings Act of 1883 did not give the tenant
the right to have his interest in unexhausted improvements valued
and the amount charged on the purchase money. And here the fact
that tenants shared in making improvements carried out by their
landlords in doing the haulage and unskilled labour was an added
frustration. Many of the complaints made against Welsh landowners
in the 1890s originated in cases of this kind. Indeed, the Liberal
solicitor, Bryn Roberts, MP, conceded that difficulties arose on the
large estates between tenants and owners only when sales of holdings
occurred. (93) There was here, then, a peculiarly Welsh problem in
so far as land sales in the depression years were far more frequent
than in England, owing mainly to pressure for land keeping up capital values. In a few instances landlords recognised the hardship
often arising from changes of ownership and called for legislative
action to secure compensation. (94)

Tenurial conditions were thus favourable to the tenant farmers on
the large estates (except for the difficulties concerning land sales
which arose on some properties). A leading Radical, Gwilym Evans,
chairman of the Carmarthenshire County Council, admitted to the Land
Commissioners that on 'good estates' (i.e. large hereditary ones)
there was a

> very large amount of good feeling. I could mention an estate in
> this county - that is Lord Cawdor's estate - where the tenants
> are so situated that practically I do not believe that any land
> court or any recommendation that might be made by the Commission
> could to any extent affect the tenants to their advantage.

Such testimony from an extremely hostile yet knowledgeable witness
strongly suggests that Adfyfr's ill-considered tirades against Welsh
owners 'en masse' were nothing less than polemical indulgences.

However it is significant that Evans then added that what he
really wished to eradicate on these large estates was the tenants'
feelings of utter dependence, which he regretfully attributed to a
pervasive 'feeling of fear - uncertainty'. (95) Bryn Roberts, MP,
took a similar view:

> If I were asked whether capricious or vindictive eviction is
> often resorted to I should say no, it is not, but the power to
> resort to it is enough, and a great deal too much. It destroys
> all independence in tenants, and makes them totally unable to
> resist the will of the landlords on any subject whatsoever.

The situation was particularly evil, he contended, because of the
political and sectarian divide between tenants and their landlords.
(96) Undoubtedly, some tenants were afraid, but it is wholly untrue
to suggest that multitudes of tenants lived in fawning servility and

trembled at the thought of persecution in the 1880s and 1890s. Landlords had learnt an important lesson following the furore which
broke over the impetuous evictions of the 1860s. Subsequently landlords came under the most intense public scrutiny, and simply did
not dare to act arbitrarily. The exertion of political pressure was
totally out of the question. The complete independence of tenants
is amply demonstrated by their readiness to vote against their landlords at national and local elections.

Conditions were less satisfactory on the small estates. Many
owners were too poor to afford the luxury of treating their tenants
liberally. The fact that both parties lacked capital meant an inevitable clash of interests. Tenants felt insecure and were unwilling to improve out of fear that their efforts would be nullified by
higher rents. (This merely reinforced, though, their peasant preoccupation - shared by tenants on large estates - for farming as
cheaply as possible and therefore consciously maintaining their
rents at as low level as possible.) Small owners of hereditary
Welsh stock were seldom rapacious, however, and the worst grievances
were suffered on the estates of the new 'commercial' landlords who
felt no ties of personal obligation towards their tenantry.

In short, the Land Question was a figment of the political imagi-
nation so far as it applied to owners of large estates, though it
must be admitted that a real grievance sometimes occurred when sales
of outlying parts of these sizeable properties took place. Advantage was cynically taken of the farming difficulties of the 1880s
and the early 1890s to engender ill-feeling against the Tory, Anglican landowner who from the beginning of the nineteenth century had
increasingly ceased to understand and represent the true interests
and needs of the Welsh people. He was made the scapegoat for all
the farmers' troubles and vituperated as a hard-hearted, rack-
renting tyrant. There is plentiful evidence to show that in fact
the large owners suffered along with their tenants and viewed the
troubled situation with equal concern as partners in adversity. The
small hereditary owner was certainly more grasping, but the difficulties of his estate usually arose from lack of capital rather than
from careless extravagance or deliberate oppressiveness. The small
newcomer was the worst offender. It is therefore necessary to
challenge much of the agrarian indictment in the 'Welsh Land Question' and to see it for what it really was - a vehicle designed to
promote the Liberal cause and manufactured by a group of well-
intentioned, fiercely patriotic Welshmen. These Welsh leaders were
indeed playing a vital part in the process of liberating rural
Welshmen from a past governed by privilege, and hence were beginning
a new chapter in the history of democracy and freedom in the principality. The Land Question constituted a vital step in the drive to
modernisation. Doffing of caps to landlords became less frequent.

The backwardness of agriculture was thus only marginally a consequence of imperfect tenurial relations: feelings of insecurity on
small estates helped retard improvements and absence of compensation
for unexhausted improvements when land sales occurred from the 1870s
was a positive handicap. Other more important factors of constraint
were the poor communications with the great centres of trade and
manufacture, the barrier of language restricting the vital diffusion
of information and ideas on improved farming, the large amounts of

open, unenclosed moorland tracts foiling attempts at improved livestock breeding, the lack of capital of the majority of farmers, and,
finally, the family and social traditions of small farms and the
limited expectations of what they could or should yield.

Thus Welsh farmers had neither the capital resources to invest in
improvements nor the intellectual attitudes and equipment to do so.
Possibly unwillingness to invest was the greater drawback because,
had the wish existed, credit might have been obtained from sources
such as the country banks.   There is much evidence to strongly
suggest that the Welsh peasant mentality viewed any rise in rents
as a consequence of permanent improvements as a veritable calamity,
given their attitude of equating 'successful' farming with low
expenditure.   Rent was a major item in the structure of farm costs
which had always to remain at its traditional level.   Not only did
this attitude govern the relationship between tenant and landowner,
but it also reflected upon the tenant's own activity.   The possibility of rent increases implied that the farmer consciously refrained
from exhibiting signs of prosperity.   There was thus a total inhibi-
tion against all improvement.   The Board of Agriculture's Report on
Radnorshire in 1794 commented that the farmer thought 'that his
prosperity through life depends upon the level of his rent'. (97)
In 1860 the north Wales farmer referred to earlier wrote:

> The tenant should not expect his rent to remain stationary. Not
> in having the farm at the same rent from one generation to an-
> other, nor in even having the sum of money which he has to pay in
> the shape of rent to be very small, does his advantage consist,
> but in having his farm upon such condition, that what he can make
> from to exceed his payments. (98)

The knowledgeable editor of the 'Cambrian News' (John Gibson) commented in 1879 of the tenant on large estates: 'Although he is in
no danger of eviction, and has but little to fear from revaluation,
yet the remote possibility of a rise in his rent is sufficient to
paralyse his effort and to prevent him from manifesting signs of
prosperity.' (99) This same myopic concern for farming as cheaply
as possible explains the tenant's frequent unwillingness to pay increased rents upon improvements made by his landlord. Fear of rent
increases was the greatest obstacle to improvement, and, though on
small estates this arose in part from the tenant's justifiable fear
that improvements would automatically lead to higher rents, it
derived basically from the peasant mentality for farming cheaply.

Contemporaries chided the Welsh farmer's slovenliness and care-
lessness in his failure to attend to the ordinary upkeep of his
holding.   E.C.L. Fitzwilliams, in referring to the change of tenants
on two farms on his property, wrote in 1865:

> The state in which those farms have been left is deplorable. How
> the 'beasts' could have lived in such a state of dirt and dilapi-
> dation I cannot conceive. Neither of them laid out a single
> penny in repairs during the twenty years they have had the pre-
> mises. I am afraid that this is only a type of most of the Welsh
> farmers of the neighbourhood who speak nothing but the blessed
> 'iaith Gymraeg' (Welsh language). (100)

The 'Cambrian News' in 1874 observed:

> The most cursory glance at the filled up ditches, broken down
> hedges, encroaching gorse bushes, and dilapidated gates, is

enough to convince anyone who understands these things that no
arrangement on the part of the landlords would give the untidy,
thriftless farmer, energy and a sense of order.
It went on to point out the miles of ruined fences between Aberystwyth and Lampeter and concluded with the stricture: 'No excuse of
want of capital or absence of security can be accepted in this case
as fences only require a little labour and attention at proper times
to keep them in order.' (101) Welsh farmers were incorrigible, and
in certain instances this can partly be blamed on landlords for
their easy-going attitudes to their estates. It was the uncommercial outlook of the Welsh farmer, and his hoarding of money arising
from his fixation for keeping his rent as low as possible, which
really lay at the basis of underdeveloped farming. The 'Cambrian
News' aptly observed in 1880:

Yearly tenancies, it is to be feared, do not account for all the
reluctance on the part of the Welsh farmers to rear fat stock;
for agriculturalists who live on their own land, and many who
hold long leases, or are tenants of landlords who neither evict
nor increase rents, follow the practices of those who are less
secure, and by no means their own masters. (102)

Apart from this concern for keeping his rent at the same level as
hitherto, an important additional factor explaining the peasant's
reluctance to put money into the land was simply his lack of faith
in the development and improvement of land as a commercial speculation. (103)

CHAPTER 6

THE AGRICULTURAL LABOURER

I

There were two fairly distinctive groups below the gentry in the local community, namely, the farmers and the cottagers. Tenancy of a farm offered independence and status, and the farmer was careful of his social standing in the locality. (1) Although farmers and cottagers lived in close contact with one another - they were linked by ties of language, religion, economic dependence, friendship and often family relationships - there was a clear distinction between the two groups. Farmers shared a strong feeling of corporate identity and regarded themselves as superior to 'the people of the small houses' ('gwyr y tai bach') who comprised the farm labourers and the other non-farming cottagers. If a farmer failed and was forced to become a farm labourer the community nevertheless continued to recognise his former status: at his place of employment he sat for meals with the master and mistress apart from the rest of the farm staff. (2) Similarly, farmers' children, while performing the same work as farm servants on their parents' holdings, and sharing the same table and sleeping quarters, were recognised as 'farm children' when visiting other farms. They would then eat in the best kitchen with the farmer and his wife. (3) The most conscious assertion of this distinction came at marriage: farmers' children were expected to marry amongst their own kind just as farm labourers were expected to marry maid servants. (4) Although intermarriage was by no means entirely absent, (5) such a step normally conferred loss of caste and often rejection by the rest of the members of the farm family. Significantly, the daughter of a farmer would not lose caste if she married a labourer who had prospects of becoming a farmer. (6)

The difference was one of rank and status and not of class. Contemporaries emphasised that a characteristic feature of the Welsh farming system throughout the century was the absence of any pronounced class division between tenant farmers and their labourers.(7) This situation was basically a consequence of the small farm units whose occupants were scarcely distinguishable from their labourers in their standard of living and mode of life. The small Welsh farmer worked the land alongside his labourers, and scarcity of farms meant that farmers' sons often became labourers of the indoor

servant type on neighbouring farms. Labourers, for their part, frequently achieved their ambition of becoming tenant farmers for the
small Welsh holdings could be taken with very little capital. Often
the first stage in this process was for the labourer, while still
working as an agricultural wage earner, to acquire a small-holding.
Thus farmers and labourers shaded imperceptibly into one another.
Close contact on the social plane arose from their worshipping together in Nonconformist chapels, albeit on an unequal social standing, and their mixing in the farm-houses at meal times. Outdoor
labourers, as well as indoor servants, took their meals at the farm,
although here, once again, the master and mistress ate in the best
kitchen away from the others in the back kitchen. This general
absence of pronounced class cleavage contrasted with the situation
in many areas of England where the two categories were quite separate and distinct, and where the larger farms meant that the prospects of an agricultural labourer becoming a farmer were remote. (8)

The major exception to this state of affairs was in the Vale of
Clwyd, Denbighshire, where the general absence of small farms form-
ing so many steps in the agricultural ladder created a sharp line of
cleavage between farmers and their labourers. The farmers were a
distinct middle class and their labourers an equally distinct
peasant class. Thus farmers' daughters and their maids did not con-
fide in one another, and farmers' sons did not become farm labourers
in their localities for fear of losing status. Labourers, for their
part, stood little chance of becoming farmers, and intermarriage in
this area was extremely rare. (9)

Agricultural wage earners in Wales throughout the century were
divided into two main groups. First, there were the farm servants
of both sexes, children (entering service from ages varying between
9 and 13 years) and adults. They were boarded and lodged on the
farm, engaged at the hiring fairs (down to the last two decades of
the century) by the year or, less commonly, the half year, and unmarried. A similar situation prevailed throughout the century in
Scotland under the 'farm kitchen' and the 'bothy' systems respectively. (10) This farm servant category disappeared in many areas of
England, outside the north, however, in the first three decades or
so of the nineteenth century, giving place to outdoor labourers
hired by the week or the day. (11) The contrast between the position in Wales and much of England is revealed by the 1861 Census
Returns. Whereas in Wales and the analogous counties of Cumberland
and Westmorland about one half of the hired labour force was of
indoor servants, elsewhere in England the ratio of indoor servants
was far less, particularly in the east Midlands and south-eastern
counties.

Why did the indoor servant class survive and, indeed, become the
increasingly dominant form of hired labour on Welsh farms in the
late nineteenth century? The most important reason was that in a
primarily pastoral region livestock required constant supervision
and men at hand at any hour of the day or night. Again, Welsh farmers, possessing little capital and often lacking in enterprise,
were reluctant to part with money and considered it cheaper to pay
their labourers partly through board and lodge. It is significant
that on the larger Welsh farms more men were hired by the week and
correspondingly fewer were boarded and lodged. Indoor servants, too,

in some cases, may have been forced upon the farmers in face of the
shortage of good, comfortable cottages (provided by the landlords)
for married labourers, an expression of the lack of capital in Welsh
agriculture. Finally, the continuance of the indoor system in Wales
may be explained to some extent on sociological grounds in so far as
the line of demarcation between the farmer and labourer did not
exist in Wales as in England. (12)

The second class of wage earners were the outdoor married labourers renting cottages either on the farms or, increasingly in the
late nineteenth century, in villages, and engaged by the week. But
unlike their English counterparts, who lived on their own find,
Welsh outdoor labourers were generally given their meals at the
farms as part of their wages. Significant exceptions to this practice were to be found in the English areas of south Pembrokeshire,
the Vale of Glamorgan and the eastern parts of the border counties
where they lived on their own find. (13) This peculiarity of
labourers of the Welsh areas receiving board at the farms may once
again be explained partly on sociological grounds, and, perhaps more
important, farmers considered it cheaper than paying full money
wages.

Two further smaller categories of Welsh farm labourers should be
noted. In the first place, in south-west Wales a common type of
labourer was the 'bound tenant' who rented a small holding of three
to five acres attached to a particular farm. The tenancy of this
small holding was on condition that the tenant worked for the farmer
whenever required at 6s. a week regardless of the season. Sometimes
these small holders were given no work in the winter months so they
went to Glamorgan to the 'works' leaving their families at home in
the cottages, returning home only in the summer to work for the
farmer in the harvest. The farmer assisted the tenant with his team
at ploughing and harvest, while in return, to repay the debt, the
tenant's wife and family worked for the farmer at harvest. (14)
Second, there was a very small group of casual labourers who, relying on their superior skills, took work by the day from farm to farm
or, less frequently, did piece-work. They would often engage themselves for a period during harvest. Frequently, they were men who
possessed small holdings of their own and who supplemented their incomes by performing odd days' work for different farmers. (15)

The total agricultural community was composed basically of farmers, their sons and relatives, and of hired agricultural wage
earners. An important feature in the Welsh situation was the high
amount of family labour employed. Whereas in England in 1891 the
ratio of labourers, farmers and their relatives was $73:20\frac{1}{2}:6\frac{1}{2}$ the
corresponding figures for Wales were 48.4:38.9:12.7. (16) This low
ratio of hired labour on Welsh holdings is not surprising, for, as
shown earlier, farms were basically family-run units with the occupier and his family, which tended to be large, working alongside
what extra hired labour force was required. Indeed, the formula
stated for many small farms of up to fifty acres in the Enumerators'
Returns of 1851 was: 'farmer of x acres employing only his family'.
Furthermore, the custom of co-operation among small farmers in operations throughout the year requiring extra hands, as at harvest, permitted the farmer to work his holding without recourse to additional
hired labour. The hired labour force was also restricted because

the amount of labour employed (including here family as well as
hired labour) in relation to the acreage was small: the pastoral
character of the farming demanded less labour per acre than arable
cultivation, and Welsh farmers were prevented by lack of capital
from running up high labour bills.

The small size of holdings meant that men were not assigned
special work. Accordingly, married labourers were styled 'all-round'
labourers. This situation, where the labourer adapted to every farm
operation contrasted with that obtaining in many areas of England,
where labourers undertook special tasks as foremen, shepherds, stock-
men, carters and spademen. (17)

Figures for the numbers of agricultural wage earners are unavail-
able before the 1851 Census Returns. However, it is clear that in
the early century the agricultural labour force grew rapidly, for
between 1801 and 1851 the population of rural Wales outside the semi-
industrialised counties of Glamorgan and Monmouth rose from natural
increase by 64 per cent. But numbers of agricultural wage earners
began to fall from around mid century. Thus, between 1851 and 1911
there was an overall decrease in male agricultural wage earners of
45.7 per cent. The recorded fall in the female labour force over
the same period was 94.9 per cent. Even if the figures for 1851 are
inflated by the possibility that some who were simply domestic servants in farm houses were included among the total of indoor servants and excluded from later censuses, a substantial decline of
female labourers was evident to contemporaries.

This fall in numbers of agricultural wage earners was part of the
overall decline in numbers of persons engaged in Welsh agriculture
from 1851 onwards. It has been shown that between 1851 and 1911
there was a fall in total agriculturalists of 45.8 per cent, the
fastest drop occurring between 1851 and 1871. But this fall was not
shared equally among all the different categories. Numbers of farmers and graziers declined by a mere 6.6 per cent and here decline
set in late, for before 1891 their numbers had increased by 25 per
cent. The fall in male relatives totalled 20.2 per cent between
1851 and 1911. The largest drop, therefore, occurred in the hired
labour force, the number of males falling by 45.7 per cent and
females even faster. It was a decline of the labour force, including both hired wage earners and farmers' sons and relatives, therefore, and not of farmers, which accounts for the decline in numbers
of total agriculturalists in late nineteenth-century Wales. (18)

As is well known, this decline came about owing to migration to
industrial areas of England and Wales and, to a much lesser extent,
emigration overseas. Of great importance here was the growth of the
iron industry around Merthyr in the early century and the independent development of coal mining in the valleys of south-east Wales
from about the mid century, a development which replaced the declining iron industry in importance as a source of labour demand. (19)
The higher wages offered in the industrial areas, together with the
shorter hours of work and the social attractions offered by town
life, led in many areas to a 'deliberate and calculated abandonment
of rural labour'. (20) A trickle of migration to the iron works at
Merthyr from relatively distant areas of south and south-west Wales
was under way in the 1820s, 1830s and 1840s. Although some of this
was seasonal migration during the winter slack farming season, there

was, too, permanent migration to the 'works' in search of higher
wages. A.H. John has drawn our attention to the long-distance
character of this movement and explains the contrast with the English type of 'drift' migration on the grounds that the typical Welsh
hill farm employed little hired labour. When members of the family
left for industrial areas the poverty of the family was such that
the vacancy had to remain unfilled. This situation, therefore, in
which 'replacement did not keep pace with the removals', was 'not
conducive to a gradual centripetal movement of population'. (21)
The coming of railways to Wales from mid century greatly facilitated,
and therefore helped to accelerate, the exodus from the Welsh countryside, an exodus which was now being given an important additional
'pull' by the opening of the Welsh coal valleys.

   Labour migration was caused by other factors besides the paramount 'pull' of the industrial areas. To a certain extent the agricultural wage earner was 'pushed' out of the Welsh countryside by
adverse conditions. This was obviously so during the difficult
farming years after the French wars, when the supply of farm wage
earners far exceeded the demand. These years witnessed a fast
growth in the population, and the growing numbers could neither be
absorbed by alternative employment nor by the traditional subsistent
agricultural economy. Indeed, farmers were retrenching their labour
in the face of depressed prices. David Williams rightly stressed
that railways served to defuse this potentially explosive situation
in the Welsh countryside. (22) Even with the improved farming fortunes of the third quarter of the century there remained strong
'push' incentives to migrate from the rural areas. Cottage accommodation improved after mid century, but it remained so defective and
scarce that married labourers became highly dissatisfied with their
situation. (23) Furthermore, the social limitations of the countryside and the lack of reasonable prospects of advancement in life
were instilled into younger generations by the system of elementary
education after 1870 in the rural schools which fitted the children
not so much for agricultural work as for clerks, shop assistants and
railway porters. The Elementary Education Act, also, by restricting
juvenile labour and consequently reducing the aggregate amount of
family earnings, tended to make the married labourer readier to
migrate. (24) Finally, from the 1890s boys from reformatory and
industrial schools in England were employed on Welsh farms, particularly in the south-west, as a cheap form of labour to counteract
agricultural depression. Such a policy to some extent drove married
labourers from the countryside and accounts for the progressively
increasing ratio of indoor servants to outdoor labourers in the late
nineteenth century. (25)

   These factors explaining the fall in the number of agricultural
labourers affected principally male wage earners. Certain peculiar
factors operated in causing a decline in the number of female labourers. This fall was essentially one in female field labour which had
been a regular feature until the third quarter of the century, although private gangs of women and children had not been generally
employed as was the case on the large arable farms of eastern England. By the close of the century, female farm labour in Wales came
to be restricted to harvest time, with the exception of the south-
western counties, where it was still employed in the lighter field

operations. The growth of humanitarian and religious feeling in
society produced a repugnance towards the employment of females in
field labour. There was, however, a decline in the female agricultural labour force in general, so that even for dairy work female
servants were difficult to engage. As men's wages rose in the late
nineteenth century there grew up among the labouring class a greater
desire to see the wife remaining at home to look after the family
rather than neglecting the latter for the sake of a few extra shil-
lings. Again, the attraction of the towns in employment in dress-
making, millinery and service in business drew women away from farm
work. At the close of the century, women were more engaged in agriculture in Wales than in England generally, but not to the extent
that they were in Northumberland and certain other northern counties.
(26)

With migration occurring on such a scale, it is important to ascertain the state of the farm labour market at the close of the
century. Migration was being felt by the 1870s in the growing
scarcity and dearness of rural labour which led farmers to reduce
their demand. Thus, from the early 1870s farmers deliberately econo-
mised their labour by increasingly laying their corn lands down to
pasture. The fall in grain prices from the mid 1870s accelerated
this switch to grass (the fall in labour costs involved in the process also playing a part in this decision) and in this way the
demand for labour was further reduced. Less manual labour, too, was
needed with the introduction of agricultural machinery. In these
ways, therefore, the diminution in supply of agricultural labour was
paralleled by a restriction in demand. By the 1890s no part of
Wales had a surplus of labour, while in certain areas near the industrial centres, in particular the Vale of Glamorgan, there was a
scarcity. (27)

II

Having examined the constitution and size of the agricultural labour
force, it is now necessary to inquire into the condition of the wage
earner in relation to hours of work, wages and general material comfort. Until the 1870s there appears to have been little progress
made towards shortening the excessively long working day of the
agricultural wage earner. Indoor servants worked indefinitely from
early morning till late at night, while the married labourer's
average day was from 5 a.m. to 8.30 p.m. It will be shown that the
gradual curtailing of working hours from the 1870s down to the close
of the century was for the most part achieved by natural adjustment
and without organised agitation by the labouring class. While a
reduction in working hours was implemented generally, there was wide
variation in the hours of labour in different parts of Wales in the
last decade of the century. They were normally shortest, as were
wages highest, around the industrial and mineral centres. The usual
day for the married labourer ranged between $10\frac{1}{2}$ and $11\frac{1}{2}$ hours during
the summer, exclusive of mealtimes, while in the winter months he
worked from dawn to dusk. Indoor servants in charge of livestock
worked longer hours. With the exception of Anglesey, where labour
agitation had gained them a twelve-hour day, inclusive of meals,

they normally worked from $12\frac{1}{2}$ to $13\frac{1}{2}$ hours, exclusive of meals.
Sunday work was confined to winter time and involved only the indoor
servants looking after the animals. The longest hours were worked
by the maidservants, who were the first to rise in the morning and
the last to retire at night. Small wonder that the greatest scarcity of labour at the close of the nineteenth century was felt among
this particular group of farm workers. Although children were employed far less after the Elementary Education Act of 1870, those
who were had to work the same hours as normal indoor servants. (28)

Although there were no fixed holidays or half days before 1914,
most farm servants were readily granted three or four days, or even
a greater number of half-days, a year for attending a wedding or a
funeral, an eisteddfod, preaching festival or a fair. Farm servants
working in the direct employ of Mrs Owen, the imperious mistress of
Glansevern, were forced to attend the established Church, however,
and one was dismissed for going to a Nonconformist chapel. (29) It
is doubtful whether this applied in general to farm servants working
directly for a landlord. By the late nineteenth century a day-trip
to the seaside or to some large town had almost become a recognised
annual event, often in connection with a Sunday school. Easter and
Whit Mondays particularly were often spent at a local fair or some
other social activity. One or more days of the year were always set
aside for time off at the hiring fairs. The scarcity of labour in
the two closing decades of the century led to a decline in the real
purpose of these fairs, for farmers endeavoured to engage servants a
few weeks prior to the fair. When hiring had been done, it was completed in the mornings, the rest of the day being given to pleasure.
Even after hiring ceased, these fairs continued as major social
occasions. Before the religious revivals of the early century they
had been the saturnalia of the whole community, but revivalism ended
the music and dancing on such occasions. Drinking and fighting at
hiring fairs only gradually lessened with the impact of the temperance movement. (30)

It is difficult to provide any general account of the wages of
this class in Wales over the period under discussion. Wide diversi-
ties in labour rates existed between different areas. Local factors
were to a large extent responsible for this lack of uniformity,
especially the distance from competing industries. A more general
reason for such diversity, however, was that agricultural wage
earners were so closely attached by tradition, sentiment and habit
to the practice of a particular area that they were unaware of the
conditions under which their counterparts in neighbouring districts
were engaged. This tendency was exacerbated as far as Wales was
concerned by the fact that there was little interchange of ideas
between them and no form of permanent organisation bringing them together for common purposes. Besides this problem of diversity,
there is the added difficulty, especially for the years before 1870,
of attempting an assessment of the money value of the agricultural
workers' earnings, for they were generally composed of payment in
kind as well as in cash. With these difficulties in mind, the
amount and movement of agricultural labour rates in the nineteenth
century will now be discussed.

Cash wages for the greater part of Wales, as elsewhere in Britain,
rose during the Napoleonic wars, so that by 1814 the outdoor labourer

on his own find in south-west Wales received daily 1s. in winter and
1s.6d. in spring and summer. Already proximity of the iron works
was advancing the price of rural labour in the south-eastern areas,
where the outdoor labourer on his own find earned from 8s. to 10s. a
week in winter and from 9s. to 12s. in the summer. (31) The drastic
fall in farm prices which set in after the war led to a reduction in
cash earnings. Walter Davies observed in 1816: 'Labourers in ·hus-
bandry are much out of employ. Some even without children have in
consequence applied for parochial relief. Others offer their labour
for food only; some at half last year's wages, and most at a diminution.' (32) And cash wages for the greater part of Wales only gradually increased before mid century. Mr Clive, the poor law commissioner for south Wales, commented in 1837 that wages were 'generally
low' in the agricultural areas of south Wales. Outdoor labourers on
their own find received between 6s. and 8s. a week: the whole of
Cardiganshire and the south and west parts of Carmarthenshire and
Pembrokeshire inclined to 6s., while the rest of the district
averaged from 7s. to 8s. Wages were naturally highest in the parishes near the 'works'. Thus, in the Vale of Glamorgan wages of
outdoor labourers on their own find were 10s. in winter and from 12s.
to 14s. in summer. (33) The advance of wages in the agricultural
districts of north Wales between 1814 and the middle of the century
seemed to have moved just as slowly as those in south-west Wales.
Once again, however, a faster increase occurred in areas adjacent to
the coal mining operations in Denbighshire and Flintshire. (34)

    The significant increase in agricultural rates for Wales as a
whole came with the construction of railways from mid century. The
actual labour required for railway construction to some extent affected the local labour market, as, for instance, in the districts
about Haverfordwest and Carmarthen in 1845 and 1846 respectively.(35)
It was the easy conveyance from the rural areas afforded by the railways, however, which made the vital difference to agricultural
labour rates. The consequent thinning of the rural market naturally
increased agricultural wages. In 1869 William Phillips, Returning
Officer of the Narberth Union, Pembrokeshire, testified to the much
improved wages of the farm labourers of south-west Wales over the
previous twenty-five years, commenting: 'I believe the turning
point in the labourers' advanced condition was about the making of
the south Wales railway.' (36) Culley estimated that wages in south-
west Wales rose by between a third and a half of their previous
level with the coming of this railway. (37) Labour rates continued
to increase throughout Wales till 1879, when agricultural depression
set in. From then until 1885 or 1886, cash wages fell as the depression took its bite, but a gradual recovery took place from the late
1880s. (38)

    The extent to which agricultural rates had increased by the close
of the century is shown in table 6.1 which represents the weekly
rates of cash wages of married labourers on their own find in 1870
and 1898 respectively. The figures are too crude for precise calculations, but roughly speaking cash wages rose over most of Wales
by as much as between 20 and 40 per cent in the closing decades.
The rates for both years clearly reveal the influence of competitive
industries on agricultural earnings.

    Cash wages of the outdoor labourer on his own find, however, by

Table 6.1 Cash wages of married labourers on their own find

County	Weekly cash wages in 1870		Weekly cash wages in 1898		
	Range of wages		Predominant rates		Average of summer and winter
			summer	winter	
Anglesey	11s.	12s.	15s.	15s.	15s.
Brecknock	12s.	15s.	16s.	15s.	15s.7d.
Cardigan	9s.	11s.6d.	14s.	14s.	14s.
Carmarthen	9s.	11s.6d.	16s.	16s.	16s.
Caernarvon	12s.	14s.	17s.	16s.	16s.7d.
Denbigh	12s.	14s.	17s.	15s.	16s.2d.
Flint	12s.	14s.	16s.	16s.	16s.
Glamorgan	12s.	15s.	18s.	18s.	18s.
Merioneth	12s.	15s.	16s.	15s.	15s.7d.
Montgomery	10s.	12s.	15s.	14s.	14s.7d.
Pembroke	9s.	11s.6d.	15s.	14s.	14s.7d.
Radnor	13s.	14s.	13s.	13s.	13s.

Source: P.P., LXXXII (1900), p.58.

no means reflected actual earnings, for outdoor labourers (both those receiving board and those on their own find) received extra allowances and perquisites in kind on top of their money wages. These varied widely from district to district and were far more numerous in the first half of the century when cash wages were low. For, with the increase in cash earnings later in the century, the former perquisites gradually disappeared. (39) In the early part of the century common perquisites had been a cottage and garden free or at a low rent, a potato plot on the farmer's land, corn at a standard price and fuel free of charge. Such perquisites were still widely granted in south-west Wales down to the close of the 1860s and their cash value was estimated as follows: leadage of fuel, 26s. a year; potato land, 26s. a year; rent free cottage and garden, 52s. a year. In this way the earnings of the outdoor labourer on his own find in south-west Wales, where his cash wages were 9s. a week, were raised to 11s. a week. By the 1890s perquisites in kind had almost disappeared throughout Wales. (40)

In this discussion on cash wages it was convenient for obvious reasons to examine the earnings of the married labourer on his own find. However, as has been shown, in Wales indoor servants received part of their wages in kind in the form of board and lodge, and similarly most outdoor labourers received board at the farm. Calculations of labourers' earnings are therefore made even more difficult than usual. The first attempt at a computation of the money

value of board and lodge in Wales was made by Culley for south-west
Wales in 1870. He calculated that the married labourer boarding at
the farm earned between 5s. and 7s.6d. a week. With the value of
his food computed to be worth 8d. a day, this class received a wage
worth from 9s. to 11s.6d. a week. With extra perquisites in kind
his rates were raised accordingly to 11s. to 13s.6d. a week. The
board and lodge of the indoor servant was estimated to be worth 6s.
a week. Therefore, with this class earning from £12 to £15 per
annum, varying according to capability and locality, weekly wages
ranged from 10s.6d. to something over 13s.6d. (41) Those indoor
servants who were sons of the employer merely received board and
lodge, for instead of being paid money wages they were normally set
up in a farm upon marriage. (42) It will be readily appreciated
that as the value of board and lodging payments in kind, as well as
perquisites, varied from farm to farm, let alone from district to
district, no such 'average' wage of the agricultural labourer can be
stated. A further additional cash payment for married labourers,
though not for indoor servants on a fixed yearly or half yearly wage,
was in some districts made during harvest. Thus wages of permanent
outdoor labourers in some districts were raised at harvest while in
others a premium of 10s. or £1 was given to each man. (43)

The important problem remains as to real wages. The more fortunate farm worker in England and Wales, located in areas of agricultural improvement or in areas of growing agricultural activity,
probably gained some increase in real wages during the Napoleonic
War years. Increases in real wages very likely occurred, for instance, in the eastern counties of south Wales where, as already
noted, 'an earlier attention to improvements in agriculture and,
more than that, the opening of very extensive collieries and iron
works' produced a rapid rise in labour rates. (44) Suffering must
nevertheless have been felt even by these prospering labourers
during years of dearth. In less fortunate areas of Britain real
wages sometimes lagged badly, and in the interior, isolated agricultural areas of much of the principality where there was a low level
of activity it is likely that labourers did far from well. On the
other hand, the large element of living-in at Welsh farms (outdoor
labourers themselves ate at the farms) meant that labourers were far
less exposed to the crisis high-price years. The receipt by many
outdoor labourers (as in south-west Wales) of bread corn at a fixed
rate per bushel all the year round, which was generally far below
the market price, similarly worked to their advantage. (45)

The want of regular employment was the chief malaise affecting
the labouring class after 1815 for, although wages were reduced,
they seem to have fallen less drastically than food prices. (46)
The bleak tragedy of rural unemployment down to mid century is
richly documented. (47) The problem was naturally at its worst
during the slack winter months owing to the small amount of cropping
in the principality. In the upper part of Brecknockshire, for instance, the farmers scarcely employed anybody in the winter months.
(48) A few married labourers were engaged in improvements made by
the gentry in planting, but most, under the old poor law, were
forced onto the parish for relief. Poor rates mounted. Whereas in
1776 poor relief cost Cardiganshire £1085, by 1819 this had increased to £20,418, a sum which was roughly maintained down to

1834. (49) The payment of cottage rents out of the rates was a
particularly common form of relief given married labourers in Wales.
(50) Although the Speenhamland system did not operate in the principality, Welsh vestries nevertheless adopted the allowance system in
so far as they granted financial assistance to large families on low
or irregular earnings in order to maintain the children. Relief was
based not on a fixed scale but rather on individual needs. (51)

Able-bodied labourers found it more difficult to get parish
relief under the new poor law. This stipulated that outdoor relief
was to be refused and that labourers could obtain support only upon
entering a workhouse, where conditions were worse than those of the
lowest paid workers outside. Undoubtedly this meant more suffering
for those who could not find work. There was, however, some easing
of this situation by the practice of the guardians in granting outdoor relief to some at least of the able-bodied who applied because
they were unemployed. Certainly this practice was widespread in
Wales as in many areas of England as late as 1846. In fact, in most
of the Welsh Unions in 1845-6 far more able-bodied workers were in
receipt of outdoor than indoor relief. (52)

Besides parish relief, the sale of stockings knitted by the wives
and children of outdoor labourers was often vital in warding off
destitution. Gleaning persisted as a recognised custom well into
the late nineteenth century in certain areas of England and Wales
(in Carmarthenshire, for example), whereby the farmers were obliged
to leave the harvest gleanings for the poor and orphans. A similar
practice in Wales was wool-gathering or wool-gleaning: as soon as
shearing was over small groups of cottagers' wives would gather
little bundles of wool put by for them at local farms within three
or four miles radius about their cottages. (53) Cottage children,
too, in Merioneth, went about collecting lichen off the rocks which
they then sold for $1\frac{1}{2}$d. a pound. (54) Those few married labourers
who (in the years before the railways) were near enough to make the
journey, often went to the iron works at Merthyr in the winter
months, returning to the farms in the summer. Another way in which
a small number of this outdoor class increased their earnings was
through migration to corn-growing areas of the English midlands and
Glamorgan for harvest work. (55)

The rise in wages of the agricultural wage earner from mid century was to some extent cancelled by the rising cost of living. The
outdoor married labourers faced not only the rising prices of these
years but also, in many cases, an increase in rents for their newly
acquired village cottages. It was out of the question, therefore,
for this outdoor group to save to any significant extent. The
indoor servant was in a better position to save in the third quarter
of the century, but he seldom did so. (56) When the depression set
in from the late 1870s the labourer's condition was not adversely
affected. Although his money wages fell slightly, he was in real
terms better off through a sharper drop in food prices and other
commodities.

Two rough indices for measuring the labourer's standard of comfort at this time are his food and accommodation. Before mid century he had virtually subsisted on oaten or barley bread, potatoes
and milk. Fresh meat was a rare luxury. While the outdoor labourer
frequently kept a pig, he mostly sold it. (57) In 1849 Clare Sewell

Read blamed the low standard of work done in general by the Welsh
farm worker as compared with his counterpart in eastern England upon
a coarse and undernourishing diet. By 1870, however, some improvement had come about. It was now reported of south-west Wales that
wheaten bread was commonly used, although the high price of butchers'
meat was still beyond the labourer's means. At the same time, in
north Wales it was reported that wheaten bread was almost universally used and potatoes and green vegetables were regularly consumed.
Again, meat and bacon were eaten only to a small extent. Buttermilk
was used plentifully. (58) Further improvements were reported in
the 1890s. Now meat was eaten more regularly, on an average once a
day in north Wales, although fresh meat was restricted to Sundays
and harvest time. But the diet, despite improvements, was still
deficient; green vegetables were little eaten compared with potatoes, and fruit was hardly ever given to labourers. (59)

The aspect of the labourer's condition which came in for most
criticism by contemporaries was his accommodation. The worst conditions were perhaps those which prevailed on the farm premises
among the indoor servants and here the situation actually deteriorated in the late nineteenth century. Indoor servants slept either
in the farmhouse itself or more generally, so far as the males were
concerned, in the lofts over the stable or cow house. Male farm
servants preferred sleeping in the outbuildings because they were
free to come and go as they pleased. These outhouses were badly lit
and ventilated, while sanitary conditions were atrocious. (60) Accommodation within the farm house was criticised because of the lack
of strict division of sleeping quarters separating menservants from
the maids, the latter always sleeping in the farm house. Farm servants ate their meals in the farm kitchen and for most of the century
they were allowed to share the kitchen with the farmer's family for
a time after supper. But this last concession was being withdrawn
increasingly during the last quarter or so of the century when the
hitherto close relationship between employer and servant was fast
disappearing. (61) The lack of supervision of farm servants was
blamed throughout the century for inducing moral laxity. Indoor
male servants were free to roam the countryside at night in pursuit
of farm maids who were allowed to admit them to the farm houses.
Here the custom prevailed of 'sitting up' all night courting in the
kitchen or, less commonly, of 'bundling' or courting in bed. Permission to practise this last custom was often insisted upon earlier
in the century by indoor servants when engaging themselves for farm
service. By the late century the custom had become far less prevalent in north Wales, while still remaining popular in Cardiganshire,
Carmarthenshire and north-west Pembrokeshire. However, even in
these areas of survival decline had come about through the influence
of Nonconformity. The custom was common, too, in Lancashire, Scotland, Norway, Sweden and America. (62)

Much dissatisfaction also existed throughout the century with the
cottages of the married labourers. In the early nineteenth century
these were mostly attached to the farms and held by the labourers
directly from their employers. Walter Davies, writing at the opening of the century, described the majority of the mud-walled and
thatched-roofed cottages in south Wales as 'huts of the most humble
plans and materials' and those of north Wales as the 'habitations of

wretchedness'. (63) Cottages in Wales and the north of England were
far inferior to many of those found at this time in the southern
English counties. (64) Some improvement in structure in Wales had
been achieved by the late 1840s, for now the walls were being made
of stone and mortar and the roofs of slate. They were, nevertheless,
still darkly lit, poorly ventilated and too confined for health or
comfort. (65) The isolation of the farm cottages, their growing
scarcity arising from both the landlords' and farmers' policy of
allowing them to fall into disrepair, and the greater independence
of living in cottages not tied to the employment, led farm labourers
increasingly in the late nineteenth century to look for cottages in
or near the villages. This latter trend, however, should not be
exaggerated, for at the close of the century, with the major exception of the Vale of Glamorgan, village life was said to be 'not a
marked characteristic of rural Wales'. (66) There is little readily
available information about the ownership patterns of Welsh villages,
except that there were no 'close' villages in the Union of Builth
and only a very small number in which one proprietor owned nearly
all the cottages. (67) In both the old farm cottages and the village ones, despite improvements arising from the creation of sanitary districts by the terms of the Public Health Act of 1875, there
were inadequacies, particularly the lack of separate sleeping accommodation and defective sanitation. Little, reporting in the 1890s,
singled out the housing of the labourer in both England and Wales as
the most grievous factor in his condition. But landowners in many
areas of England were improving cottage accommodation on their
estates, a tendency notably absent in Wales. Little concluded: 'It
would seem that bad as the cottage accommodation is in some parts of
England, it is far worse in Wales. The general standard of accommodation is lower, and there is much less evidence of progress and improvement.' (68) The wretched accommodation in certain instances
can be explained by the fact that cottages in many districts had
often originated in squatters' settlements. (69)

   Evidence from farm labourers themselves concerning their accommodation and other matters is difficult to obtain. The Land Commissioners came across one labourer, however, who was prepared to give
evidence, in the person of David Williams of Burry Green, Gower,
Glamorgan. He maintained that the scarcity of married labourers in
his area was caused mainly by inadequate cottage accommodation. In
particular, he, like so many others, condemned the normal practice
of tied cottages, because under this system if a man lost his job on
a particular farm he lost his house as well. Landlords, he protested, should erect cottages and let them directly to the labourers.
(70)

   Summing up on the general condition of the agricultural wage
earner over the course of the century, it is clear that until about
the middle of the century he lived a harsh, impoverished existence:
hours of work were strenuously long, wages low, accommodation harsh,
and his diet meagre and undernourishing. Indoor servants, however,
comprising up to a half of the hired labour force early in the century, were relatively more secure than the married labourers: once
engaged they enjoyed a certain amount of employment throughout the
year and their living-in meant that they were protected from the
price fluctuations of necessary foods in the years before the repeal

of the Corn Laws. Although their accommodation, food and hours of
work all made for a miserable existence, records of their spending
clearly reveal that some at least were able to purchase essentially
luxury items and, rather than save, spent in pursuit of pleasure
mainly at fairs and weddings. (71) The worst conditions were undoubtedly those experienced by the married labourers, who were uncertain of employment and, particularly in the winter months, were
often forced onto the parish or Union for relief. For those who
were able to make the journey, seasonal migration to the iron works
or to the corn harvest, involving family separation, were means of
riding hard times and of warding off the threat of the hated workhouse. Of vital importance to the outdoor labourer's survival was
his potato plot, and when this crop failed, as for instance in 1847,
terrible suffering ensued. The slight advance in wages which had
occurred in south Pembrokeshire, we are told, was 'nothing to be
compared to this loss'. (72) Old age was a daunting prospect, many
no doubt preferring to die of starvation than to suffer the humilia-
tion of the workhouse. The general picture here presented of an
impoverished, degraded class of outdoor labourers was not true for
the whole of Wales, however. Able-bodied pauperism was largely
absent in Monmouthshire and Glamorgan in the 1830s and 1840s outside
periods of recession in the iron trade. (73) The drain of surplus
rural labour to the iron works left the remaining labourers on the
land relatively well off. (74)

Although crimes of violence were 'almost unknown' among the rural
population in these early years, it is hardly surprising that petty
theft, poultry stealing, sheep stealing, horse and cattle stealing
(though not cattle maiming), and theft of barley and turnips, should
have featured as the typical crimes in this impoverished society.
Poaching of the streams for salmon and the moors for game was a form
of self-help by which the labourer procured fresh meat and fish for
his table. (Sometimes he salted the salmon and sold it.) Farm servants, too, went poaching, probably for the sport and diversion it
provided. In the Denbigh area, for instance, they used to steal
straw from the farms and go along the banks of the river Clwyd with
torches and spears to catch salmon. Similarly, in south Pembrokeshire they used to lime the local streams. Sometimes gangs of
poachers offered open defiance and violent clashes with the authorities inevitably resulted. One such affray took place on the night
of 3 July 1830 at the fishery of Blackpool on the river Cleddau,
Pembrokeshire, when a large poaching gang, led by John Llewellin, a
labourer, clashed with and beat up the steward of the local Slebech
estate and five others. Farm servants, interestingly following the
lead of farmers and their sons, were members of the poaching gangs
which openly defied the authorities along the banks of the Wye and
its streams in the 1850s. (75)

The condition of the agricultural wage earner improved steadily
from the mid 1850s, the all-important factor for change being the
railway. Down to 1870 or so the improvement was basically an advance in wages. And, in this respect, the proximity of coal and
iron works in the south and of slate quarries and lead mines in the
north meant that, on balance, the wages of the Welsh labourer were
higher than those in many of the southern counties of England,
though not so high as in the northern and eastern districts. (76)

From the 1870s improvement lay primarily in an amelioration of the
general environment. Thus, the educational provisions of the 1870s
made education compulsory for the labourers' children who could no
longer be put to work in the fields and farmyards as before. Higher
earnings meant that the labourer's wife, too, need no longer go out
to work. And shorter hours enabled the outdoor labourer to spend
more time with his family. The labourer's diet, too, was improved,
although the system of boarding the outdoor labourer meant that the
wives and children suffered through receiving a smaller cash income.
Small wonder, then, that poaching was still an important means of
providing for the family, although the chance of excitement in join-
ing the poaching gangs with their blackened faces, and also the
growing feeling of resentment towards the Game Laws and the odious
sporting tenants, no doubt largely explains why game offences were
on the increase from the late 1860s. (77) Some improvement had
taken place in cottage accommodation but this, along with that of
indoor servants, remained abysmal throughout, and worse than elsewhere in Britain. The influence of the Nonconformist pulpit and the
temperance movement led to an increase in sobriety among farm workers later in the century. Furthermore, a new self-respect was
afforded the labourer by his gaining the vote in 1884 and by the
changes in local government from 1888. What was lacking above all
at the close of the century were adequate recreational facilities
both of a physical and an intellectual kind. Also, relatively few
Welsh labourers throughout the century were members of benefit
societies and in times of sickness they were dependent on the meagre
provision of the parish. (78)

III

Finally, we must discuss the incidence of disturbances and combinations among Welsh agricultural wage earners in this period. Although this class, especially the outdoor labourers, lived an impoverished existence in the early nineteenth century, they did not rise
in widespread revolt in the autumn and winter of 1830-1 as did the
labourers of the south and south-eastern counties of England.
Labourers there rose for higher wages, better working conditions
and, above all, against the hated threshing machine which had led to
a loss of winter employment. (79) Barns, ricks and poor houses were
burned, and threshing machines were smashed. David Jones has shown
that in Wales threatening 'Swing' letters appeared, and disturbances
and burnings occurred, mainly in east Glamorgan, on a small scale, and,
to a more serious extent, in Monmouthshire, where threshing machines
were threatened. Threatening letters were also sent to the owners
of the Stackpole, Orielton and Brownslade estates in the corn-
growing area of south-west Pembrokeshire. Special Constables were
sworn in not only in these three counties, but also in Montgomeryshire and Flintshire to put down any violence. (80)
    It is significant that disturbances in Wales were confined to the
corn-growing areas of the south-east. Dissatisfaction with low
wages also played a part in causing unrest in this area in 1830-1.
There can be no doubt that labourers in the Vale of Glamorgan, who
generally lived on their own find, must have been miserably

impoverished in 1829 and 1830, when wet summers brought high corn
prices. There is evidence of some agitation for higher wages in the
Vale in the winter of 1830. Lord Bute's agent, E.P. Richards, wrote
to him on 10 December 1830 that he had been told 'there had been a
meeting of Labourers at Boverton to obtain an Increase of Wages but
that the Meeting passed over without any disturbance or tendency to
mischief'. Again, on the same day, Talbot of Margam wrote to his
estate steward: 'Let me hear if there is any further intelligence
of meetings of Labourers to raise wages.' On the night of 10 December a rick of hay belonging to Grey of Dyffrin House, in the parish
of St Nicholas, was set on fire and a letter addressed to him was
found near the spot charging him to lower his rents. Other papers
were circulated in the neighbourhood 'urging the farmers to compel a
reduction of rent that the Labourers might be better paid'. Besides
hatred of the threshing machine and a reduction in real wages in
1829-30, excitement among the labourers was possibly also engendered
by the Reform crisis. E.P. Richards wrote to Lord Bute on 4 December 1830:

> It is pretty evident that the language nightly made use of in
> both Houses of Parliament by the late opposers of the Administra-
> tion has had its effect both here and throughout the Country in
> raising an opposition to the existing order of things and the
> consequence has been that disaffection and disloyalty have gained
> ground most rapidly, though in this county fortunately it has not
> gained head sufficiently to show itself in open acts of hostility.

Undoubtedly a crucial factor in raising the level of excitement
among the labourers in the Vale was the premature swearing in of
Special Constables. E.P. Richards and Talbot of Margam both condemned such action among the magistrates as likely to inflame and
arouse the labourers. It was stated later of the parishes of Llandaff and Radyr: 'The few Riots and Burnings which took place in
this part of the country I believe were increased by a degree of
excitement which was unnecessarily produced by the Swearing of
Special Constables.' (81)

Even within the arable area of the south-east, however, the
really significant feature was not so much the degree of damage to
property but rather the general lack of disturbances. Part of the
explanation, of course, is that even in the Vale of Glamorgan farming was essentially of a mixed kind rather than wholly arable.
Again, farm wages were not so wretchedly low here as in the south of
England. Thus, Talbot, in his letter of 10 December quoted above,
after inquiring about meetings to raise wages, added 'They have not
the excuse of the poor devils in England who only get 7s. a week,
and pay £3 a year for their miserable cottages, besides the expense
of fuel.' In this last comment, there lies an important clue to the
explanation for the general lack of disturbances in Glamorgan and
Monmouthshire in 1830-1, even though labourers' wages were depressed
at this particular time. As already shown, there was no significant
surplus population in Glamorgan and Monmouthshire with the result
that labourers were usually employed and wages were 'as compared
with most English counties, above an average rate'. In 1831 a sympathetic address to the Glamorgan farm labourers commented: 'You
may think yourselves poor; but you can only form a faint idea of
what poverty is in the Eastern and Southern counties of England.'(82)

There is no problem in explaining the complete absence of labourers' disturbances elsewhere in Wales in 1830-1. The fundamental
reason was that Wales was for the most part a region of pastoral
farming. Again, 'the seditious works from the London Press' had
little chance in influencing many of the monoglot Welsh-speaking
labourers. (83) Important, too, was the mode of living in scattered
farm houses over most of the principality which prevented easy combination of effort between members of the labouring classes. It is
doubtful, however, if there was any widespread ill-feeling on the
part of the Welsh labourers against their employers at this particular time or at any other time in the miserable, impoverished years
up to mid century. In the years of severe hardship, tension understandably crept in. Thus, in the years 1841-3, the return of
labourers from the iron works to the rural parishes of Glamorgan
meant considerable discontent among the labouring population. In
west Wales labourers in the late summer of 1843 abandoned their
former support of the farmers in the Rebecca Riots and began to hold
their own meetings to press for better wages and allowances. (84)
But for the most part, as I have argued throughout, institutional
and social relations between farmers and their labourers were close
in these years up to mid century - a veritable patriarchal system.
Thus, labourers, though greatly impoverished (particularly the married ones) did not view their employers as a class apart and unsympathetic towards their plight.

The improved condition of the agricultural wage earner in Wales
after 1850 was accompanied by the growth of a greater feeling of independence on his part than formerly. Symbolising the growing gulf
between farmer and labourer was the substitution around mid century
of the formal address 'Master' and 'Mistress' for the kindly old
terms 'uncle' and 'aunt'. (85) Greater opportunities for alternative employment naturally strengthened his bargaining position and
made him less easy to manage. Feelings of discontent, too, were
aroused among the indoor servant class by the withdrawal of previous
privileges, like sitting in the kitchen after supper and drying wet
clothes. It has been stressed that great dissatisfaction was felt
over accommodation. Yet, given the new spirit of independence and
discontent with conditions, there was a singular lack of labourers'
unions to agitate for improvements. The Labourers' Union of the
1860s and 1870s which grew up in England under Joseph Arch had no
parallel in Wales. The Lleufer Thomas report on Welsh agricultural
labourers in 1894 spoke of a 'total absence' of farm labourers'
unions in Wales. Some combinations of labourers for shorter hours
were from time to time attempted, but upon gaining small concessions
these soon disbanded. The strongest combination came in Anglesey
and Caernarvonshire in 1889-91 and obtained a substantial reduction
in working hours. With this much achieved, however, the movement
fell apart, despite the fact that the farmers appeared helpless to
oppose their demands, and the desire for a trade union on the part
of the leader of the movement, John Owen Jones, did not materialise.
At Michaelmas 1891 the labourers of south Pembrokeshire, encouraged
by certain delegates from England, proposed to join a labourers'
federation in order to gain a wage rise of 2s. a week. In most districts the farmers compromised and granted a 1s. rise, whereupon the
proposed union came to nought. (86)

The reasons for this lack of labourers' unions in Wales resemble some of those explaining the quiescence of 1830-1. Thus, the scattered nature of the labour force was an important factor earlier in the century, but in the 1860s and 1870s was of even greater importance for it greatly reduced the influence of the press, which was so vital to labour agitation in south-east England, (87) and so isolated Welsh labourers from external events and trends of opinion. Again, as earlier, the small size of Welsh farms meant a high degree of family labour where the interests of employers and workers were not in conflict. Furthermore, with regard to the labour force outside the family circle, down to the end of the century, notwithstanding the decline in the old semi-patriarchal system, there were strong ties between the employer and workers, particularly with regard to indoor servants. In this way, feelings of a separate identity as a class were hardly likely to take strong root. J.P.D. Dunbabin has demonstrated for the whole of England a close correlation between trade unionism and the absence of indoor servants. Unionism was virtually absent where the ratio of outdoor labourers to indoor servants was less than 3 to 1. (88) In Wales the ratio in 1871 was 0.9 to 1 for the north and 1 to 1 for the south. Again, as far as Wales was concerned, married labourers generally boarded at the farm and thereby feelings of a separate identity were retarded. Farmers and labourers in the principality, as stressed throughout, were hardly distinguishable in their mode of life and had a common sympathy for one another's position. Many farmers had risen from the ranks of the labourers and many labourers aspired to become farmers.

To a limited extent hiring fairs reduced the need for organised trade unions for the growing scarcity of labour in the last quarter of the century or so meant that such fairs served as a kind of labourers' trade union. It was the reverse of the previous situation of plentiful labour when the hiring fair had resembled a combination on the part of the farmers for the purpose of keeping wages low. A Caernarvonshire labourer was of the opinion in the 1890s that 'on the whole, the hiring fair is advantageous to the labourer'. Here, in Caernarvonshire and Anglesey, the hiring fair remained down to the end of the century the typical mode of engaging farm servants, and there existed a kind of understanding among them not to engage themselves outside the fairs. The Land Commissioners concluded in the 1890s that the hiring fairs helped servants to secure both greater uniformity and advances in the rates of wages than they could otherwise have achieved. But such fairs were of declining influence in this respect, for, as noted, farmers outside of the two counties mentioned were tending increasingly from the 1880s to engage servants at home. They were responding to the growing scarcity of labour and to the mounting criticism from the respectable members of society that hiring fairs were dens of vice and immorality. (89)

Down to the close of the century, to repeat, farmers and labourers lived and worked side by side in reasonable harmony. The crucial change in relations came only during the war years of 1914-18, when increases in labourers' wages failed to keep pace with the rising cost of living. Labourers felt that farmers were not allowing them a share in the big war-time profits. This feeling of hostility was especially pronounced in the industrial areas of

Glamorgan and Monmouthshire, where contact with industrial trade unionism provided added militancy. The growing gulf between the classes led to the formation of Agricultural Labourers' Unions in many Welsh counties during the war years. (90)

CHAPTER 7

MARKETING

I

The marketing of agricultural produce depended in part upon what
could be produced. As shown above, physical and climatic factors
dictated that Wales should be essentially a country of pastoral
farming with the major items of output comprising cattle, sheep,
pigs and horses, and livestock products like wool, butter, cheese
and eggs. Other important conditions of trade were the absence of
large local markets for consumer goods and the imperfect communications linking rural Wales with external markets in the years before
railways were built. This meant that coastal shipping played an
important role in the marketing of Welsh agricultural produce, particularly in the shipment of produce to Bristol. In the early nineteenth century Bristol's traditional function as the metropolis of
south Wales was to some extent altered towards becoming the entrepôt.
Shipments of agricultural produce from south Wales to Bristol were
increasingly transhipped to Cardiff and Newport en route to the
mining valleys of south-east Wales.
    It is impossible to quantify the internal trade in agricultural
produce, and any attempt to do so for the external trade runs into
difficulties because of a lack of reliable statistics. However,
some evidence exists to give a partial impression of the volume of
external trade in the early nineteenth century. Walter Davies in
1810 stated that 8000 head of cattle were exported from Anglesey
every year. Later, in 1848, the number yearly exported from Anglesey to England was reported to have risen to between 10,000 and
12,000. At the same time 5000 to 7000 cattle were annually sent out
from the Llŷn peninsula. It was estimated that on the eve of the
coming of railways 13,000 cattle left Carmarthenshire, 10,000 left
Pembrokeshire and 7000 left Cardiganshire, for English markets.
Estimates also survive for numbers of sheep sent out of Wales. It
was claimed in 1849 that from 5000 to 7000 sheep annually left
Anglesey for English fattening areas. In 1845 it was estimated that
20,000 sheep a year were driven from the Llŷn peninsula and another
20,000 from the district around Caernarvon. (1)
    Second, information about quantities of livestock and other agri-
cultural produce shipped from the coastal regions either to Bristol

or Liverpool is provided in the Bills of Entry for those ports. Produce shipped from the ports in the south went to Bristol and from
those in the north to Liverpool. No trade in livestock between the
ports of south Wales and Bristol was recorded, but regular shipments
were made from the ports of north Wales to Liverpool. Only small
numbers of cattle and sheep were shipped. For example, in 1835 only
103 cows, 88 calves, 24 bulls, 255 sheep and 84 lambs were sent out
from north Wales. In marked contrast, some 12,385 pigs were shipped
to Liverpool in that year, mainly from Beaumaris, Holyhead, Amlwch,
Bangor, Porthdinllaen and Pwllheli. Numbers sent out in other years
were:

1832   6,444
1837   10,484
1847   12,072
1855   65

These pigs were shipped in fat condition. (2) The figures recorded
for both cattle and pigs show that the volume of trade was increasing between 1815 and 1850 in response to the growing demand for meat
from the rising centres of industry.

    Some indication of the volume of dairy produce and corn shipped
from Welsh ports is provided in tables 7.1 and 7.2. Substantial

TABLE 7.1 Shipments of dairy produce from selected Welsh ports,1847

Port	Butter*	Cheese**	Eggs
Carmarthen	422 casks 1 pot	674 cheeses	24 boxes
Haverfordwest	891 casks 50 pots	827 cheeses 15 cwts	4 boxes
Solva	373 casks	454 cheeses	nil
Cardigan	7 casks	69 cheeses	4 boxes
Beaumaris	19 crannocks	nil	nil
Pwllheli	66 cwts	nil	500 eggs
Porthdinllaen	45½ cwts 77 pots 46 crannocks	nil	4100 eggs 12 panniers
Mostyn	10 cwts	242 cwts	nil

Source: Bristol and Liverpool Bills of Entry.
* Cask = 100-120 lbs.
** Cheese = 20-130 lbs.

quantities of dairy produce were shipped from south-west Wales. Exports of grain were mainly of oats followed by barley and, in much
smaller quantities, by wheat. A marked fall-off in shipments of
both dairy produce and corn occurred from the mid 1850s owing to the
more efficient transport afforded by the railways.

    Agricultural items in this land and sea export trade were collec-
ted by the system of fairs and markets and private transactions at

TABLE 7.2 Shipments of corn from selected Welsh ports, 1832 and 1835

Port	Wheat (bushels)		Barley (bushels)		Oats (bushels)	
	1832	1835	1832	1835	1832	1835
Aberthaw	3,568 +280 sacks	1,200	13,424 +70 sacks	6,920 +180 sacks	64	nil
Carmarthen	2,539 +60 sacks	914	15,989 +40 sacks	4,543	152,567	105,891
Haverfordwest	9,696	1,884	7,768	4,146 +40 sacks	84,048	81,643 +102 sacks
Cardigan	1,248	nil	1,384	733	35,648	27,712
Beaumaris	nil	nil	680	896	14,280	26,088 +7 sacks
Pwllheli	nil	448	3,776	9,776 +4 sacks	200	360
Amlwch	976	144	4,752	9,160 +26 sacks	29,512	67,304
Caernarvon	80	nil	nil	80 +16 sacks	960	1,680

Source: Bristol and Liverpool Bills of Entry.

farm houses. Fairs, primarily for the sale of livestock, were held
in many Welsh towns and villages on average three times a year,
often on feast days. Small villages like Wiston in Pembrokeshire
and Cynwyd in Merioneth had only one fair a year, while large towns
like Carmarthen and Aberystwyth had as many as seven. They were
held throughout the four seasons but there was greater concentration
in the six months between May and October than in the six between
November and April. Thus, of the combined 341 fairs of all the
towns and villages of south Wales held during 1814, some 226 took
place between May and October and 115 between November and April.
The timing of the fairs was determined partly by the needs of the
English farmers for store cattle (grass-fed animals being needed in
the spring and stall-fed ones in the autumn), partly by the need to
rest store cattle immediately after the rigours of over-wintering,
and partly by the deplorable state of transport facilities in the
winter months. Oxen, steers and barren cows were thus sold off in
the greatest numbers in the spring and autumn fairs. Sheep sales
were mainly transacted between June and September. In June and July
the trade was mostly in wethers, while in August both wethers and
draft ewes were sold. September sales were mainly confined to ewes.
The most popular horse sales were in May and June, while pigs were
sold between November and February. The larger fairs extended over
two days, and in some places even three. Whereas cattle and horses
were sold first in the fairs of the south, followed by sheep and
hogs, this order was generally reversed in the north, reflecting the
importance of sheep farming in the area. (3)

The average fair-area in Wales in 1818 extended over thirty
square miles. (4) Despite these considerable travelling distances,
farmers took their livestock to a number of fairs in their localities, sometimes deliberately withholding their stock from sale at
one fair in the hope of realising better prices at the next. It has
been shown that in difficult years delays in rent payments were
often granted by agents who fully understood the necessity for this
practice of trying different fairs. Between 1818 and 1836 David
Thomas of Llan-y-Crwys, near Lampeter, Carmarthenshire, bought and
sold stock at the fairs of Lampeter, Cayo, Llanwnon, Llanybyther,
Llandovery and Llansawel. The tenant of Market Gate farm, in the
parish of Jeffreston, Pembrokeshire, bought and sold stock at the
fairs of Narberth, Maenclochog, Monkton and Pembroke between 1849
and 1861. (5)

Markets were held once a week at most small Welsh country towns
and bi-weekly in larger ones like Carmarthen, Cowbridge, Brecon and
Denbigh. Farmers brought to them their supplies of butter, cheese,
eggs, fowls, butchers' meat, wool, corn and knitted stockings. In
the pre-railway era, and, to a great extent afterwards, they conveyed their produce by horse and cart, or on foot.

Welsh store cattle assembled at the local fairs were purchased by
English or Welsh dealers for sale in the English markets. These
beasts were mainly three years old or more and were driven to the
fairs between spring and autumn. Cattle sold at various fairs in a
particular locality were collected together at one place by a dealer
in readiness for the tramp eastwards. The dealer employed hired
labourers, known as drovers, to drive the cattle to the English
centres. He himself normally followed by coach or on horseback the

day after and took charge of the sale of cattle upon their arrival.
The major routes reflected the location of the two great seasonal
markets. In the spring and early summer the main batches were
driven to the rich grazing districts around Northampton and Leicester for sale at the important market centres of Rugby, Northampton,
Leicester, Market Harborough, Uppingham and Daventry. Dealers with
adequate capital resources were able to draft their beasts into the
markets under the most favourable conditions, while others lacking
this advantage were forced to sell indiscriminately at the first
opportunity. During autumn and winter, cattle were driven to the
south-eastern counties where they were needed for yard or stall-
feeding. The chief market centres here were Chelmsford, Colchester,
Bromtree, Romford, Brentwood, Hertford and Bedford. (6)

The most important drovers' routes crossing Wales to the English
border avoided wherever possible the turnpike roads in order to
escape toll charges. In addition, these roads were hard and tiring
for cattle. The drovers, therefore, made across country following
the old prehistoric and packhorse tracks and Roman roads. However,
R. Colyer shows that certain drovers chose to use the turnpike roads,
calculating that the advantages gained in having the pick of the
markets would offset the toll charges. (7) The routes from the
Welsh border to Northamptonshire naturally varied with the points of
entry to England. Those entering England from Kington made their
way across the border through Pembridge, Leominster, Bromyard, Wor-
cester, Stratford-on-Avon, Warwick, Daventry and on to Northampton.
Droves entering through Shrewsbury followed Watling Street through
to Lutterworth, Rugby and onwards to the Northampton district.
Cattle crossing the border at Kington or Shrewsbury destined for the
south-eastern counties normally followed the same route to Northampton and thence through Bedford to Chelmsford, Ongar, Brentwood or
Romford. (8) The journey from west Wales to Northamptonshire took
from fifteen to twenty days, while twenty-five to thirty days were
necessary to reach the markets of the south-east. Cattle, on average, were able to walk between twenty and twenty-five miles a day.
It has been estimated that even with careful driving cattle from
north Wales would lose up to a hundredweight en route to the Midland
grazing areas. (9)

Little is known about the profit margins of the dealers, but some
indications are provided in the records of the Jonathan family of
Dihewyd, south Cardiganshire. (10) Between 1862 and 1864 their
accounts reveal that the gross average margin per head was fairly
constant at about 16s., which meant a profit of ten per cent on the
cost price of the animal. Listed expenses were more variable, from
8s. to more than 12s., and so the net profit fluctuated between
3s.4d. and 8s.9d. per head. Expenses differed considerably from one
journey to the next owing to inclement weather sometimes involving
the purchase of hay and grain on the road. At other times there
were difficulties in selling, a reflection of rudimentary market
intelligence and time lost on the road which meant added expense in
maintaining the cattle on purchased hay and grass. Summer trips
involved less expense than at other times. Expenses were made up
chiefly of toll-payments, the cost of grass for the animals on the
journey, shoeing the beasts, beer and lodgings for the drovers and
the dealer, and the drovers' wages. In the case of the drover

Roderick Roderick of Lampeter, Cardiganshire, the daily wage was 2s.
with all expenses paid. (11)

Until the close of the eighteenth century Welsh drovers (12) had
obtained the means of purchasing cattle from various sources, including advances by the receiver of taxes. (13) Afterwards, much of the
necessary capital was supplied by the private banks which had grown
up in the late eighteenth century. Thus by 1840 Wilkins and Co.,
from their first establishment at Brecon in 1778, had extended their
business over most of south Wales. They would advance sums of up to
£2000 for two or three months on the joint promissory note of a
drover and his surety. The money would then be used to pay the
farmer for his cattle. In granting accommodation to the drovers
they were more cautious than certain other banks, demanding that
'some responsible person' should vouch the good faith of their
drover-client. Indeed, banks like the 'Black Ox' of Llandovery, and
Waters, Jones and Co. of Carmarthen, would advance a drover about
four times as much as the Brecon bank without collateral security.
(14) It is doubtful whether drovers could have conducted their
business without such accommodation from the banks. Thus, when Wilkins and Co. withdrew £1 notes from 5 February 1829, accommodation
to drovers in particular was reduced, and many were consequently
'thrown out of business'. (15)

Many drovers were Welsh and small-time, and it was customary for
them to sell on a commission system. This extra risk sometimes fell
on the farmer, for if the drover failed to realise the price in England which he anticipated, he contrived to get 5s. a head or so
allowed him at the time of settlement. Sometimes he absconded with
the money, or became bankrupt, whereby the farmer got only a minimal
return. (16) Bankers were not immune from the bad faith of their
drover-clients as David Lewis, a banker at Newcastle Emlyn, Carmarthenshire, found to his cost when, in 1792, he advanced £500, albeit
on collateral security, to William Jones for the purpose of buying
cattle at Newcastle fair. Jones defaulted. (17) It is not surprising, then, that a commonly used epithet at the time was 'Not only a
drover but a rogue'. A report on Anglesey in 1807 bitterly attacked
the 'swindling drovers' whose characters were 'not worth a chew of
tobacco'. It also blamed the niggardliness of the farmer, who preferred to risk all his property on credit rather than accept money
in hand from some other dealer because the latter would not give the
5s. or 6s. more for the beast which the 'swindler' offered him. 'But
to their sorrow,' adds the report, 'the bait has too often ruined
them.' (18)

Sheep, both ewes and wethers, were also sent out of Wales in
store condition. In the pre-railway age they were similarly driven
to the English markets, the most important of which were in the
neighbourhood of London, at Pinner, Watford, Harrow, Stanmore and
Barnet. Middlesex farmers had a great liking for Welsh mountain
ewes. Although there is ample evidence that some of the sheep were
purchased for the English markets at the local Welsh fairs, it often
happened that jobbers bought sheep off the farms and conveyed them
directly to the English fattening areas. K. Bonser informs us that
sheep usually followed the same routes as cattle and were dispatched
in flocks of 1500 to 2000. The journey to the south-east took from
twenty to twenty-five days, sheep on an average covering twelve
miles a day. (19)

The gross profit margins of the sheep-droving business of the Jonathan family varied between 2s.2d. in 1862 and 1s.2d. in 1864, yielding an average of about 1s.8d. per head to meet all expenses and to make a profit after allowing some interest on capital. There was thus a 15 per cent profit on the cost price of the animal. Expenses over the three seasons 1862-4 remained fairly constant at from 9d. to 10d. a sheep. The net profit in 1862 was 1s.5d. a sheep, in 1863 9d. and in 1864 4d. (20)

Pig droving was also an important business. Large numbers of lean hogs from west Wales were sold in the Bristol markets. They were driven across the coastal lowlands of south Wales, finally taking the Passage across the Severn. Although, as will be shown later, increasing numbers of fat pigs were being sent out of west Wales to Merthyr, the Bristol market remained the primary one for pigs reared in that region down to mid century. (21) Pigs were also taken out of north Wales by drovers for the English markets. They were generally sold in fat condition. Dolgellau had an important pig market whence fat pigs were driven to Shrewsbury, Bridgenorth, Wolverhampton, Dudley, Bilston and Birmingham. The routes followed were roughly the same as those used by cattle. (22)

Much of the grain, butter, cheese and eggs was sold mainly to satisfy the limited local demand, and the marketing organisation was accordingly even more rudimentary. For instance, the small amount of dairy produce that found its way to external markets from inland Wales was easily handled by higglers. They bought up the heavily salted tub butter in the interior regions of north Wales and sent it to the Chester and Shrewsbury markets. Thus, in the spring and summer about three tons of butter a week were sent from Bala to Chester. Cheese bought up in the local markets of north Wales was sent to the fairs at Chester, Wrexham, Shrewsbury, Bridgenorth and Wolverhampton where it was purchased by buyers from London, Liverpool and Manchester. It will be shown that considerable quantities of butter were, however, sent from inland areas of south-west Wales to the iron manufacturing areas of Glamorgan and Monmouthshire, but here also, part of the trade was handled by higglers. Farmers themselves often carted their own supplies to external markets. (23)

Only in the coastal areas was corn and dairy produce exported in sufficient quantities to justify a merchant organisation. Figures quoted earlier emphasise that Carmarthen and Haverfordwest were especially important in sending out large shipments to Bristol. In 1830 there were nine butter merchants resident at Carmarthen, one of whom also dealt in cheese, while in 1844 there were fourteen. There were six butter merchants at Haverfordwest in 1830 and two more in 1844. The same merchants in both ports also handled corn and flour. The large exports of grain from Amlwch in Anglesey justified the operation there of five corn merchants in the 1840s. (24)

The development of the iron industry in Glamorgan and Monmouthshire created for the first time a huge internal demand for agricultural produce. It was estimated that Merthyr alone in the 1840s had upwards of 2000 horses and these, as well as others elsewhere, had to be fed with hay, straw, oats and beans. (25) The 200 horses kept by John Nixon at his Mountain Ash coal works in the early 1860s consumed nearly 400 tons of hay a year. (26) The working population required wheat, flour, bacon, meat, butter, cheese and potatoes.

This growth of industry in its early stages made use of the eighteenth-century marketing pattern based on Bristol because, until the
South Wales Railway linked west Wales with the coalfield, transport
facilities were designed to link the inland towns with the ports.
Produce thus shipped to Bristol from west Wales increasingly finished up in the growing industrial towns of the south-east. Evidence given before the Select Committees of both Houses of Parliament on the South Wales Railway Bill in 1845 amply demonstrates this.
The 'want of direct communication' from Carmarthenshire and Pembrokeshire to the industrial areas of Glamorgan and Monmouthshire meant
that a 'considerable portion of it' was sent in sailing vessels and
steamers to Bristol. Most of it was 'resold in Bristol for the
eastern parts of south Wales' and then 'reshipped at Bristol for the
supply of those parts'. The same applied to Irish produce ultimately destined for the same markets. (27) Very large quantities of
provisions shipped from the southern ports of Ireland to Bristol
were resold there by Bristol middlemen to merchants from south-east
Wales, and then transhipped to Cardiff and Newport in order to reach
the mining districts by the canals. The 'small amount of intermediate traffic between one port and the other' in south Wales was
the main reason why Bristol continued to exercise the function of
entrepôt, developing a steamer service between itself and Cardiff.(28)
     Further evidence as to the continued importance of Bristol was
provided in 1846 at the hearing concerning the Vale of Neath Railway
Bill. William Young, a flour and provision merchant of Neath, testified that the mining population about Merthyr was largely supplied
with food through the port of Bristol and the Cardiff route. Edward
Morgan, a Merthyr corn merchant, agreed that a small quantity of
corn was sent from Pembrokeshire and other parts of south-west Wales
to Merthyr via the roundabout route of Bristol, Cardiff and up the
Taff Vale railway, or the canal. (29) Again, John Williams of
Cardiff observed in 1860:

     From the latter of the two ports above named /Carmarthen/ were
     exported considerable quantities of barley, oats and butter,
     principally conveyed to market at Bristol: and up to a very
     recent period, previous to the extension of railway communication,
     it was a very common occurrence for the corn merchants of Glamor-
     gan visiting the Bristol markets to purchase there the produce of
     counties adjacent to their own, bringing it by water to Newport
     and Cardiff. (30)

Difficulties of inland transport between the Vale of Glamorgan and
the industrial area to the north in the pre-railway era meant that
even corn grown in the Vale was marketed along traditional lines to
Bristol. From here, once again, it was often returned as flour or
malt to Cardiff to be forwarded to Merthyr via the Glamorgan canal
or the Taff Vale railway. (31)
     The growing industrial market of south-east Wales, therefore, did
little to change the traditional Welsh marketing organisation in the
years before the South Wales Railway. Some modifications did occur,
however. Edward Morgan, the Merthyr merchant, testified in 1846
that large quantities of butter, pigs and poultry reached Merthyr by
cart from Pembrokeshire, Carmarthenshire and Cardiganshire. (32)
These carts were known as 'Cardy' carts (most of them coming from
Cardiganshire) and left the south-western areas in groups of about a

dozen on Mondays, usually led by the farmers themselves. They went
as far east as the iron towns of Monmouthshire. (33) Fat pigs were
sometimes driven from the fairs of west Wales (stretching as far
north as that of Towyn in Merioneth) to the industrial markets of
the south-east. (34) Butter from Glamorgan and Brecknockshire was
also sent to the mining towns. Corn, too, was sent from Radnorshire
to Merthyr which, by 1814, was its 'best market though at a distance
of upwards of 50 miles through Builth and over the Wye at Glasbury'.
(35) The demand for butchers' meat led to the rich pastures of the
Vale of Glamorgan being utilised towards the production of fat
cattle and sheep. Most of Merthyr's potato supply also came from
the Vale. (36)

Transport costs, however, severely limited the influence of
industrialisation upon Welsh farming in the years before the railway.
Butter from south-west Wales, for instance, was brought over the
hills to Merthyr in one-horse carts - distances covering from 57 to
70 miles - at a cost of £5 14s. a ton for 50 miles or 2s.3d. a ton-
mile. The journey both ways took up to a week and the cart usually
returned empty, though sometimes small quantities of coal were carried. The estimated cost for the carriage of a ton of butter over
the same distance by rail was 3d. a ton-mile. Again, the cost of
sending a ton of flour from Neath to Hirwaun was 12s. and from Neath
to Aberdare 14s., amounting to about 9d. a ton-mile, a cost which
allegedly prevented Neath merchants from sending farm produce drawn
from Ireland, Devonshire and Pembrokeshire to the mining districts.
(37) Difficult access to markets explains why the horses of the
Dowlais works were fed with grain imported from Ireland, for to
obtain oats from Brecknockshire 'would be too expensive', involving
as it did conveyance over the highest land in south Wales between
the Usk valley and Merthyr. (38) In a similar vein it was testified
in 1846 that most of the flour consumed at Merthyr came from Ireland,
partly because of the high transport costs involved in obtaining
corn supplies from south-west Wales. (39)

Even after the South Wales Railway was constructed across the
coastal plain, farmers from the Vale of Glamorgan found the continuing poor transport facilities to the iron works a severe drawback.
Accordingly, in 1862 a railway directly linking Cowbridge with Merthyr was advocated to prevent livestock from the Vale being driven
from the important Cowbridge market to either Bridgend or Llantrisant and then carried by the South Wales Railway westwards to Neath,
and finally up the Vale of Neath Railway to Merthyr, an overall rail
journey of 54 miles. Because of this roundabout route and its repu-
tation for delay, dealers preferred to have their livestock driven
from Cowbridge by road to the 'works'. The distance from Cowbridge
to Aberdare was 24 miles, involving two or three days on the road.
Sometimes this journey proved too much for the fat cattle, and
dealers had to slaughter them on the route. (40) Aberdare and Merthyr in the early 1860s formed the chief market for farmers in the
region about Cowbridge in hay, straw and oats. For this to reach
the mining area, it had either to be carted to Llandaff station and
so up the Taff Vale, or it went from Bridgend to Llantrisant westwards to Neath and up the Vale of Neath Railway. This westerly
route was used, for example, by Thomas Wilson, a farmer and hay merchant in the Cowbridge area, who sent from 600 to 1000 tons of hay

and about 100 tons of straw a year to Merthyr and Dowlais. He submitted that although the fifty miles journey (compared with the pro-
jected direct route of 24 miles) incurred extra expenses, it was the
loss of time and of trade under existing conditions which really
frustrated him. (41) Clearly, then, before the construction of an
adequate rail network the impact of industrialisation upon farming
in south Wales was restricted.

   Although lack of adequate transport facilities hindered the
farmer in the marketing of his produce, certain pre-railway improvements should be mentioned. Thus better roads in north Wales in the
early nineteenth century led to the decline of the great traditional
March fair of north Wales at Wrexham, as English dealers were enabled to travel to the interior regions of the west. Nevertheless,
conveyance along these roads - by waggons, carts and pack mules -
remained slow and expensive. (42) The construction of canals and
tramroads did something to improve access to markets. Thus, the
Montgomeryshire canal, completed in 1819, and the Brecon and Aberga-
venny canal, completed in 1811, the latter linking Brecknockshire
with the Bristol channel, were highly beneficial. The Hay tramroad
was opened in 1818, linking Brecon with Hay and with Eardesley, in
Herefordshire, and this facilitated the conveyance of farm produce
from Brecknockshire to the mining districts of the south. (43) River
transport, too, served particular areas. Thus corn was conveyed in
vessels down the Dee from Holt to Chester, and vessels were naviga-
ted up the Severn as far as Pool Quay until the construction of the
Montgomeryshire canal, when much of the traffic was transferred. (44)

II

The essential railway network was built piecemeal in Wales during
the third quarter of the nineteenth century. The Chester to Holyhead line, together with the connecting line from Caernarvon to
Bangor, was opened in 1852. In the same year the South Wales Railway reached Carmarthen; by December 1853 it had been extended to
Haverfordwest. A branch line from Llanelli to Llandeilo was opened
in January 1857 and was carried on to Llandovery by 1 April 1858.
By 1868 this line was extended via Llandrindod Wells to Shrewsbury.
The Tenby and Pembroke branch lines opened in 1863, and in 1864 and
1865 two lines were respectively opened from Carmarthen to Pencader
and to Llandeilo. The line from Pencader to Aberystwyth was opened
in 1867, and in the same year Aberystwyth was linked by rail to
Pwllheli. The mid-Wales line from Shrewsbury to Aberystwyth was
completed in sections between 1859 and 1866. In 1869 a connection
from Ruabon via Corwen, Bala and Dolgellau was made with the west
coast line. (45)

   One basic limitation in the transport network remained, however,
for the physical contour determined that the direction of Welsh
railways should be east to west; in this way the traditional problem of linking north and south Wales remained unsolved. This, together with the absence in mid and north Wales of any considerable
internal urban market, meant that farmers of these regions continued
to export, finding their new opportunities for their finished produce in the industrial areas of the Midlands and the northern

counties of England. In south Wales, on the other hand, it was the
domestic market of Glamorgan and Monmouthshire which provided farmers with new possibilities. But while different markets were imposed on north and south Wales, they presented the Welsh farmers of
all areas with the means of breaking away from the traditional
pattern of semi-subsistent agriculture.

In the first place, railways brought the same advantages to the
Welsh farmer as to the English by cheapening costs of transport.(46)
The droving system now came to an end, although it did not entirely
cease in so far as south Wales was concerned. Here, small numbers
of cattle still left on foot as late as the 1880s. (47) Hawke
points out that the benefit of railways in providing cheaper transport was even more considerable than at first sight because droving
in the nineteenth century was 'an industry of increasing costs'.(48)
Railways also provided speedier access to new and better markets.
The 'Welshman' in 1871 remarked that: 'The Manchester and Milford
railway has done as much good to Cardiganshire as if an immense town
had sprung up in the midst, with thousands of population requiring
to be fed. The railway carries off all the surplus produce to the
best markets of England.' (49) Fairly equal rates as between rail
and sea carriage, (50) together with the advantage of speed that
railways possessed over sea transport, meant that shipments of livestock from north Wales, as around the coast of Britain generally,
also declined sharply from the 1850s. Whereas 12,072 pigs were
shipped from the combined ports of north Wales in 1847, a mere 65
were shipped in 1855. Again, whereas 1148 sheep and 1771 lambs were
shipped from north Wales in 1847, by 1855 numbers shipped had fallen
to 90 and 170 respectively.

Besides benefiting the farmer by cheapening the marketing of
livestock and providing easy access to new and better markets, railways also remodelled the marketing of livestock in Britain by influencing a decline of the fairs. Those on or near railways flourished
at the expense of those at a distance. Thus, in Wales, for example,
the Llanbadarn fairs were merged with those of Aberystwyth; Lampeter
fairs in south Cardiganshire grew at the expense of a number of
neighbouring ones, and Bridgend grew at the expense of the hitherto
more important market town of Cowbridge. (51) Another way in which
railways influenced this decline was by allowing dealers to purchase
more easily at farms. The same tendency was felt in the Chard district of Somerset, and no doubt elsewhere. (52) Dealers calling at
farms was a traditional practice in Wales and one which might have
operated to the detriment of the Welsh farmer. Thus it was observed
of the neighbourhood of Machynlleth in the pre-railway era: 'It
were well for the farmers, we presume, if they were not in the habit
of disposing of their stock to buyers who go round the farm houses
in a clandestine manner, to purchase cattle at almost their own
prices.' (53) By 1913 it was stated:

There can be no doubt railways have to a large extent done away
with the need for markets as that need existed when sheep, cattle,
horses, and other animals had to be driven on foot to the popu-
lous centres. In a sense the modern farmer's market is wherever
he can find a buyer, and postal and railway facilities have
enabled him, by means of middlemen, to sell his stock in any part
of the country. (54)

It was stated in 1905 that 'some good fairs have become practically
extinct because of this disastrous practice'. Not only did travelling (often local) dealers stand to gain by private sales at home,
but the farmers themselves myopically clung to this mode of business.
'Cattle look better at home,' it was claimed by farmers, and there
was less loss of time and trouble involved. (55) Also, farmers were
often attached to local dealers for personal reasons. Moreover,
according to the 'Cambrian News', railway companies preferred the
system of private sales on farms to the open stock markets. Less
demand was made upon rolling stock and railway company rivalry and
competition were avoided. (56)

Although reduced in number, the old, periodic fairs in Wales survived the coming of the railways. (57) In many fattening regions of
England and Scotland, as, for example, in the Chard and Wellington
districts of Somerset, railways induced a catastrophic decline in
the traditional fairs through the growth of monthly, fortnightly,
weekly and bi-weekly auction markets on or near railroads for the
sale of fat stock. (58) But in rearing areas like Wales, specialis-
ing in stores, the traditional, periodic fairs remained dominant.
D. Alexander states: 'Fairs were still the most efficient means of
assembling buyers and sellers for the transfer of animals from scattered rearing grounds to the grazing areas near the towns and
cities.' (59) Thus, in Wales monthly and more frequent fat stock
auction markets did not supplant the old fairs as happened in so
many other areas of Britain. Railways did, however, influence the
growth of monthly livestock markets in Wales at certain towns
through which they passed, and such markets led to a decline in the
old fairs. (60) But these monthly markets, with the exception of a
few towns like Carmarthen where fat stock were sold in large amounts,
did not sell by auction, for store-rearing farmers in Wales, as in
England, were reluctant to pay a commission to the auctioneer. (61)

A further change brought by the railways was that areas far
removed from the main centres of demand could now fatten their animals rather than send them as stores to be fattened near the towns
and cities. (62) But this switch to grazing from rearing did not,
for the most part, take place in many parts of Wales. An authority
on Welsh agriculture argued in 1879: 'The rearing of frames for
English graziers to cover with flesh is a most unprofitable and
thankless labour, and yet this is the work that Wales does for English farmers.' (63) One obvious reason for this was that the natural poorness of the grass over much of the principality did not
easily permit farmers to finish their stock for the butcher. But it
is arguable that, with more enterprise, Welsh farmers could have
gone in for fattening to a greater extent with the coming of the
railways. The 'Cambrian News' stated impatiently in 1880: 'We have
contended for many years that land in Wales, if properly treated, is
as capable of fattening stock as land in many parts of Scotland,
where little else is done by ordinary farmers.' (64) A particular
requirement for cattle fattening was adequate housing and shelter,
and this was sadly lacking on most Welsh holdings. It has been
shown that the poverty of many small Welsh squires and the certainty
of even run-down farms being readily taken by land-hungry tenants
meant that they neglected to provide such essential facilities.
Tenants, on their side, desired to farm as cheaply as possible, and

this, as well as lack of capital, explains their reluctance to purchase the necessary feed inputs. The conservatism of the Welsh
tenants, too, explains their persistence in growing white crops at
the expense of turnips, swedes and mangolds necessary as cattle feed.
Welsh farmers clung to the view that they should produce everything
needed at home, and in this way semi-subsistence farming continued
as a feature of Welsh agriculture after the coming of the railways.
Rearing of store stock, therefore, continued predominant. Thus,
while railways fundamentally altered the means by which farmers marketed their produce, they did not lead to any basic change in the
system of farming.

Cheap transport, however, led to some extension of livestock fattening in south Wales to serve the industrial market of the south-
eastern valleys. In the Castlemartin area of south Pembrokeshire
farmers from mid century increasingly fattened their cattle for the
butchers, and at Pembroke in the 1870s could be seen the best and
largest show of fat stock in all three counties of south-west Wales.
(65) Further east, St Clears and Carmarthen were important marts
for the sale of fat cattle. (66) Many farms in the Vale of Glamorgan were managed on noticeably improved lines when compared with the
rest of the principality, (67) and one aspect of this was the feeding of Herefords and Shorthorns for the butcher. (68) The railway
also opened up the towns of the north country to the Welsh farmer
and so encouraged him in the fattening of some of his cattle. It
was reported of mid Cardiganshire in 1871: 'Every week the agents
of the north country butchers come down the Manchester and Milford
Railway and ... they sally forth, and going across country, snap up
the finest cattle they can lay their hands on.' (69) In north Wales,
the Vale of Clwyd, particularly, went in for cattle fattening. (70)
Moreover, as the drop in the demand for heavy prime fat beasts set
in from the 1880s onwards, the traditional trade in store cattle of
three years old and above began to decline. The growing demand for
smaller and leaner animals meant that Welsh farmers could now, in
some cases, mature their animals sooner.

Railways no less affected the marketing of other farm produce.
Overland carriage was greatly facilitated and the coastal traffic in
butter, cheese and corn declined as a result. Produce from south
Wales rural areas was mainly sent directly to the south Wales industrial towns, and Bristol's role as an agricultural entrepôt now
ended. In mid and north Wales, on the other hand, the purely local
markets for finished produce declined relative to those across the
border. As with the fairs, some local markets decayed because of
the absence of railways. Thus, the markets at Newcastle Emlyn, in
north Carmarthenshire, were in decline by 1883, a railway reaching
the town only in 1895. (71) But even when certain towns were provided with railways, they nevertheless declined because railways encouraged a few great centres. Thus, cheap transport meant a decline
in the Brecon markets in favour of larger places like Neath and Swansea, and Lampeter's Saturday market lost out to Carmarthen. (72)
Another reason for the gradual decline of many Welsh weekly markets,
despite rail facilities, was the increased farmgate sales to dealers.
(73) The latter tendency was helped, as already shown, by the
railways.

Railways opened up for the first time the industrial markets of

south-east Wales and the Midlands for Welsh butter, but not London.
In 1871 the 'Milk Journal', commenting upon the small quantity of
Welsh butter that reached the capital, stated that

> The country merchants in the Principality send all their butter
> to the 'black country' in the neighbouring counties; or, as in
> South Wales, to what they call 'the hills' viz. the mountainous
> iron districts of Glamorgan and Monmouth. The price obtained
> there is equally as high as could be given for it by London
> butter factors.

The proximity of these places and the big demand for it from the
mining population partly explains why it was not sold in the London
markets. (74) Of greater importance, however, was the fact that
Irish, Danish and New Zealand 'creamy' butter came to replace the
heavily salted tub butter in English markets. Railways played an
important role in facilitating the introduction of foreign butter,
and thus they not only opened Wales and the rest of rural Britain to
better markets but increased foreign competition. Despite changing
consumer tastes and a consequent falling off in sales in the principal English towns of the Midlands and elsewhere, Welsh farmers persisted in their traditional product. (75) Thus, sales of heavily
salted tub butter from Montgomeryshire fell at the Shrewsbury and
Oswestry fairs in the 1880s and 1890s. (76) Farmers of south-west
Wales were slow to adopt new methods of butter manufacture, partly
because of their innate conservatism but partly also because the
Glamorgan colliers continued their preference for the highly salted
Welsh butter. (77) But even here the native product gradually lost
ground to foreign competitors from the 1890s. (78) Further handi-
caps to successful marketing of Welsh butter lay in poor packaging,
the lack of a single unit of sale, and the absence of a brand indi-
cating the quality of the product. This latter deficiency contrasted, for instance, with the efficient branding system in the Cork
butter market. (79) Wholesalers in the large towns favoured the
standardised sources provided by Irish and foreign suppliers. Welsh
farmers were not alone in this lack of standardisation, however, for
English farmers from the late 1860s lost out to foreign and Irish
competition in both butter and cheese manufacture because of 'the
variety in quality, in the units of sale and in the containers
used'. (80)

Improved transport also opened up new markets for British cheese
while simultaneously increasing competition from abroad. Welsh
cheese manufacture did not respond to the need for improvement in
quality and uniformity, and decline set in from the 1870s. The
industrial market of the south-east did not lead to increased cheese
production in the neighbouring counties. The reason lay in the
poorness of native Welsh cheese, which, according to one contemporary, was 'seldom fit to eat'. (81) The market was supplied mainly
from imported American cheese. (82) One native cheese, however,
which remained popular with the Glamorgan colliers because it did
not crumble easily, was the Caerphilly cheese, made chiefly in the
hill districts of Glamorgan. By 1902, however, it was claimed that
even this seemed 'to be fast disappearing'. (83)

Railways, then, brought advantages and disadvantages to the
British farmer in the marketing of his finished produce. Certainly
farmers were presented with new and better markets. Equally, better

transport facilities ended the artificial protection which Britain
had previously enjoyed in spite of the removal of protection in the
1840s. Railway companies were accused by British farmers of short-
sightedness in allowing foreign producers to send commodities to
British markets at lower rates than were payable over short distances by the home farmer. The 'Cambrian News' commented sourly in
1909:

> To the great bulk of farmers in Cardiganshire, Montgomeryshire
> and Merionethshire railways are more a hindrance than a help, for
> it is far easier and cheaper to send meat and other produce from
> the Continent and the Colonies to Wales than to send meat and
> other produce from Wales to the centres of large population in
> England. (84)

Railway companies countered that cheaper rates would be possible if
farmers co-operated in selling their produce jointly. (85) The unwillingness among Welsh farmers to establish co-operative butter and
cheese factories explains much of their failure to develop dairy
husbandry in the late nineteenth century. Besides cheapening the
cost of marketing their produce, such factories were essential for
achieving a better quality and uniformity of product in face of
Irish and foreign competitors whose standardised produce was at-
tained precisely through factory production. Co-operative factories
for butter and cheese, particularly the latter, and privately owned
creameries were developed in certain areas of England like Derby-
shire, Staffordshire and Cheshire from the 1870s. (86) In Wales the
one significant attempt to establish a co-operative butter factory
at St Clears, Carmarthenshire, in 1891, ended in failure in 1905.(87)
The main reason for the failure of co-operative dairies in Wales, it
was said, lay in the farmer's reluctance to allow his neighbours to
know the extent of his investment in a factory for fear of arousing
the real or supposed desire of his landlord for increased rent, and
(on the small estates) for fear, also, that his neighbour might
offer higher rents for his farm. (88) It was this fear, reasonable
or unreasonable, which lay at the bottom of the tenant's unwillingness to improve, and this fear was especially fatal to progress on
co-operative lines. In contrast to Wales, the Irish situation was
conducive to co-operation, for there tenants, after Gladstone's Land
Act of 1881, practically owned the land, and the increase in profits
was secured to them and not channelled off in higher rents. (89)
This applied even more so to Denmark and the Netherlands, countries
of peasant ownership.

More important than co-operative factories in certain dairying
areas of England in countering foreign competition was the increasing shift to liquid milk production. (90) With an expanding home
population enjoying rising incomes, and with rising labour costs,
farmers found that liquid milk, protected by its perishable nature
from foreign competition, was a more profitable enterprise than
either butter or cheese production. Railways were all important in
allowing farmers to exploit this growing urban demand for milk. In
Wales, as in upland areas elsewhere in Britain, opportunities for
milk production were restricted by the large areas of poor hill and
moorland pastures suited to the production of store animals and the
ancillary seasonal manufacture of butter and cheese. In low-lying
areas of Wales a switch to liquid milk did occur, but as for the

west and south-west of England, the distance of many of these areas
from large industrial markets, incurring extra transport costs and
the risks of milk souring on the journey, meant that this switch-
over was on a small scale. A further factor here was that railway
coverage of Wales outside the industrial areas was relatively sparse.
Thus, even after rail construction there were many remote areas with
poor transport facilities. Under these conditions it was easier to
market butter and cheese once a week, or even less frequently, than
liquid milk twice daily. It was only with the advent of the motor
lorry in the inter-war years and the institution of the Milk Marketing Board in 1933 that Wales went in for liquid milk production on a
large scale. (91)

Earlier, the switch occurred only in particular areas. By the
1890s some north Wales farmers were producing liquid milk for the
north Wales coastal resorts and Liverpool. (92) The industrial
market of the Glamorgan hill district and Cardiff down to the end of
the century was supplied with milk mainly from Somerset and Monmouthshire. (93) Except for farms immediately adjacent to the 'works'
and the large towns like Cardiff and Swansea, liquid milk was not
marketed from the farms in south Wales with easy access to the industrial area. One reason for this was that in both butter and cheese
the south Wales farmers found that their traditional variety of product, albeit losing ground elsewhere to foreign competition, was
popular with the Glamorgan colliers, many of them migrants from
rural Welsh areas. Sales of milk off the farms of south-west Wales
to the Glamorgan market came only in the first decade of the present
century. (94) Significantly, these milk-producing areas were adjacent to the railway, notably in the Towy valley and along the
Carmarthen to Whitland line. Although by 1914 the quantity of milk
sent from the Towy valley to south-east Wales 'had reached a considerable volume', no evidence has been found of milk reaching
London from Wales before this date. (95)

CHAPTER 8

FARMING PRACTICES

I

The farming methods used to supply these demands gradually changed
as the century advanced and also differed widely according to the
scale of the business. We have stressed that there was a fundamental distinction between the usual type of family farming and the
occasional practice (particularly in the Vale of Glamorgan) of large-
scale commercial farming. Farming methods in both cereal and livestock departments reflected this basic distinction. For the most
part farm operations in Wales over the whole period were backward,
but on the few large farms progressive high-farming techniques were
increasingly in evidence.

Peasant tenant farmers preferred their position to that of labourers on account of the status and independence which a farm-holding
bestowed. At the same time they were often obliged to work harder
than ordinary labourers and also to put their children to work at a
very early age. (1) Such farmers, despite their unflagging industry,
lacked the capital, education and enterprise to farm skilfully and
scientifically. Consequently, on these small holdings the farming
was poor, unskilful and slovenly, characterised always by a fundamental distrust of money and a consequent drive towards subsistence.

Artificial manures were but little used throughout the century,
the small farmer relying mainly on home-produced animal manure and
the purchase of lime. Until the mid century these were virtually
the only manures used on the small Welsh holdings. Lime was used
increasingly from the late eighteenth century, and in the early nineteenth became more widely applied than farmyard manure. In the pre-
railway era great expense was incurred by the farmers in carting
their lime and coal, often from long distances, and this was a
serious handicap to agricultural improvements in Wales. In Radnorshire, for instance, farmers had to restrict their tillage because
of the cost of procuring lime. (2) Farmyard manure became the chief
fertiliser on small Welsh holdings in the second half of the century:
more was now available because of the increased stock kept on the
farms, and it improved in quality as more and more corn came to be
used as animal feed rather than being sold. The use of lime, in
contrast, fell off markedly from the 1870s owing to its high price,

the cost of carting and distribution, the decrease in wheat acreages, and the gradual spread of cheap artificial manures. (3)

Ignorance and particularly expense had minimised the use of guano and bone manure as artificial fertilisers on Welsh holdings, and only with the introduction of superphosphates in the 1880s did Welsh farmers enthusiastically adopt artificials.   It was relatively cheap at £2 10s. to £3 per ton, compared with £10 a ton for guano in the 1840s, and £6 a ton for bone manure in the 1870s.   Even more popular was basic slag, which was the cheapest of the artificials and excellent for grasslands.   From the early 1890s thousands of tons were sold throughout Wales with highly beneficial results.   In particular it supplied the soil with phosphoric acid, which was essential to the Welsh situation where concentration on store stock rearing drained the soil of its phosphoric acid content.   This exhaustion was not compensated by a certain amount of nutritional input through the fattening of cattle upon the same soil. (4)

Thus all through the century the need for a liberal manuring of Welsh soil was urgent.   But this was not forthcoming.   Farmyard manure (derived from animals fed on straw) was poor, but the situation was worsened by the farmers' constructing the dunghills on slopes, thereby causing the rains to wash away the best properties.   Again, Welsh farmers mismanaged the application of quick lime by over-exposure to the air.   The actual export of bones by dealers from Wales to England for manufacture into manure was another disservice to Welsh agriculture. (5)

As with the provision of manure, the small farms largely supplied their own animal feed-stuffs consisting chiefly of oats, barley and hay.   All through the century there was little linseed and cottonseed cake purchased onto the small Welsh holdings.   Furthermore, root crops, especially turnips and mangolds, were insufficiently grown.   Poor farm management was clearly displayed in the persistence with home-grown wheat from the 1870s at the expense of roots.   This dependence on the traditional kind of feed-stuffs meant that any significant extension of cattle fattening was impossible.

The desire to farm cheaply again meant that grass seeds brought onto the farms were of poor quality.   From the 1870s scientific research led to significant improvements in the purity and germination of commercial seeds.   Yet Welsh farmers usually ignored the new strains, and continued to employ an admixture of hay-loft sweepings and minor purchases of cheap seed varieties. (6)   The 'Cambrian News' commented in 1883: 'in this, as in other matters, farmers have a tendency to go in for cheapness /rather/ than for excellence, the result being a rapid and luxurious growth of weeds instead of luxurious grasses'. (7)   This reluctance to use new seed varieties partly explains the low average yields per acre in 1886-8 of hay from clover in Wales - 23.75 cwts compared with 28.31 cwts for England, and 29.73 cwts for Scotland.

The methods of performing the principal farm operations with respect to cropping on these small farms were backward, although some improvements set in from mid century.   Crop rotations spread only slowly: as late as 1859 the Carmarthen Farmers' Club passed a resolution condemning the poor state of farming in the district, and among other causes blamed the restricted area of green crops and the growth of three or four white crops in succession. (8)   Similarly it

was reported of north Wales in 1858 that husbandry was fifty years
behind the best managed counties of England: turnips were but
rarely cultivated and corn crops taken two, three or four years in
succession exhausted the soil. (9) At mid century the small upland
farms of north Wales in particular were characterised by the scanti-
ness or almost non-existence of green cropping. White crops were
the rule, green crops the exception, and summer fallowing was practised to revivify the land after exhaustion from over-cropping with
barley and oats. (10) This slovenly course of cropping on lowlands
and uplands alike, with a fallow at the commencement, was still widespread in 1872. An observer wrote: 'The system of farming is by no
means uniform. A four-course rotation, or some modification of it,
is sometimes met with. More commonly, the seeds are allowed to lie
for several years and, when ploughed up, wheat is taken, followed by
barley, and that occasionally by oats.' Here in this latter instance can be seen only a bare adherence to a cropping system (it
will be recalled that most farmers were forbidden in their agreements to take more than two corn crops in succession). Sometimes
there was an entire absence of any cropping system. Thus, the same
observer in 1872 remarked:

> Indeed, the old rude practice still clings to some of the out-
> lying districts - the land is broadcasted with oats and barley
> until it scarcely pays expenses, then with scarcely the apology
> of clover seeding it is permitted to remain in the natural grass
> and squitch for a few years, until it gets rested and capable of
> again bearing a course of cropping. (11)

Welsh small farmers down to the 1870s were reluctant to grow
green crops and roots because of the labour and expense of cultivation (see chapter 1). But even on these small holdings progress in
root cropping (turnips, swedes and mangolds) did occur between the
1870s and 1890s, in contrast to the fall off in the other green crop
and corn constituents within the arable sector. This was partly because more livestock were now kept, and partly because the introduction of superphosphates greatly facilitated root cropping. (12) This
increased growth of roots, along with the wider application of artificial fertilisers, meant that the previous system of summer fallowing fell into disuse. Nevertheless, as late as the 1890s summer
fallowing at the season of vegetation between barley sowing and hay
harvest was still practised in some parts of Wales. (13) Increased
amounts of roots also led (especially in Pembrokeshire) to the decline in 'fogging', whereby grass was kept from being fed upon from
about mid summer to the following February or March. (14)

Backward husbandry techniques were reflected in the type of agricultural implements used. Until the mid nineteenth century agricultural implements in Wales were simple, clumsily designed, and ill-
calculated for improvement. In tillage operations the plough and
harrow were the only two implements in general use, and, although in
the more accessible and fertile regions the iron swing plough had
become general by the mid century, the awkward old wooden plough
prevailed in the remote areas of the west. The many contemporary
descriptions of the old Welsh plough, considered to be one day's
work for a carpenter, reveal how backward one of the principal farm
operations must have been. Thus Maculloch stated: 'The Welsh
plough, which is still in common use is a wretched implement: it

does not cut, but tears the ground by main force. The land is frequently, indeed, not more than half ploughed.' (15) These wooden ploughs were still to be found in remote areas among the Welsh hills as late as the 1870s, but over most of the principality they had by this time been replaced by more efficient iron swing ploughs. (16) At first these were produced by local blacksmiths whose initials would be embossed on the mould board. But their heavy and cumbersome design led to their being fast replaced by the 1890s with lighter and more efficient patent iron ploughs made by English firms. Changes also occurred in the traction of the plough. At the opening of the century oxen were generally used, but they were gradually replaced by horses in the decades that followed. Up to the 1860s the plough was drawn by three or four horses in single file, whereas by the 1890s the usual method of draught was by a pair of horses abreast. (17)

The harrows used for breaking the ploughed land into a tilth were in the early century virtually useless. They were made of wood and rectangular in shape, and their clumsiness in design was rendered even more of a disadvantage by the inefficient mode of ploughing. Unlike the plough, the harrow was little improved over the course of the century. Small farmers in the 1890s still clung to the traditional wooden oblong implement. (18)

Seed was broadcast by hand on the small farms throughout the century, the farmer sowing with both hands at a good walking pace. This primitive system was nevertheless accomplished with skill for the seeds sprouted remarkably evenly. Corn drills remained too expensive for the smaller farmer. (19) Harvesting implements and techniques likewise were often rudimentary on these small farms. Down to the end of the 1870s hay was mown with the scythe. This primitive method meant that at every hay harvest a certain amount of grass was unavoidably left uncut until much of its goodness was lost by overripening. Although as late as the 1890s the scythe was still in use on many small holdings (especially on sloping, uneven ground), it was nevertheless being replaced increasingly from the 1880s onwards by light one-horse mowing machines. By 1906 these were very common even on the small upland farms. For most of the century, too, the hay was worked and pitched with a fork. By the 1890s, however, 'tedders' (haymakers for tossing the hay) and horse-rakes were gradually coming into use in the more advanced lowland districts, although implements of this kind were unsuitable for the many farms in Wales situated on slopes. By the early 1900s considerable improvements were being made to those implements and they were becoming increasingly used on Welsh holdings. (20)

The hay was 'made' differently from area to area, but a common feature was the collecting of it into small cocks before carting to the stack-yard. Down to the close of the century and beyond in the very hilly districts horse-drawn sleds were used for carrying hay and corn. (21) The sled in these hilly regions was safer and more efficient than wheeled carts. On steep slopes hay cocks were arranged in parallel rows along the slope and not down it, because a horse was never worked up and down such gradients. A wheeled cart taken along a slope would always have been in danger of overturning. The sled was in no such danger and, in addition, could easily be turned round at the end of each row. (22) In the less hilly regions

the gambo became the usual harvest cart, and was to be found too in
the border counties of Hereford, Shropshire and west Gloucester. It
generally consisted of a flat oblong platform some ten feet long by
five feet wide and fitted with a pair of shafts which were rigid
continuations of the frame. The wheels were about four feet in dia-
meter. The body was either fitted with fore and tail ladders or
with a pole in each corner. There were no sides to this vehicle.
In the last quarter of the century the sideless gambo was replaced
as the harvest vehicle in west Wales by the long cart. Its framework was similar to that of the gambo but side supports were now an
added feature. What characterised these carts from the tumbril of
the English Plain was their lightness and one-horse traction. (23)

Up to the last decade or so of the century, oats and barley were
cut with a scythe over which a cradle was attached, in order to
gather and hold the cut stalks, and to facilitate in laying them in
a neat swath convenient for binding them into sheaves. One man
could cut an acre of barley or oats in a day. The typical harvest
tool for cutting wheat in Wales down to the 1890s was the reaping
hook. (This was used rather than the scythe chiefly because wheat
grows taller than oats or barley and therefore did not lie so easily
in a scythe's cradle.) Mowing with a reaping hook was a slower process than with the scythe: a man with a scythe could cut as much
corn in a day as could two or three men with a reaping hook or a
sickle, while one man with a machine could perform as well as six
men using scythes. The scythe and reaping hook were not replaced by
the self-binder in the late nineteenth century on the small Welsh
holdings because of the restricted acreage under corn, uneven ground,
and the wet climate which frequently twisted the crops. (24)

The reaping completed, the corn was left for a few days to mature
before being bound into sheaves. The latter were then collected
into bundles, often by the children, and the men then built them up
into 'mows', called in some places of Cardiganshire 'Cardiganshire
Cocks'. These were constructed to withstand the wet weather, and
were thus hauled at leisure to the yard where they were built into
stacks. (25) Threshing on the small farms was done in the first
fifty or sixty years of the century by flail. This comprised two
parts, the handshaft and the swingle, and required skill in its
operation. The threshing of two measures of oats with a flail was
considered a good day's work. The process continued from Michaelmas
to the following May. (26) Although the flail remained in use in
the outbuildings of a few small farms as late as the 1890s, it had
generally disappeared two decades earlier, and even remote hilly
areas had quickly adopted the threshing machine driven by horse or
water power. Winnowing (the process of separating the grain, the
offal and the chaff) was in the early century done with the old-
fashioned winnowing fan, but from around mid century this was gradually replaced by the winnowing machine. This in turn went out of
use when steam threshing machines were introduced, but the small
headway made by the latter in Wales meant that winnowing machines
were prevalent, especially in upland areas, at the close of the century. Water-power was widely utilised on the hill farms for driving
the threshing and winnowing machines. (27)

Steam power was used only to a very small extent in Welsh farming
operations in these years. Steam ploughs, which were a common

feature in certain areas of England from the 1850s, were rarely
found in Wales as farming conditions were totally unsuitable. Fields
were small and irregularly shaped (a result of piecemeal early enclosure), the land often steep and uneven, and - more fundamentally
- the soil was generally too thin to permit of deep ploughing involved in steam tillage. (28) Again, steam threshing machines were
little used in Wales. Most farms were too small to require the purchase of such elaborate machinery. In fact many of the 'commercial'
farmers simply hired steam threshers from a machine proprietor, but
here again the small tenant was under certain inconveniences. These
included the accumulation of too much litter at a time and the consequent waste of it; the inexpediency of employing it for threshing
out small parcels of corn required regularly for feeding purposes;
and, finally, the small upland holdings, with the roughness of the
roads and steep slopes, were difficult to reach. Small farmers sometimes solved the problem by bringing their corn to the large farms
to be threshed by a hired machine before the latter was removed.(29)

Thus, farm machinery remained primitive for most of the century.
It only really made significant headway, if remaining far from widespread, after 1880. With falling prices for their produce, farmers
were now trying to cut their costs of production by reducing their
labour bills. One way of doing this was through the extension of
labour-saving machinery, and by the first decade of the present century this was most noticeable in the case of hay harvest. A number
of factors operated throughout the century towards retarding the
introduction of machinery. It has been shown how the physical characteristics of Welsh holdings rendered them unsuitable for many of
the new types of machinery. The sparse coverage by railways meant
that implement makers and agents did not canvass the country
thoroughly, and the agents were handicapped by not knowing Welsh.(30)
The farmers themselves were unable or unwilling to meet the considerable cost of farm machinery, especially in those many instances
where depreciation was great. (31) They were also typically scepti-
cal of the advantages of the new machinery over traditional implements. Thus the introduction of hay mowers into south Cardiganshire
in the 1890s was stubbornly resisted by the local farmers: some
perversely argued that hay would not grow again along the track
marks left by the mower's iron wheels, while others naively predic-
ted that cows would not eat hay cut by machine! Many small upland
farmers, too, were not concerned about time-saving. Indeed, the
notion involved a total reorganisation of the traditional routine,
and they were simply not equal to it. (32)

The increased use of machinery not only reduced the demand for
labour, particularly at harvest, but also largely contributed to the
increase in the work efficiency of farm organisation in Wales between 1871 and 1921 as measured in terms of efficiency per person engaged. Investigations carried out at Aberystwyth in 1926 revealed
that had the standard of work accomplished (work efficiency) which
prevailed in 1871 continued till 1921 then some 37 per cent more
labour or of labour time than was employed on the farms in 1921
would have been needed. This increase of 37 per cent was in effect
an increase in work performance per hour of labour. (33)

As the increase in efficiency per person engaged was made possible mainly by an improvement in mechanical equipment, it obviously

required also the aid of increased power mainly for tractive purposes. This was obtained chiefly from horses. Between 1871 and
1921 the number of working horses per 100 acres of cultivated area
in Wales and Monmouthshire increased from 2.6 to 3.2. This increase
is all the more striking when it is realised that it occurred at a
time when there was a decrease in the proportion of land under
arable which required much the greater application of horse power
per unit acre. (34)

The small labour forces on Welsh holdings, the absence of labour-
saving machinery for much of the century, and limited capital meant
that co-operation between neighbouring farmers was an essential
element in the major farm operations. Each small farm in north Carmarthenshire needed at least nine or ten hay scythers. (35) This
mutual help system was a very old one in Wales and was most likely a
survival of the old Welsh custom of 'Cymortha'. In Brecknockshire
pooling of labour by groups of neighbouring farmers occurred at hay-
making, corn harvest and sheep shearing. With regards to the latter,
each sheep farmer had certain days allocated to him, and neighbouring farmers and their labour forces co-operated over two or three
weeks. (36) Similarly, in the western districts of Radnorshire farmers co-operated during hay-making and corn harvest and again during
sheep-dipping and shearing seasons. (37) In Merioneth farmers rendered mutual help on threshing day, either by going themselves, or
sending their servants to do so, and when an incoming tenant entered
a new farm (about 25 March) it was customary for several neighbours
to send men with their teams to do his ploughing. Similar assistance was given in carting and spreading manure. (38) In the Welsh-
speaking areas of north and east Pembrokeshire, in Carmarthenshire
and south Cardiganshire, small farmers likewise pooled their labour
at harvest periods, especially during hay-making. About a dozen
farms co-operated as a local group for hay-making, and such a group
had been long in existence. David Jenkins points out that such
groups were not exclusive; rather each farm was the focus of its
own group, the farms that co-operated with it not necessarily co-
operating with one another. One particular farm in the group always
started off, the rest following in a set order, and no farmer was
foolish enough to break the rule. Members of the group thus waited
until the leader sent out the call for scythers or, later, for machines. The farmer whose holding was being worked would act as the
foreman, setting the pace for the next scythers and judging the distances for sharpening. Co-operation in the hay harvest also occurred during carting. When the hay was carted to the rickyard each
farm within the group was expected to contribute a horse and gambo
along with pitchers in the field and rickyard. (39) Although farmers continued to co-operate after the scythe went out of use in
sending hay mowing-machines to neighbouring holdings, and co-
operation in carting lasted until the coming of the baler after the
Second World War, it is clear that the introduction of machinery at
the turn of the century was directly responsible for restricting and
eventually destroying the ancient practice of co-operation in the
hay harvest. Thus, in 1919 it was observed of Carmarthenshire farming that whereas formerly the entire labour force of one farm was
drafted on the busiest day - carting - to another holding, by the
present time only one or more of the men was loaned by one farmer to
a neighbour on hauling days. (40)

A particular feature of the rural economy of south-west Wales was the large number of small holdings of three to five acres attached to farms, let with the farms, and sublet by the farmers to labourers. This system of 'bound tenants' helped solve the problem of extra labour at peak seasons for, as shown in chapter 6, in return for help given the tenant by the farmer at ploughing and harvest (by sending his team and machinery), the tenant's wife and family helped the farmer at turnip hoeing and harvest. Besides this group of team-less smallholders, the wives of both farming and non-farming cot-tagers played a vital role in helping in the corn harvest in the Welsh-speaking areas of south-west Wales. David Jenkins has rightly emphasised that farmers did not co-operate in corn harvest. This was the climax of the farming year when crops vital for house and animals had to be garnered in uncertain weather conditions. Harvest-ing of corn, even on a small farm working with simple implements, was a lengthy process: at least a hundred working days were needed to harvest forty acres of corn. (41) Farmers thus harvested their corn independently and derived the extra labour required from the system of 'setting out potatoes', whereby farm and non-farming cot-tagers (like railwaymen and road menders) set out rows of potatoes in a farmer's fields. In return for the manure provided by the farmer for each row, they gave free labour, usually performed by the cottagers' wives, at corn harvest. This was the 'work debt', and the basis of payment was determined by the formula 'for each load of manure one day's work'. (42) A specific potato setting group was attached to each farm. Ultimately, the corn binder did much to fragment the cohesion of these close 'face to face' communities by dispensing with the need of the harvest work debt. (43)

Potato plots were common elsewhere in Wales, but payment in money was usually given for the privilege in the closing years of the cen-tury. In a few instances, however, as in the areas about Llanfyllin and Derwenlas, Montgomeryshire, harvest work had been performed by cottagers' wives as a 'labour debt' earlier in the century, and down to the 1890s in the Pwllheli region of Caernarvonshire potato grounds were to some extent paid for by the wife giving 'a little help in harvest'. But here the labourer concerned supplied the necessary manure. Thus, in the area outside the south-west nothing like a highly systematised potato 'work debt' was in existence. (44)

Another type of labour debt which helped to solve the extra sea-sonal demand for labour arose from the interdependence between small holdings of 5 to 30 acres and larger neighbouring farms. It was pointed out in chapter 4 that a Welsh farmer below the upland frin-ges needed at least 30-40 acres to make a living for himself and his wife from his farm, independent of any form of supplementary income. 'Farms' proper, then, were of 30 acres and above. The many smaller holdings in receipt of some additional income were numerous through-out the principality. Holdings of between 15 and 30 acres in south-west Wales could maintain a horse and were referred to as 'one-horse places', while holdings of under 15 acres kept cows instead of horses and were classified as a 'one', 'two' or 'three' 'cow place' according to the number kept. A cow needed roughly 4 acres. (45) Such holdings were dependent on 'farms' for vital services. It was reported of the Builth Union in 1893: 'There is constant inter-change of services between regular farmers and small-holders also,

who supply each other's wants as occasion offers without any payment
of money.' (46)   While farmers provided small holders (who were not
the 'bound tenants' of south-west Wales referred to above) with
teams for ploughing, and carted their manure and hay, they extracted
in return a labour debt at harvest time.   Many small holders in all
regions of Wales, it has been shown, were craftsmen-smallholders,
and thus as late as 1900 the local shoemaker, the blacksmith, the
carpenter, the weaver, the mason and the tailor could be found in
the corn harvest in north Carmarthenshire discharging their 'debts'.
(47)

Farms of between 30 and 80 acres could provide a living, but were
seldom able to function as independent units even in operations outside of peak harvest periods.   The concentration on store cattle and
butter on most Welsh holdings meant that the services of a bull were
vital.   Upkeep of bulls was expensive, and consequently they were
kept on very few farms of less than 80 acres and on none below 60,
which in south Cardiganshire meant that only one farm in four kept a
bull.   Thus 75 per cent of the farms there were dependent on the
remaining 25 per cent for this vital service.   The summer months
therefore saw a constant trafficking of cows between the smaller
farms and their larger neighbours.   Similarly, only one farm in
eight in south Cardiganshire kept a boar, and the importance of
bacon pigs to most farmers of this pastoral economy meant once again
that co-operation between large farms and their smaller neighbours
was essential.   No cash payments were made for these essential services, for the debt was paid once again by a day's labour on the
large farm concerned either at a peak period such as hay harvest
(though not at corn harvest when the smaller farmer was fully engaged with his own crop), or in mixing culm for the fire. (48)

Welsh farmers depended largely upon the breeding and rearing of
the native Black Cattle as a useful 'dual purpose' meat- and milk-
producing animal.   Given the general absence of suitable outbuildings for winter housing on Welsh holdings and the thin - often
barren - soils, these were the most profitable to the majority of
farmers.   Calves were housed during their first winter, but owing to
the deficiency of farmyard accommodation for stall-feeding and of
shelter, young cattle were kept afterwards in the fields throughout
the winter months.   However, dairy cows of all ages were generally
housed at night. (49)   On the extensive mountain farms where usually
a few cattle were kept along with the sheep, cattle of necessity had
to be sheltered during winter.   They were not, however, brought to
the homestead for winter shelter, but were housed in detached buildings some distance from one another.   The absence of tillage and
good meadows meant that a farmer could not collect at one place sufficient food to last the cattle throughout winter.   He was obliged
to erect winter shelters in those favoured spots where he could collect the greatest quantities of food.   Usually from six to eight
were housed in one place.   So harsh were conditions in the mountains
of north-west Wales that each winter yearling heifers were drafted
off and sold to lowland Welsh farmers further east.   Adverse physical and climatic conditions, together with inadequate outbuildings,
clearly debarred the successful introduction of the improved Shorthorns and Herefords. (50)

In areas apart from upland sheep grazings, the most vital element

of the farmer's wealth consisted of dairy cows, which were the very
basis of the whole livestock enterprise. Milk cows were kept on
every farm, and around mid century in south-west Wales were usually
in a ratio of 2:3 with other cattle. (51) The characteristic feature of Welsh farming below the mountain sheep-runs was the combination of calf-rearing with butter-making. The cows calved in the
spring, and the milk, surplus to what was needed for rearing the
calves and pigs, was made into butter and cheese in the summer
months between June and October. Most of the calves reared on the
farms were eventually sold off as stores when three or four years
old - though younger later in the century - while a few were kept as
milk cows and finally disposed of to the butchers.

During the first three-quarters of the century the native Welsh
Blacks degenerated in form and symmetry owing to very poor management. By the 1870s they could only be described as 'herring-backed
mongrels'. (52) Welsh farmers took their best heifers to the fairs
and sold them to dealers, and breeding was done therefore through
the worst stock. The situation was aggravated by a failure to
select the best bulls, farmers too often contenting themselves with
the service of mongrels. (53) Too little attention was given to the
young stock at every stage of their development. Calves were half-
starved on separated milk, buttermilk and oatmeal gruel, and were
cheated of the cream content of the milk owing to the practice of
turning as much milk as possible into butter. Yearlings were neglected, and two-year-olds were left to take care of themselves. Winter
keep was very inadequate, being confined to hay with or without some
small allowance of crushed oats or meal, and this limited winter
keep on the small farms was to prevail down to the close of the
century and beyond. (54)

The Blacks also suffered before the 1870s from a lack of interest
in their improvement on the part of the Welsh landowners. Their
money and attention were increasingly given to the fashionable Shorthorns and Herefords, and their example was slowly taken up by the
more progressive tenants. The new breeds gained real ground in
south Wales with the coming of the railway, so that by 1871 it could
be stated of south-west Wales 'the Shorthorn daily increases and
multiplies amongst us'. (55) Fortunately, in the second half of the
century certain landowners came to realise that the native Blacks
were the best suited to the physical and climatic conditions of the
region, and shrewdly switched their energies into improving the
breed.

Efforts to improve the Blacks were first made in 1867 by Morgan
Evans, who proposed the establishment of a Black Cattle Herd Book
and a Black Cattle Improvement Society. No support was immediately
forthcoming, but from 1871 onwards a new interest began to develop.
In that year James Bowen, owner of Llwyngwair in north Pembrokeshire,
suggested a champion prize for the best black bull open to the three
counties of south-west Wales. By 1874 some twenty good bulls had
been found. From these efforts and those of R.H. Harvey of Slade
Hall, Haverfordwest, there successfully materialised in 1874 the
first Black Cattle Herd Book. Its aim was to improve the breed by
encouraging the selection of the best young cattle for stock purposes. (56) This led to drastic improvements in the Blacks of both
south and north Wales, though the mistaken belief of many farmers

that mongrels were the more profitable remained a constant check to progress. (57) In 1878 prizes were awarded for the first time for Black Cattle at the Royal Agricultural Society's Show at Bristol, largely owing to Lord Cawdor's influence combined with the existence of the Herd Book. In 1885 a South Wales Black Cattle Herd Book Society was formed 'to maintain the purity of the South Wales Black Cattle, and to promote their improvement'. (58) For some years the cattle of north Wales were included in the Welsh Black Cattle Herd Book, but a disagreement led in 1883 to the first volume of the North Wales Black Cattle Herd Book, edited by William Dew of Bangor. Especially prominent in promoting the native Blacks in north Wales were Lord Harlech, John Platt of Bodior (near Holyhead), Major Platt of Gorddinog (Bangor) and Assheton Smith of Vaynol (Caernarvonshire). From 1883 down to 1904 the breeders of north and south Wales kept their separate institutions, but in that year the two societies amalgamated to form the Welsh Black Cattle Society. A still more important stimulus to improving the Welsh Black Cattle breed came in 1914 with the Livestock Improvement Scheme instituted by the Board of Agriculture and Fisheries. (59)

Despite all these efforts, the native breed in south Wales on large and small farms alike gave place increasingly from the 1890s to the Shorthorns even in Pembrokeshire and the Vale of Towy, traditional strongholds of the Blacks. They more than held their ground, however, in north-west Wales in the counties of Anglesey, Merioneth and Caernarvon. Significantly, in this region were to be found many upland tracts where no other breed of cattle could survive. (60)

Butter-making was the responsibility of the female contingent of the farm family and staff. The separated cream was turned into butter in various kinds of churns, the three most common in north Wales in the third quarter of the century being the revolving churn, the barrel and knocker type and, most primitive of all, the swing churn (which was an oblong box swung on pivots). Down to mid century in north Wales, churning by dogs was practised by means of a dog wheel. (61) The butter was then stored with heavy salting in casks or tubs made by local coopers, weighing when full about a hundredweight. These often remained on the farms until the following spring when they were sold to higglers. Under this system of calf-rearing and butter-producing a cow was expected on average to produce about $5\frac{1}{2}$ lbs of butter a week, or over the four to five months grass season about 100 to 120 lbs of butter, enough therefore to fill a cask or tub. (62) The quality of Welsh butter remained poor throughout the century and little improvement followed new marketing opportunities or educational instruction. Dairy Schools were implemented by the County Councils from the close of the 1880s, and Aberystwyth and Bangor Colleges taught dairying both internally and in their travelling dairy schools. Welsh farmers nevertheless persisted in over-salting and were slow to utilise cream separators. One drawback to improvement was the deplorable dairy facilities on most small Welsh holdings. Thus milk was frequently and inappropriately kept in the parlour. (63)

Cheese manufacture occupied a secondary place to butter-making on most Welsh holdings, and much of it was produced for home consumption. The cream of the milk went for butter, and after the calves had left off feeding on the skim-milk the latter was then used in

cheese manufacture. (64) The cheese consequently lacked fat and was
of inferior quality. It was rendered even worse in some areas of
west Wales by the milk being kept too long in order to make a large
cheese. Such cheeses weighed, according to the season and the
number of cows, from 20 to 130 lbs. (65) The cheese press used on
farms in north Wales in the third quarter of the century was simple,
merely a box filled with large stones, with a screw to bring it down
on the cheese vat to press the moisture out of the cheese. (66)

Swine husbandry was also an important item on most Welsh farms as
it complemented the prevailing pattern of rearing of store cattle
and butter manufacture. Yet, the breeding and management of pigs
were deplorably neglected. There were many varieties in the different areas of the principality, all the result of continuous - and,
in many instances, injudicious - crossing. Montgomeryshire produced
the best pig, and this variety found a big demand in the English
market. Pure breeds such as the Berkshire and the Tamworth were
kept only by the landowners on their home farms and by the 'fancy'
breeders. As for management, little attention was given to correct
siting of styes and to the cleanliness or warmth of the litter. (67)

Mountain sheep farming was throughout a special feature in Wales.
The small mountain farms with their often extensive sheep-runs were
occupied by men who could be styled shepherds rather than farmers.
Flocks varied in size from 50 up to 2000. (68) The sheep were the
small, hardy native breed, admirably suited to the rigours of the
climate. A few cattle and ponies were kept in addition on these
holdings. It has been shown earlier that in some cases the sheep-
walks were let exclusively to particular farmers, while more frequently farmers grazed their sheep in common on the open wastes.
For convenience those occupiers of farms which grazed in common had
drawn up imaginary boundaries, but these were often ignored by the
stronger, more aggressive flock masters. The lack of fencing on the
sheep-tracks, together with the neglect of roots, largely accounted
for the unimproved nature of the flocks. Absence of fences allowed
rams to come too early to the flocks, which resulted in lambs being
dropped in early March rather than at the latter end of April. Such
early yeaning meant that ewes had no milk for their lambs, and inevitably many lambs died of starvation or perished with cold. Had
mountain ewes been timed to yean about four to five weeks later in
the season, they would have been in much better condition and able
to provide milk. If a particularly severe winter was followed by a
slow and late spring, the sheep farmer suffered drastic losses from
dead lambs, as happened, for example, in the springs of 1879, 1881
and 1883. Farmers themselves were partly to blame, for they made
little effort to provide their ewes and lambs with food or shelter.
They considered that any attempt to protect and feed their stock
would be unremunerative, and too readily left such vital matters of
management to chance. Some of the failure to provide food arose
again from the unenclosed nature of the land which made it difficult
to grow hay and turnips. The feeling also existed that any food
provided would surreptitiously be utilised by the occupiers of neighbouring farms. (69) It goes without saying that absence of fences
meant that all attempts to improve the breeds of sheep, cattle and
ponies were doomed to failure. Thus, the 'Cambrian News' correctly
pronounced in 1906: 'One of the ways by which almost all the ills

of mountain sheep farmers could be got rid of would be by enclosing sheep farms.' (70)

Welsh mountain flocks received little attention from the time of lambing until their leaving the uplands. They were left to fend very much for themselves against snow, storms and rain and were given (as already shown for ewes and lambs) little shelter and food like hay and turnips. Lambs were allowed to follow the ewes till late in October, and then were generally sent down for winter either to the valley farmstead and its enclosed fields, or to the lowlands to some farm which had a grass 'run' for letting. They returned to the upland 'walk' in April and were henceforth expected to take care of themselves. A few of the oldest and weakest ewes were brought down from the mountains in December and grazed until their return in spring either on the homestead or further afield. For example, Merioneth flocks sometimes wintered in the Vale of Clwyd, and Mont-gomeryshire flocks on the banks of the Menai. (71) (Such downslope movement in winter from upland farms was the reversal of the old upslope migration in summer from lowland farms to upland grazings - from 'hendre' to 'hafod' - which ended at different times in differ-ent places between the sixteenth and the early nineteenth centuries. Summer dwellings had been essential while cows had been the chief animals on the moorlands (they had to be milked daily and butter and cheese prepared regularly) but when sheep and store cattle became the dominant stock in the eighteenth century they were no longer necessary. Sheep husbandry required far less constant attention. Furthermore, the reclamation of high marginal land with the spread of enclosures resulted in the old 'hafod' (temporary summer dwelling) becoming a self contained farm.) (72) This downward movement in winter was limited, however, for the wethers and hardier ewes were left on the mountains. This was partly owing to the fact that the small homestead farms in the valleys did not possess sufficient pas-turage to carry all the ewes in winter. (73) Small wonder that up to a third of the flock died when weather conditions were especially severe. Until the advent of the new consumer preference for leaner joints in the 1880s, the wethers and ewes remained on the mountains until they were drafted for sale as stores in the autumn at $4\frac{1}{2}$ years old.

Below the mountain sheep-farm zone came the hill or 'half hill' farms. These had sheep-walks attached which were usually fenced, and to avoid the expense of wintering it was arranged that the walk carried in summer the number of sheep the enclosed farmstead was able to accommodate in winter. Normally the walks were stockless from December until spring. The bringing down of all the ewes during winter ensured a much heavier sheep than the mountain farms produced. (74) The sheep kept at the close of the century were generally, in south Wales, a cross between the best Radnor Forest and native mountain breed and, in the north, a cross between the Kerry Hill and Shropshire Down. Cattle rearing and butter produc-tion, however, were at least as important as sheep rearing on these numerous hill farms. (75)

The wool of the mountain and hill sheep was unavoidably poor, given the damp atmosphere and severe winters. Once again fences and the provision of sheds for shelter and better feeding would in many cases have improved the fleece. Furthermore, the Welsh farmer

valued his sheep for mutton and neglected the management of wool.
Washing was done only partially; shearing was carried out in the
unclean surroundings of farm yards, stables, cowhouses or barns; and
the fleeces were stored in bedrooms or barns for long periods and
often mutilated by rats and vermin. Dealers vociferously complained
of unclean Welsh wool, and this negligence contributed to the univer-
sal preference for colonial clips late in the century. (76)

Sheep kept on small lowland farms were larger, and produced by
various crosses of the native stock with English breeds. Almost
every lowland farmer in south Wales in the 1840s kept a few ewes,
from 10 to 60, depending on the size of the holding. However, fewer
sheep were kept than conditions warranted, because of the small farmers' obstinate refusal to grow more root crops. In districts where
turnips were grown the sheep were not folded on the land, but the
turnips were thrown on the pastures for them. Lack of winter feed
meant that the lambs were sold off before winter set in, most farmers being obliged to buy their sheep in spring and sell them to the
butchers in autumn. (77)

If the small Welsh farmer reared indifferent cattle and sheep,
this criticism could not be levelled at the horses he bred. Dealers
from all over Britain looked favourably upon the quality of Welsh
horses. The breeding of carthorses was a popular if secondary pursuit of the small farmers of the lowlands. The one-horse farmer
normally kept a mare rather than a gelding, so that with careful
management a foal could be produced every year and sold in the
autumn. Carthorse breeding was highly suited to the lowlands of
Montgomeryshire, and throughout the century the region was noted for
its excellence in this department. From its foundation in 1876, the
Montgomeryshire District Entire Horse Association did much to improve the breed by introducing superior sires from England. (78)
Similar societies and associations were set up in other districts.
Landowners, too, played a vital part in introducing the best sires
at a low cost for the use of their tenants. Local autumn shows for
the encouragement of breeding of carthorses sprang up in many areas
in the 1880s and 1890s, and special horse fairs were established at
centres like Aberystwyth and Welshpool from the mid 1870s to attract
the best buyers. (79) The great demand for the smaller kind of carthorse in the coal mines of Glamorgan and Monmouthshire meant that
farmers in Brecknockshire and Radnorshire paid considerable attention to breeding such typically Welsh horses. (80)

Tenants of higher lands concentrated (profitably) on breeding
Welsh cobs and ponies. The short-legged, short-bodied compact cob
was valued for its lightness of foot combined with strength, and was
especially suitable for work on hilly ground. (81) It was particularly prominent in Cardiganshire, and, following the deterioration
of the breed through sales of the best animals during the Crimean
War, it underwent notable improvement as a result of the work of the
Cardiganshire Horse Show Association established in 1872. Its aim
was to improve the native breed by importing the best sires from
outside Wales, and much of the credit for its success before closing
down in 1877 was due to Vaughan Davies of Tanybwlch, Cardiganshire.
(82) However, by 1890 the Cardiganshire cob was a deteriorating
breed, the best stock having been allowed to leave the county in the
1880s. A similar decline was evident elsewhere in Wales. (83) No

attention was paid to the breeding of the Welsh mountain ponies, commonly called 'Merlins'. They ran wild on the mountains until three years old, when they were caught and brought down to the fairs like flocks of wild sheep in July and August. They were eagerly purchased by dealers, many for work in the mines. (84)

II

Certain areas of Wales were fertile and suited to progressive farming. These were found in the Vale of Clwyd and east Flintshire in the north, along the eastern borderlands and the valleys leading into them as the Severn, the Wye and the Usk, and, in the south, in the Vale of Glamorgan, the Towy valley, the region running westwards from Carmarthen to St Clears and Laugharne, and the Castlemartin area of Pembrokeshire. Not all farmers in these fertile regions farmed for the market. But many were occupiers of sizeable holdings and possessed the capital and enterprise to farm along improved lines. Thus there were many farms in the Vale of Glamorgan of between 200 and 300 acres and a few from 500 to 800 acres. In the lower parts of Monmouthshire, again, farms were frequently from 300 to 400 acres. Tenants of these farms were just as ready to adopt new machinery and new methods of cultivation as their counterparts in England. (85)

Most of these large farms practised mixed husbandry, but arable was usually predominant in the Vale of Clwyd, east Flintshire and the Vale of Glamorgan. In the latter, as late as the 1880s, two-thirds of the area was under arable. Rotation of crops in various courses, using roots and clover or other grass seed breaks, was introduced on these large holdings during the early nineteenth century. Often the four-course system was followed. (86) By the last quarter of the century, however, farmers and landlords came to see that a strict adherence to the Norfolk course was counter-productive, the soil in time becoming clover sick. To remedy this two white crops were frequently taken in succession. (87) Manures were liberally applied and artificials were purchased in large amounts. The lead in using artificials was taken by the landowners who in the 1840s bought supplies of guano, which was an excellent supplement to farmyard dung in the growth of roots. (88) Their example was followed by the large farmers who began to purchase it in the 1850s, as, for example, did the tenant of Market Gate Farm, in the parish of Jeffreyston, south Pembrokeshire. (89) Dissolved bones at £7 a ton, nitrate of soda at £13 or £14 a ton, and mineral superphosphates at £6 10s. a ton were the most extensively used artificials in Wales in the 1870s, and large farmers as well as landowners purchased them from the manure agents located in the local towns. An excellent example of liberal manuring with artificials for root crops was afforded by the tenant of the 419 acres farm called Eglwysnunyd, near Aberavon, Glamorgan, who spent about £100 a year on artificials in the early 1870s. The farmstead even contained a special shed for artificial manure. (90)

Roots and green crops were carefully cultivated on these large farms for fattening stock. Mangolds were sown in April on ground which had been prepared by ploughing, harrowing and rolling since

the previous autumn. The seed was sown in drills well manured with
farmyard dung and dissolved bones or mangold-manure. The produce of
an acre was seldom less than 35 tons and the crop was trimmed with a
reaping hook, pulled and carted for storing, at the end of October.
When properly stored they kept fresh and juicy until after mid
summer, and helped to meet the spring demands of the cattle and
sheep. Swedes were sown between the middle of May and early June in
drills which again had been well manured with dung, dissolved bones
and mineral superphosphate. They were pulled in November or December, a third to a half being carted home for the use of the cattle
stock, while the remainder which was left on the swede-land was, for
convenience in penning the sheep, thrown into heaps and protected
from frosts by a covering of soil. Turnips sown in June or July
were grown for the maintenance of lambs in October and November, a
few being, if possible, spared for the ewes in hard weather. They
were all consumed on the ground. Turnips were usually sown on the
flat - rather than raised drills - after vetches, white mustard,
trifolium and other such catch crops had been consumed. These were
sown in the previous autumn after the corn harvest, and they formed
valuable supplements to the spring food. (91)

The most up-to-date machinery was employed in planting and harvesting the grain and root crops. Steam cultivation was largely
absent, however. Demonstrations as at Tan y lan, Holywell, in 1861
and at Borth, Cardiganshire, in 1875, failed to win over the larger
tenants to steam ploughing. (92) The one farm in the Vale of Glamorgan that adopted steam cultivation in the 1880s was Boverton Farm
(735 acres). (93) In the north, a steam cultivation firm from
Birkenhead was doing contract work in Denbighshire in 1884 and
ploughed, for example, at Pwllhalog farm. But its scale of business
was too small to attract general notice. (94) Even on large farms
the fields were frequently too small and irregularly shaped to
permit of steam ploughs being used to advantage. (95) Horse-drawn
'diggers' or 'chilled' ploughs made of chilled steel came to replace
the swing ploughs on the large farms in the better agricultural districts in the last two decades of the century. (96)

Drill husbandry for corn, clover and roots was practised on the
well-managed farms by the early 1870s. Grain crops in the Vale of
Glamorgan were usually sown with a Suffolk drill, while clovers and
roots were sown with a broadcast drill. (97) A wide range of labour-
saving machinery was introduced in harvest operations on the sizeable holdings from the late 1860s. The horse-drawn mowing machine
and the self-delivery reaping machine both gained increasing popularity on the large farms in the Vale of Glamorgan from their introduction in the 1860s. An even greater labour-saver was the self-
binding reaper which came into use in the Vale in the mid 1880s. It
was estimated by the occupier of Boverton Farm that the self-binder
saved the farmer at least 4s.9d. an acre. (98) Other implements
used at hay harvest in the last quarter of the century were the
tedder (or haymaker), the horse rake and the elevator. On these
large and low-lying farms waggons were generally used for carting
corn and hay. The horse- and sometimes the water-threshing machine
became a common feature on the large holdings from the 1840s.
Whereas in 1841, for instance, there was not a single threshing
machine on the Peniarth estate, Merioneth, by 1853 there were eleven

located on the largest farms. (99) By 1872 large farms in south
Wales were using the portable steam-threshing machine. Either there
was one belonging to the farm or, more commonly, the work was done
by an itinerant firm which in the 1870s charged $2\frac{1}{2}$d. or 3d. per
bushel for wheat and barley, and 2d. per bushel for oats. Steam
threshing, usually by hiring, came into general use on the well-
managed farms throughout Wales in the last quarter of the century.
(100) Other machines like chaff cutters, cake crushers and root
slicers and pulpers were also driven by steam. (101)

Livestock management on these substantial holdings also stood in
sharp contrast to the general neglect of the small family-farms.
Instead of a number of ill-bred store animals being produced, the
livestock was often fattened for the butcher on roots. Scientific
breeding was carefully attended to, and the animals were given the
proper amount of shelter and feeding. Local breeds of cattle like
the Glamorgans, the smoky-faced Montgomeryshire variety and the Pembroke Blacks were from the mid century increasingly abandoned by the
substantial tenants in favour of the 'improved' breeds like the
Herefords, Shorthorns, Devons and Ayrshires. (102) Cattle on those
sizeable holdings which practised feeding were fattened off at $2\frac{1}{2}$ to
3 years old. Young cattle were wintered in loose yards and fed on
cut straw and pulped roots. Fattening beasts of 2 years old were
grazed outdoors in the summer on the rough meadows, and in addition
received daily supplies of cotton and linseed cake. The fattening
process was seldom completed till the winter, and for this purpose
the heifers were tied in stalls and steers were placed in a warm
fold-yard. They were fed on cut swedes, linseed or cotton cake,
mixed meal (wheat, barley and pea) served with chopped clover. Some
farms of this nature did little breeding, but preferred to buy 2- or
3-year-old steers in the autumn, and then fattened them for the
spring market. Sizeable holdings in the Vale of Glamorgan parishes
of St Athan, Llantwit Major, Llanfihangel, Llandow, Monknash, Wick
and onwards to Colwinstone and St Bride's Major were characterised
by this type of excellent management. Here the response to the
demand for beef, mutton, clover-hay and wheat-straw from the mining
valleys was clearly in evidence. (103) This superior farming was
exceptional, however, even within the small number of lowland farms
that practised fattening. It was largely confined to the better
farms of the Vale of Glamorgan and south Monmouthshire. Many farms
within the Vale which fattened stock lacked the housing facilities
for stall-feeding, and this, too, was the situation among the large
feeding farms of south Pembrokeshire. (104)

Not all the large farmers, even of lowland areas who invested
money in their business, were able to finish their cattle for the
butcher. The soil was often too poor. Thus in the typically Anglicised parish of Kerry, near Newtown, in east Montgomeryshire, some
of the best Hereford cattle were bred in the 1890s, but these had of
necessity to be finished in the English Midlands. (105) Again, much
of Pembrokeshire outside of the Castlemartin area remained a breeding and rearing county. We referred earlier to the accounts of the
farm of Trefayog in the northern parish of St Nicholas, near Fishguard, for the years 1867-81. (106) The annual rent was £126 until
the end of 1872 when it was raised to £156. The occupier, a winner
of prizes at a cattle show in 1874, concentrated on store cattle and

TABLE 8.1 Income from sales off Trefayog farm, near Fishguard, Pembrokeshire, 1872-6

Commodity	1872			1873			1874			1875			1876		
	£	s.	d.	£	s.	d.	£	s.	d.	£	s.	d.	£	s.	d.
Wheat	28.	6.	7½	8.	0.	6	6.	15.	6	0.	19.	6	19.	19.	6
Barley	50.	0.	0	16.	14.	1½	55.	8.	0	1.	2.	6	28.	7.	5
Oats	10.	10.	0	10.	6.	4	0.	0.	0	22.	5.	9	27.	10.	6
2-year-old steers and heifers	161.	4.	0	194.	16.	6	161.	10.	0	118.	15.	0	154.	15.	0
Cows	98.	16.	6	15.	10.	0	14.	0.	0	39.	10.	0	32.	15.	0
Bulls	0.	0.	0	31.	10.	0	5.	0.	0	14.	10.	0	0.	0.	0
Sheep and lambs	90.	5.	0	86.	0.	5	46.	3.	0	64.	5.	7	71.	0.	4
Pigs	22.	5.	6	64.	14.	6	66.	14.	8	41.	18.	9	34.	0.	4
Colts and mares	35.	0.	0	59.	0.	0	22.	12.	6	27.	10.	0	45.	0.	0
Butter	89.	18.	3½	97.	15.	5	116.	9.	9	83.	0.	6	102.	19.	3
Cheese	4.	10.	1	0.	0.	0	0.	0.	0	0.	0.	0	0.	0.	0
Wool	6.	4.	8	6.	18.	4	4.	17.	6	9.	1.	6	8.	3.	6
Potatoes	3.	8.	6	3.	18.	0	9.	8.	6	2.	8.	9	7.	12.	0
Ryegrass	0.	0.	0	3.	3.	0	25.	13.	6	1.	10.	0	4.	2.	0
Swedes	0.	0.	0	0.	15.	0	0.	0.	0	0.	0.	0	0.	0.	0
Cowskin	1.	10.	0	0.	9.	0	0.	10.	9	1.	19.	6	0.	17.	9
Total	601.	19.	2	599.	11.	1½	535.	3.	8	428.	17.	4	537.	2.	7

Source: N.L.W. MS. 6642A.

butter production (see table 8.1). Improved husbandry was clearly
in evidence. In 1874, for example, expenditure included £5 4s.8d.
for clover seeds, 4s.8d. for mangold seed, 18s.9d. for oilcake for
calves, £7 11s.0d. for 24 cwts of phosphate, £8 8s.0d. for 12 cwts
of nitrate, £2 8s.0d. for 6 cwts of mangold manure, £18 18s.0d. for
58 cwts of bones for turnips, and £1 16s.0d. for $4\frac{1}{2}$ cwts of potato
manure.

   Sheep farming was skilfully managed on the large low-lying farms.
With the growth of turnips and green crops on these holdings in the
early nineteenth century, the small native breed of Welsh sheep
became gradually replaced by crosses with larger kinds from the
neighbouring English counties. (107) Increasingly during the second
half of the century the large farms of the fertile lowlands and valleys came to carry flocks of Cotswolds, Oxford Downs, Leicesters and
Shropshires. The Shropshire Downs made noticeable gains over the
rest from the 1880s, as experience taught the Welsh farmer that the
long-woolled varieties, like the Leicesters and the Cotswolds, were
not so suited to the moist climate of the principality. (108) Two
systems of management were followed on these low-lying farms. First,
there was the 'flying' stock system, under which ewes were purchased
onto the farms in autumn for breeding and fattening early lambs,
which were disposed of in June, the ewes in turn being fattened for
the butcher in the autumn. The process was then repeated. (109)
Second, there was the system of regular breeding and rearing. Great
care was taken to select purely bred, healthy tups, and many of the
leading breeders in south Wales regularly attended the Gloucester
September fair for this purpose. Ewes were put to the ram about
1 October and the lambs were dropped at the beginning of March. The
best breeders taught them to eat cake at an early age, in September
they were put on white turnips, and in early December on cut swedes.
As time advanced the feeding stuffs became more varied. Peas, linseed or cotton cake, Indian corn and crushed oats not only matured
the animals quickly, but also kept up the condition of the land and
reduced the manure bills. At thirteen to fourteen months old the
wether tegs, and those of the non-breeding ewe tegs, were fit for
the market. Ewes were as well treated as the lambs during the
winter months. Hay was liberally dealt out and roots, usually white
turnips, were fed them, mainly on the pastures. (110)

III

Farming practices in nineteenth-century Wales for the most part
remained backward. Agricultural output was consequently even lower
than the limited levels imposed by soil and climatic factors. The
preponderance of small occupiers explains this lack of improved
techniques. They were disinclined or unable to adopt the modern
methods which their neighbours with large farms were practising.
Yet the important fact remains that the small unexperimenting Welsh
hill farmers frequently succeeded where English and Scottish newcomers failed. The key to the Welsh farmer's success lay in his
willingness to work relentlessly and to live frugally. It was
stated at the time that whereas the Englishman when proposing to
take a holding generally put himself the question: 'Can I make a

living here?' the Welshman simply asked himself: 'Can I pay the
rent?' Still, by dint of parsimony, money was saved over the years
even by these peasant hill-farmers. (111)

CHAPTER 9

CONCLUSION

I

The role of agriculture in the Welsh economy declined over the
course of the century, particularly from the 1850s onwards. Whereas
a fifth of the total labour force in Wales in 1851 was employed in
agriculture, by the close of the century the ratio had fallen to a
twentieth - a decline of 75 per cent. Agriculture's traditional
pre-eminence was replaced by the iron and coal industries located in
the south-east. Labourers, rather than farmers and their relatives,
left the peasant holdings in large numbers from mid century, a high
percentage settling in the industrial valleys of Glamorgan and
Monmouthshire.

   Physical factors - the wet climate and thin, unforgiving terrain
- dictated that the farming was essentially mixed, with an emphasis
on store animals and dairy produce. Sheep husbandry predominated on
the mountain and high moorland farms. Furthermore, economic conditions in the second half of the century influenced a still greater
emphasis on grass farming. Thus, the relatively more remunerative
livestock prices from mid century saw a quiet shift from cereals to
livestock. But only with the high labour costs and (slightly later)
falling cereal prices of the last three decades of the century did a
dramatic switch to grass occur. The scale of the movement is shown
by the Agricultural Returns. Between 1870-2 and 1912-14 the area
under permanent grassland rose from 57 per cent to 75 per cent of
the total cultivated area of the principality. This total cultivated area (some 59.8 per cent of the geographical area in 1894) had
grown appreciably since the beginning of the century under the combined stimuli of enclosures, the rise in the level of industrial
demand and the coming of the railways.

   The production of almost every type of commodity on the small,
largely self-sufficient family-holdings - a few sheep and a few
cattle were kept, butter was made, oats and barley were grown, and
even a little wheat was sown - shielded the Welsh farmer from the
drastic fluctuations experienced in the Midlands and south-eastern
counties of England. The season had to be bad indeed that hit him
in every department of his business (1842-3 was such a year and,
significantly, brought its well-known dire social consequences).

This is not to state that there was absence of hardship in the three
decades or so before mid century and during the 'great depression'.
Welsh farmers were generally poor, able to scrape a living only by
dint of hard work and a frugal style of living, and adverse economic
conditions brought distress and sometimes failure. Still, mixed
farming (together with minimal labour costs) staved off ruin on a
scale experienced, for instance, by the corn farmers of the English
Midlands.

Welsh farming - apart from the few favoured lowland areas - could
never have been a handsomely profitable business. Store livestock
could yield only limited profits, for the turnover was too slow and
labour contributed too small a share to the value of the product.
However, it was less profitable than it need have been. Husbandry
techniques remained unimproved throughout: drainage - the foundation of all good farming practices - was deplorably inadequate,
green crops and roots were sparsely grown, scant attention was given
to livestock breeding, and agricultural implements were crude. It
is important to stress that this low state of farming persisted
despite the undoubted improvements in fertilisers, seed varieties,
farm machinery and livestock breeds which began to feature from the
1870s as farming became more capital-intensive. The railways, while
altering the system of marketing, did not administer the anticipated
vital injection of enterprise and capital into Welsh agriculture.

It is generally accepted that agriculture was in a bad state but
there are widely differing explanations for this. Contemporaries
and later generations of Nonconformist-biased Welsh historians
blamed the landlords for failing to establish favourable tenurial
arrangements, thereby depriving the tenants of the necessary confidence to farm with enterprise. This study has argued that such an
interpretation, though containing an element of truth, is strewn
with pitfalls. It is contended that the 'Welsh Land Question' - the
agrarian indictment against the landowners - was largely the inven-
tion of Welsh Nonconformist Radicalism towards achieving political
democracy and national fulfilment, and that while the Radical
leaders were sincere men, dedicated to achieving their goals, they
often pressed anti-landlord allegations which had no basis in fact.

The cultural, religious and political differences between landlords and tenants did not have the unfortunate economic consequences
that the Radicals claimed. Hereditary Welsh owners, large and small
alike, far from being wholly out of sympathy with their tenants,
possessed an inborn sense of responsibility for their welfare. They
did not conduct their dealings with them on a purely commercial
basis, nor did they allow political and religious sentiments to
influence the way they selected and subsequently treated them.

Tenants on the large estates farmed under positively favourable
conditions. Although they held under yearly agreements they were
usually tenants for life. Indeed, virtual hereditary family succession obtained in a century of acute land hunger. (At the same time
such hereditary succession, we have seen, was itself a factor producing a craving for land since it meant far fewer holdings becoming
available to 'outsiders' than would have happened in its absence.)
Tenants felt no strong sense of insecurity. They were charged fair
and often lenient rents, competition for holdings not being the
decisive factor in determining rents. Their landlords also carried

out substantial improvements - particularly from the late 1860s -
with only small returns on their outlays. Tenants were also
cushioned in difficult years by being permitted to run up high
arrears and to pay their rents in driblets, and by the grant of rent
abatements. Large owners adopted the attitude that they and their
tenants were partners in the business of farming. It is fair to
state that the tenants on large estates were throughout more favourably placed than were the small owner-occupiers.

Conditions were far less propitious on the small estates. Tenants
paid competitive rents (very likely feeling insecure in the process)
and received little in the way of improvements to their holdings.
Their owners were anxious to take as much from the land and to
return as little as possible. An enlightened Anglesey curate struck
a right balance in 1840 when addressing landowners about their
responsibilities:

> It is true that tenants are much to be blamed for out-bidding one
> another in their avidity to obtain any farm which might become
> vacant. But the fault of letting to the highest bidder is yours,
> the evil therefore commences with you, and it is an evil which
> you ought never to encourage. (1)

On the other hand, lesser landlords of Welsh stock were seldom rapacious: their poverty dictated that they took what rents were
offered, but it is doubtful if they squeezed the last penny. The
continuance of many families on the same holdings over long periods
on these small estates suggests otherwise. Similarly, poverty prevented small owners from maintaining their estates in good repair.
Exploitation was rather the unpleasant characteristic of the newcomers from business who felt none of the traditional ties and sense
of responsibility, but instead regarded landownership as a commercial enterprise and as an avenue to sport and amusement. They were
out of step, claimed H.M. Vaughan, with 'the old simple life of
their predecessors'.

If grossly exaggerated in the past, it is readily acknowledged
that tenurial relations did to some extent hinder improvements. The
fact that both small owners and their tenants lacked capital meant
that their interests were usually in conflict. Land hunger, here,
was an inevitable source of friction and tenants were unwilling to
invest partly because they feared their outlays would be swallowed
in higher rents. Lack of compensation for unexhausted improvements,
too (although never the vital constraint it was made out to be), was
a genuine grievance when properties of under 1000 acres of large and
small estates were being sold from the 1870s. But there were other
far more basic obstacles to improvements like poor communications,
the language barrier, wide tracts of unenclosed moorland which hindered improvements in livestock breeding, tenants' lack of capital
on large and small estates alike, and the peasant mentality which
was unwilling to invest. The last was the crucial factor of constraint. Peasant tenants were preoccupied with farming as cheaply
as possible, which stemmed only in part from a concern for low-risk
farming. Low expenditure mainly involved keeping rents at a level
charged in the past. Thus they were determined to do as little as
possible to manifest signs of prosperity. Although large owners
neither evicted nor raised rents as a matter of course following
tenants' improvements, yet the remotest 'possibility' that rents

might be raised was sufficient to paralyse all efforts.   There was thus a total reluctance to improve.   Fear of rent increases was therefore a crucial obstacle to improvement, and, though on small estates it was partly the consequence of landowners' conduct, it derived basically from the peasant belief that their well being constantly depended upon the level of their rent.

The peasant mentality, too, was suspicious of innovation and change, believing the old tried methods to be the best.   Land was not regarded as a commercial speculation but simply as a means of providing a livelihood.   Thus farms were thought of by the local peasant community as units that should carry a certain number of livestock only, and if a farmer exceeded that number he was looked upon with question and even disfavour as overreaching himself, and perhaps tempting fate. (2)   There was in this way a discouragement of improvement by the local community as a whole.   Attitudes towards new machinery as valuable time-savers were similarly conservative and quaint.   Such a non-improving outlook was to some extent allowed to persist owing to the easy-going, distinctly uncommercial attitudes of many landlords.

II

The squires and gentry were not an organic part of nineteenth-century Welsh rural society.   Although resident for much of the time, they lived apart from the rest of the community.   By the close of the eighteenth century the long, gradual process of alienation of the squires and gentry from their native society was virtually complete.   They spoke the English language and had come to despise the Welsh peasant culture as inferior.   The spectacular growth of Non-conformity in the early nineteenth century and its offspring, political Radicalism, imbued - indeed indoctrinated - the common people with a new set of values that posed an inevitable challenge to the traditional political and social ascendancy of the landlords.   Although deference (a mixture of habit, ignorance, fear and genuine loyalty) persisted down to the 1860s and beyond, the Chapels were continually gaining ground, and in 1868 the first revolt of the people against the oppressive twin-dominance of squire and Church achieved a spectacular victory.   The landowners were disappointed and affronted at what they considered to be the ungrateful behaviour of people whose welfare they had always sought to promote.   They undoubtedly felt 'betrayed' and strongly resented the perfidy of the meddling preachers.

A few of the more impetuous and arrogant struck back crudely, and so inadvertently furnished the Radical cause with the convenient myth of oppression and martyrdom which so pervaded and influenced the course of Welsh politics down to the close of the century. Nevertheless, such bludgeoning behaviour was wholly unprecedented, and comparable fits of pique never recurred.   Indeed, from the 1870s the squires took great pains to ensure that they could not legitimately be charged with having influenced the voting behaviour of their tenants.   Although landed power continued to exist, it had declined to such an extent by 1888 that landlords accepted the democratic implications of the Local Government Act with an air of calm

resignation. They rightly attributed such persuasive pressures to
the Nonconformist preachers. The 'chapel screw' was a power which
landlords could not hope to meet; in fact spiritual influence
replaced economic sanctions as a subtle form of coercion.

During the 1860s and 1870s longstanding criticism of the gentry
as political leaders ripened into a total attack on their very existence as a class. Against a 'favourable' background of depression
in the 1880s the preachers and editors orchestrated this earlier
criticism to a majestic crescendo. The Land Question became a burning issue. To legitimate grievances like the Game Laws, sales of
property on large and small estates from the 1870s without provision
of compensation to tenants, and marriage of holdings were added many
that were either without foundation or, as with competitive rents
and a consequent feeling of insecurity, were applicable only to
small estates, more particularly those of under 1000 acres. As a
result the old ties of loyalty and respect were seriously impaired.
Tenants became far more critical. They now questioned conditions
which they had hitherto accepted as the natural order of things and,
pinched by depression, many supported land reform (though not Free
Sale which would have led to rack renting of future tenants) as a
means of gaining immediate reductions in their rents. Yet the
degree of collapse arising from the Land Question can be overstated.
There was no spontaneous, mass tenant movement for land reform, and
it is clear that the party of agitation had grossly overestimated
the extent of the decay of the old tenant-landlord ties. Many landlords were personally liked and respected even after they had been
rejected as political leaders and replaced by prominent members of
the Nonconformist denominations.

Government legislation from the late 1860s onwards gradually
diminished the political and social prestige attached to landownership. Unlike their counterparts in England, Welsh owners were enabled to sell parts of their properties in the last quarter of the
century because pressure for land sustained a favourable land market.
The significant break-up of Welsh estates came only after 1910, however. As in England, owners were induced to sell out of feelings of
insecurity engendered by the political climate, and, more important,
because the improvement in the land market offered them the chance
of re-investing their capital in more remunerative enterprises than
land now that its social and political fringe benefits were inexor-
ably passing. The democratic purge was more thorough in Wales,
presenting owners with even more compelling reasons to sell than
those facing their English counterparts. The full flood of land
sales was only reached in the years between 1918 and 1922. Welsh
owners took full advantage not only of the high prices prevailing
but also of their tenants' keen desire to purchase their ancestral
homes.

Welsh agricultural society lacked a well-defined and sizeable
middle class. (The rising commercial and professional middle
classes of rural Wales belonged to the towns.) This meant that
below the squires and gentry there was only one other main class,
namely, the peasantry, who were all linked together by the one paramount factor in their lives, the land. However, it is more accurate
to think of the peasantry as divided into two distinct groups: at
the top were farmers, and, below them, the cottagers or the 'people

of the little houses'. This last group comprised farm labourers,
non-agricultural labourers as road menders, quarrymen, gardeners and
coalminers, and craftsmen as shoemakers, tailors, blacksmiths and
carpenters. Although farmers in Wales worked the land alongside
their labourers and were little removed from them in their standard
of living, nevertheless their occupancy of land bestowed status and
independence. The absence of an identifiable middle group, together
with the self-imposed isolation of the gentry, meant that farmers
were effectively the local 'aristocracy'. They possessed a strong
group sense of their superior position. Intermarriage (the vital
test of feelings of separateness) with the cottagers was uncommon.
   Yet, down to the close of the century farmers and cottagers were
linked closely together. The close-knit nature of the local communities was to a large extent a consequence of the relative poverty,
isolation (more particularly down to the 1870s), backwardness and
low productivity of the region, and the persistence of semi-
subsistence farming, since these prevented the appearance of wide
income inequalities, and encouraged mutual help with the major farming tasks. Farm labourers and indoor servants maintained close
social relations with their masters down to the close of the century.
As in other pastoral areas of the 'highland zone', a substantial
proportion of labourers in Wales were indoor servants. Moreover,
outdoor labourers in the principality (unlike anywhere else in
Britain) were boarded at the farms. There was little evidence of
conflicting economic interests between the two categories: many
servants were farm children either at home or on neighbouring farms,
and labourers realistically aimed at eventually taking farms themselves, although land hunger (admittedly partly caused by such
favourable chances of obtaining holdings) was often to frustrate
their ambitions. Labourers' protest and trade unionism were therefore conspicuously absent throughout the century (the dispersed
labour force and the language barrier were also important ossifying
forces). Nevertheless, accompanying their better bargaining position from mid century onwards there came a growing spirit of independence. Old semi-patriarchal ties were slowly weakening as commercial attitudes developed, although the crucial change in relations between farmers and labourers was only to occur during the
First World War.
   Small farms with their limited labour force necessarily relied
upon co-operation at all times of the year between farmers themselves and between farmers and local cottagers. Conversely, cottagers depended heavily upon the local farms as a means of livelihood. Indeed, agriculture throughout the century remained the
dominant force in the lives of the country people. Thus Daniel E.
Jones, writing in 1899 of the history of the parishes of Penboyr and
Llangeler in south Cardiganshire, could state of the local craftsmen:
'nevertheless they were first of all agricultural workers. The farm
was the big "spring" whence they and their families got their livelihood ... /there was/ a close link between craftsmen and cottagers.'
(3) Not only here but in all parts of Wales it was customary for a
section of the 'little people', the craftsmen-smallholders of cow-
places and one-horse places (averaging about fifteen acres) to
receive help at different times of the year from local farmers.
Teams were provided for ploughing; manure, hay and coal were carted,

and straw was given for pigs' bedding. In return the craftsman-
smallholder and his wife helped the farmer at harvest. Many cottagers had no land but a garden, and these, too, were closely linked
with the neighbouring farms. In south-west Wales a highly organised
system of potato-setting groups drawn from the cottagers formed a
vital element in the local economy, farmers and cottagers operating
the system to mutual advantage. Elsewhere the association was
looser and vaguer, but existed nevertheless. Thus in north Wales
cottagers comprising tailors, shoemakers, millers and shopkeepers
would give a helping hand at corn binding as an acknowledgment of
various kindnesses shown towards them since the previous harvest in
the form of a little buttermilk, straw for pigs' bedding, being
allowed to collect firewood, the cartage of a load of coal, planting
a row of potatoes, being given second-hand clothes and being allowed
to glean. (4)

For most of the century, then, the close economic interdependence
between farmers of varying sized holdings, and between them and
their neighbouring cottagers, together with ties of religion, language, personal friendships and family connections, gave the local
community a close intimacy of personal relationships. This was the
vital characteristic of the Welsh rural community despite its pattern of dispersed farmstead and cottage settlement. Indeed, the
Welsh neighbourhood was so closely knit by economic interdependence
that possibly not even the bitter religious divisions of the 1880s
and 1890s between Church and Chapel could rend it. Thus D. Parry-
Jones has plausibly contended (for south Cardiganshire) that the
system of co-operation and help between certain farms and cottages
was far older than the religious differences, and was resistant
enough to absorb them. (5) However, within this essentially friend-
ly and co-operative farming community there was, paradoxically, an
explosively divisive force - land hunger. The shame and torment of
neighbours secretly bidding against one another for possession of
holdings must often have created acute strains and tensions.

Poverty meant that the rural community was often under severe
pressure. There was a higher incidence of rural unrest in Wales in
the first half of the century than later, and this is mainly attributable to the remorseless pressure of a fast growing population on
a semi-subsistence economy in the grip of intermittent prolonged
depression. The peasant community of small tenant farmers and farm
labourers was deeply impoverished. On the whole, the inhabitants,
though greatly discontented, were surprisingly peaceful. The peasantry were not readily prone to violence. But the occasional enclosure riots and the Rebecca disturbances saw the peasantry of certain
areas rise up in angry protest. Freeholders, tenant farmers and
cottagers throughout the century opposed enclosures because they
removed a vital prop to their livelihood, and on a few occasions
they tore down fences. These early outbreaks of violence were clearly the expression of the popular will of the whole interdependent,
close-knit peasant community, even if, as in Rebecca, the small farmers were the leaders. As for those in Britain generally, they were
a spontaneous, 'direct action' form of protest, born of despair and
anger. (6) They were only rudimentarily organised, largely destruc-
tive of property (the small injury to persons in the Rebecca Riots
was truly amazing), concerned with invoking traditional 'justice'

and ancient customs, and given to intimidatory threats to obtain the compliance of the rank and file. (The custom in south-west Wales called carrying 'ceffyl pren' (literally the 'wooden horse') meant that the mode of getting rid of a grievance like tolls by nocturnal violence was a familiar and natural procedure.) Economic distress and a loss of traditional rights were the paramount factors underlying these outbreaks of rage, but there were other significant elements which led to a state of smouldering resentment in the community, namely, the growing lack of confidence in the upper classes as magistrates in the administering of justice and the levying of taxation of all kinds (deference nevertheless persisted well into the second half of the century) and the dislike of tithes and of the workhouse partly on religious grounds.

It has been stressed that the close economic and social ties between Welsh farmers and their labourers meant that there was little conflict of interest between them. These links were closest in the early century and largely explain the absence or, at any rate, small incidence of labourers' protest in these years of dire poverty when cottagers were enabled to survive only by dint of a 'scavenger' economy. Generally, labourers did not regard farmers as unsympathetic towards their plight. Thus there was little disturbance in Wales in 1830-1, although the pastoral nature of the farming was of course an important reason for the lack of trouble. The area most liable to insurgence, the corn-growing area of Glamorgan, was saved by the close proximity of the iron and coal industries, so that farm workers there were considerably better off than their counterparts in the southern and eastern counties of England. The severe farming crisis in the early 1840s seems to have been the only time when conflict ruptured good relations (farm outbuildings and ricks were fired in Denbighshire and Montgomeryshire). (7) Arson was the oldest form of rural protest and further research into its incidence in Wales may well modify the viewpoint presented in this study. For the moment it would seem that the only category of the labouring population that showed a strong tendency to violent protest was the squatter who fought a losing battle against the oppression of Crown agents, private landowners, tenant farmers and small freeholders.

Conditions greatly improved in the countryside from the mid 1850s with the coming of favourable farming conditions and the fall in population owing to migration. Welsh labourers were now in a better bargaining position, and discontent was rife, especially over deplorable accommodation. Yet protest - now undergoing throughout Britain a chemical change into a relatively peaceful, 'forward looking' activity, and finding its characteristic genre in trade unionism - was largely absent. Once again the scattered labour force and the continuing (if slowly dissolving) close ties between farmers and labourers hindered protest for improvements.

The significant rural protest in late nineteenth-century Wales came with the 'Tithe War' and the Land Question. The tithe disturbances, as Dunbabin indicates, were a reversion to the older direct-action type of protest. (8) Welsh farmers, pinched by agricultural distress, and, as Nonconformists, naturally reluctant at having to pay tithes, were pliable agents in the hands of the preachers and the politicians towards achieving sectarian and political goals. Farmers showed no such willingness, however, to adopt the Irish

system of 'boycotting' urged on them in the columns of the 'Baner',
the 'Genedl' and the 'Herald Cymraeg' in 1886 and 1887 as a means of
gaining reduced rents. Despite allegations in the 'Western Mail' in
January 1886 that Calvinist tenants in Denbighshire were practising
such a policy, (9) there is no evidence that this actually happened.
There were certain factors which explain this lack of direct action:
conditions on most Welsh estates were not nearly so adverse as in
Ireland, many landlords retaining the respect of their tenants; certainly as a class they were more popular than the clergy, and, of
course, they were at hand to retaliate immediately and effectively.

Besides opposition by the squatters, cottagers and small freeholders to the fencing of commons, the other community protest that
was present throughout the century was poaching. Significantly, the
gangs who tore down fences on mountain land in Caernarvonshire between 1858 and 1869 (10) and who poached salmon in the Wye and its
tributaries between the mid 1850s and the late 1870s called themselves 'Rebeccaites'. Both groups of protestors savagely brushed
with the authorities. The conflict witnessed a struggle not between
law-abiding citizens and 'deviants', but between two opposing con-
cepts of law. While the peasants appealed to ancient custom and
traditional 'rights', landowners and their agents strictly enforced
their legal rights to their property. In so doing they were frequently oppressive and insensitive to human suffering.

The local Welsh neighbourhood was represented by contemporaries
as being extraordinarily peaceful. (11) Certainly the crime figures
suggested this, (12) but it was argued in 1885 that these under-
stated the true position. It was contended that although crime was
not systematically concealed (in order to reflect credit on the
local police and magistrates) and although sentences were properly
administered, there was a disinclination on the part of members of
the community to prosecute in petty cases. The reasons were various-
ly ascribed to ties of relationship, membership of the same Chapel
or sect, and especially to the dislike of incurring the odium of
prosecution for the sake of a small loss. (13) What evidence we
have so far indicates that crimes of violence to persons were rare,
the most common offences being drunkenness and petty theft. A prevalent crime on the upland, unenclosed commons was sheep stealing.
It was regarded as a serious offence owing to the fact that sheep
rearing was vital to the economy and also because the charge was
often one extremely difficult to prove. (14) It is doubtful if
sheep stealing on the Welsh moorlands was to any significant extent
a protest crime. Poaching, we have shown, was sometimes clearly a
form of protest, but it was often motivated by the simple aim of
self-help and by the thrill of excitement it offered young lads.

Even allowing for the disinclination to prosecute in these face-
to-face communities, it still remains likely that the Welsh rural
community was relatively peaceful. The leavening influences of Nonconformity, temperance and education worked a profound civilising
effect over the course of the century. Witness, for instance, the
transformation in the social character of the community meeting-
place, the local fair. Throughout, it is likely that the moral
sanctions of these close-knit communities were strong antidotes to
anti-social behaviour. Those who transgressed the standards of the
locality did not escape lightly. (15) Conformity was a necessary

virtue in the custom-ridden, conservative-orientated Welsh farming
neighbourhood.

The vital characteristic of the local community - the close interdependence between farmers and between them and the local cottagers
- was disappearing as the century drew to a close. The common
people were by the 1880s far more independent, their economic eman-
cipation resulting from higher money incomes and the spread of far
more local shops than hitherto. (16) Conversely, farmers were increasingly freed from their dependence upon extra harvest help by
the development of farm machinery. The process of change was slow,
but with the passing of the old economic ties went, too, a rich
complex of human relationships, perhaps most fully expressed in the
merriment and banter of the harvest crowds.

APPENDIX 1

Price indices for wheat, barley, oats, store cattle, store sheep, mutton, beef and butter (average of 1839-45 = 100)

Year	Wheat	Barley	Oats	Store cattle	Store sheep	Mutton	Beef	Butter	Pigs
1811								131	
1813	208	202	200						
1814	154	148	134						
1815	125	109	125						
1816	104	82	92						
1817	182	175	161						
1818	158	158	147						
1819	142	162	144						
1820	120	119	118						
1821	87	79	82						
1822	91	78	76						
1823	81	83	82						
1824	105	121	109						
1825	105	118	98						
1826	105	109	101						
1827	106	128	133						
1828	87	98	87			91	100	91	
1829	111	107	103			91	120	77	
1830	102	103	104					69	
1831	110	110	112			83	95	100	
1832	92	95	86			100	105	91	

Year	Wheat	Barley	Oats	Store cattle	Store sheep	Mutton	Beef	Butter	Pigs
1833	86	78	72			109	110	83	
1834	78	69	82			113	105	83	
1835	77	88	92			100	100	77	
1836	74	78	89			109	105	80	
1837	99	102	103					109	
1838	101	101	96			100	115	106	
1839	122	122	119	75	133	109	110	106	105
1840	121	125	125	77	128	104	105	117	100
1841	104	97	100	129	111	104	100	111	112
1842	103	100	95	104	122	109	110	94	101
1843	83	75	76	105	61	100	90	83	86
1844	88	87	86	109	65	96	85	80	91
1845	79	94	99	99	81	91	90	103	107
1846	91	90	101	136				100	115
1847	118	128	117					109	
1848	95	100	95			113	130	111	
1849	82	87	91	89	108	113	110	89	98
1850	66	67	76	73	89			86	102
1851	70	72	84	81	96			89	
1852	66	80	91	103	104			94	105
1853	80	83	91					103	114
1854	115	122	118					120	130
1855	109	104	126			117	125	120	
1856	138	119	139	121	114	113	125	131	
1857	102	117	124	148	122	109	120	131	
1858	86	97	118	144	113	113	130	123	115
1859	67	81	112			126	130	123	114
1860	80	98	117			126	140	134	144
1861	90	117	125			135	135	123	119
1862	90	104	112	120	110	148	145	120	122
1863	78	100	105	138	125	135	140	109	
1864	68	87	94	143	136	135	140	123	
1865	70	82	106	154	143	152	145	140	
1866	84	102	126	146	196	161	160	146	

Year	Wheat	Barley	Oats	Store cattle	Store sheep	Mutton	Beef	Butter	Pigs
1867	104	124	137	150	131	165	160	131	
1868	122	125	142		92	126	140	117	
1869	92	121	137		104	143	155	160	
1870	78	104	116			148	155		
1871	91	102	121					154	
1872	102	107	132			157	195	143	
1873	101	109	106			165	205	154	
1874	108	135	145					160	
1875	81	125	145					163	
1876	84	112	133	201				160	
1877	94	115	140	203				166	
1878	90	116	123	222				149	
1879				203				126	
1880				200				151	
1881	76		99	187				149	
1882	83	96	100	218		187	215	151	
1883						187	195	149	
1884			92			165	180	146	
1885	61	95	108			183	195	137	
1886	56	80	86			161	165	126	
1887	56	70	82			161	150	126	
1888	58	80	82			161	150	131	
1889	57	73	90			157	160	137	
1890	58	76	93			152	165	126	
1891	62	79	101			152	165	137	
1892	51	73	98			157	155	146	
1893	44	67	95			148	155	143	
1894	42	67	80			143	150	126	
1895	41	63	77					123	
1896	48	64	80					120	
1897	59	71	87					126	
1898	50	69	85					111	
1899	44	69	73			152	175	129	
1900	53	69	86			152	160	137	

Year	Wheat	Barley	Oats	Store cattle	Store sheep	Mutton	Beef	Butter	Pigs
1901	46	70	96					140	
1902	47	74	92			152	165	131	
1903		70	88			148	170	131	
1904	49	70	79			148	160	140	
1905	50	69	83			143	150	134	
1906	45	67	81			143	150		
1907	53	72	99			152	155		
1908	53	74	81					146	
1909	54	75	106					143	
1910		70	76					143	
1911	52	79	87					137	
1912	58	84	105					151	
1913	56	80	100						
1914	63	78	105					154	

The corn crop indices above are composite indices of Carmarthen,
Denbigh and Caernarvon markets. The store cattle and store sheep
indices are of prices obtained in a number of markets in west Wales.
The mutton and beef indices are of prices in Bangor market and the
butter index is of prices in Carmarthen market. The various sources
are indicated in D.W. Howell, 'Welsh Agriculture, 1815-1914', ch.6.
In brief, corn prices were obtained from 'The London Gazette' except
for the years 1864-84 when they were taken from local newspapers;
the store cattle and sheep prices were taken from the account books
of the Jonathans of Dihewid, Cardiganshire, as tabulated by J. Ll.
Davies in 'Abersytwyth Studies', XIII (1934) and XIV (1936); the
Bangor mutton and beef prices were obtained from the 'Carnarvon and
Denbigh Herald' and 'North Wales Chronicle' newspapers and the
Carmarthen salted butter prices from the 'Carmarthen Journal' and
'The Welshman' newspapers.

APPENDIX 2

Price indices of steers (2-year-olds), ewes, fat cattle, fat sheep and fat pigs at Carmarthen market (average of 1877-80 = 100)

Year	Steers	Ewes	Fat cattle	Fat sheep	Fat pigs
1845			70		
1846			78		
1847			89		
1848			74		
1849			52	47	
1850					
1851					
1852			67		
1853			78		
1854			70	94	
1855			74		
1856			74		
1857			81	88	
1858			81	79	79
1859	78	68	81	76	77
1860			78	91	92
1861			81	88	97
1862		96	85	82	103
1863			89	79	80
1864			96	88	82
1865	71	98	96	94	99
1866					

Year	Steers	Ewes	Fat cattle	Fat sheep	Fat pigs
1867		75	85	71	89
1868	82	75	93	74	99
1869	90	75	104	79	110
1870					
1871					
1872			104		
1873			126	118	110
1874	86	120	104		100
1875	98	124	107	112	113
1876			96		
1877	106	118	96	112	97
1878	114	108	107	103	98
1879	86	87	89	76	87
1880	102	87	115	106	117
1881		112		100	
1882	118		107		96
1883	122	112	111	115	110
1884					
1885	90	90	81	76	83
1886	86	82	89	76	84
1887	90	80	70	71	82
1888	94	107	89	88	82
1889	106	124	85	94	97
1890					
1891	90		81		
1892	90		67	62	101
1893	90	81	74	71	90
1894	73		81	91	92
1895	90	109	89		76
1896	78	86		88	74
1897	86	99	81	88	82
1898	82	94	81		
1899	82	93	81		
1900	81		81		

Year	Steers	Ewes	Fat cattle	Fat sheep	Fat pigs
1901	78		78		
1902	84		93		
1903	94				
1904	86		78		
1905	94	99	81		
1906	78		89		
1907	98				
1908	96		96		
1909	90				
1910	106	80	93	88	
1911	67			74	
1912	82	96	89	71	
1913	98	101	111	82	
1914	102	84	96		

The years 1877-80 are used as a base because prices for most commodities are available for these years. On the whole they would represent average pre-depression prices for most types of livestock and dairy produce rather better than the unusually high years of the early and mid 1870s. For store cattle, however, they are somewhat higher than average pre-depression prices. These prices for Carmarthen were obtained from the reports of its livestock fairs carried in 'The Welshman' and the 'Carmarthen Journal'.

NOTES

INTRODUCTION

1 P.J. Perry (ed.), 'British Agriculture 1875-1914' (London, 1973), pp.xxxvii-xli.
2 'The Parliamentary Debates', 4th ser., vol.II (16 March 1892); E.J. Hobsbawm, 'Industry and Empire' (Penguin, 1970), ch.15.
3 Recent modifications, however, of the anti-landlord indictment have been made in articles by Jane Morgan, Denbighshire's 'Annus Mirabilis': The Borough and County Elections of 1868, 'The Welsh History Review', 7, no.1 (1974) and I.G. Jones, Merioneth Politics in the mid-Nineteenth Century, 'Jnl of the Merioneth Hist. and Rec. Soc.' (1968).

CHAPTER 1 The historical perspective

1 J.D. Chambers and G.E. Mingay, 'The Agricultural Revolution 1750-1880' (London, 1966), p.208.
2 'Report of the Royal Commission on Land in Wales and Monmouth-shire', P.P.,XXXIV (1896), p.45.
3 B. Thomas, Wales and the Atlantic Economy, in B. Thomas (ed.), 'The Welsh Economy' (Cardiff, 1961), p.15.
4 A.H. John, 'The Industrial Development of South Wales' (Cardiff, 1950), pp.64-5.
5 Figures provided in P. Deane and W.A. Cole, 'British Economic Growth' (Oxford, 1967), p.143.
6 K.O. Morgan, 'Wales in British Politics 1868-1922' (revised edn, Cardiff, 1970), chs 1-3.
7 'Cambrian News', 2 Dec. 1887: editorial on Farming in Wales.
8 'R.C. on Agriculture', P.P., XV (1882), Appendix, pp.18 and 377.
9 H.L.R.O., Minutes of Evidence, H. of C., 9-10 June 1845, vol.80, concerning the South Wales Railway Bill (8-9 Vic., CXC).
10 'R.C. of Inquiry for South Wales', P.P., XVI (1844), Appendix to Evidence, 3, p.445.
11 D. Davies, Welsh Agriculture during the Great Depression, 1873-1896 (unpublished MScEcon thesis, Wales, 1973), p.89.
12 Chambers and Mingay, op. cit., pp.113-14.

13 E.L. Jones, 'The Development of English Agriculture 1815-1873' (London, 1968), pp.10-12.
14 F.M.L. Thompson, 'English Landed Society in the Nineteenth Century' (London, 1963), pp.231-3.
15 Chambers and Mingay, op. cit., pp.124-6.
16 Thus in Carmarthen market wheat averaged 58s.7d. a quarter compared with its level at the beginning of the war of 43s.3d., barley 32s.8d. compared with 24s.8d. and oats 21s.8d. compared with 16s.8d. The 1794 prices are provided in C. Hassall, 'A General View of the Agriculture of Carmarthenshire' (London, 1794), p.46.
17 P.P., XXXIV (1896), p.738; J. Gibson, 'Agriculture in Wales' (London, 1879), p.53.
18 T.H. Williams, Wales and the Corn Laws (unpublished MA thesis, Wales, 1954), p.25.
19 E.L. Jones, 'Seasons and Prices' (London, 1964), p.159.
20 'Replies as to Agricultural Distress', 1816: Report of T. Gough, quoted in Appendices to the 'Report of the R.C. on Land in Wales and Mon.', 1896, P.P., XXXIII (1896), p.23.
21 N.L.W., Glansevern MS.2266.
22 The pre-war price is quoted in D. Williams, 'The Rebecca Riots' (Cardiff, 1955), p.112. For 1811 see Appendix 1.
23 N.L.W., MS.1762B: Walter Davies' Journal, no.7.
24 Glansevern MS.1053: letter of 13 Feb. 1817 of W. Jones, Court, to W. Owen, Lincoln's Inn; Harcourt Powell MS. (unnumbered): letter of 11 Aug. 1818 of H. Wilson to J. Harcourt Powell, in B.E. and K.A. Howells (eds), 'Pembrokeshire Life: 1572-1843' (Haverfordwest, 1972), p.89.
25 N.L.W., Trenewydd MS.464: letter of 13 June 1821 of J. Symmons, Haverfordwest, to W. Gwynne, London; N.L.W. MS.1762B: entries for early June and 11 Nov. 1821; Harcourt Powell MSS: letters of 13 Aug. and 30 Sept. 1821 of H. Wilson to J. Harcourt Powell, in Howells, op. cit., pp.95-6.
26 N.L.W., Lucas MS.3103; for conditions in Denbighshire see N.L.W. Longueville MSS, Bundle 1247: letter of 24 Aug. 1822, in Montgomeryshire see Glansevern MS.2317: letter of 18 Oct. 1822 of E. Jones to R.O. Jones.
27 'Carmarthen Journal', 4 June, 13 Aug., 10 Sept., 15 Oct. 1824 and 3 June, 18 Nov. 1825: accounts of livestock sales at Carmarthen fair; N.L.W., Dunraven MS.445: letter of 14 Sept. 1825 of J. Collier to R. Webb.
28 'Carmarthen Journal', 14 July, 18 Aug., 7 Nov. 1826 and 8 June, 16 Nov. 1827.
29 Glansevern MS.2097: letter of 4 May 1829 of A.D. Jones to R. Jones; Lucas MS.3240: letter of 20 July 1830 of J. Harvey to Lord Kensington; N.L.W., Nanteos MS.3: letter of 29 Aug. 1831 of J. Hughes to Capt. Ll. Philipps, Dale Castle, Pembs.; N.L.W. MS. 11,780E: letter of 26 March 1833; Williams, op. cit., p.115.
30 W. Youatt, 'Sheep: Their Breeds, Management and Diseases' (London, 1837), p.267.
31 Lucas MS.3240: letter of 27 Oct. 1832 of J. Harvey to Lord Kensington.
32 N.L.W. MS. 11,780E: letter of 26 March 1833.

33   Glansevern MS.2125: letter of 25 April 1836; Youatt, op. cit.,
     p.267.
34   The authoritative work on the Riots is Williams, op. cit.
35   The standard reference to prices in these years is provided in
     P.P., XVI (1844), Report, p.2. More precise information is
     provided in Appendix 1.
36   'The Welshman', 30 Sept., 7 Oct., 4 Nov. 1842.
37   Williams, op. cit., pp.115-16.
38   P.R.O., H.O.45/1611: letter of 9 July 1843 of W. Day to
     G.C. Lewis, Esq.
39   Chambers and Mingay, op. cit., pp.158, 177 and 180-1.
40   See D.W. Howell, Welsh Agriculture 1815-1914 (unpublished PhD
     thesis, University of London, 1969), ch.6.
41   'The Welshman', 14 Sept. 1849.
42   N.L.W. MS.6641B.
43   See Howell, op. cit., ch.6; see also Appendix 1.
44   'Carnarvon and Denbigh Herald', 26 Oct. 1872.
45   P.P., XXXIV (1896), p. 756.
46   C.R.O., Cawdor MSS, Box 141: letter of 21 Aug. 1868.
47   'Carmarthen Journal', 14 Aug. 1868, 20 Nov. 1874.
48   T.W. Fletcher, The Great Depression in English Agriculture 1873-
     1896, 'Econ. Hist. Rev.', 2nd ser., XIII (1960-1), p.419.
49   Chambers and Mingay, op. cit., pp.179-80.
50   P.P., XV (1882), p.7.
51   Cawdor MSS, Box 142: letter of 28 July 1879 to Lord Emlyn; P.P.,
     XV (1882), p.15; P.P., XXXIV (1896), p.857.
52   See Howell, op. cit., ch.6; see also Appendix 1.
53   Thompson, op. cit., pp. 309-10; Fletcher, op. cit., pp.419-20.
54   See Howell, op. cit., ch.6; see also Appendices 1 and 2 and
     Davies, op. cit., pp.83-90.
55   Thompson, op. cit., p.220.
56   Figures calculated from the rentals of the estates, all (except
     Cawdor) housed at N.L.W.
57   'Replies as to the Agricultural Distress', 1816.
58   N.L.W., MS.1762B, 8-19 June 1821.
59   P.P., XVI (1844), Appendix VI: evidence of J. Rogers, St Clears,
     Carmarthenshire.
60   C.R.O., Derwydd MS.CA 19; Nanteos MS.3.
61   For the banking crisis of 1816 see N.L.W., Aston Hall MS.320:
     letter of 28 Jan. 1817 of J. Fayel, Aston, to Mr Lloyd in
     Brussels: 'many banks gone in Wales also'; for the banking
     crisis in 1825 in Pembrokeshire see Trenewydd MS.193.
62   'Replies as to the Agricultural Distress', 1816: report of
     S. Lloyd of Bala.
63   Glansevern MS.1053: letter of 13 Feb. 1817 of W. Jones, Court,
     to W. Owen of Lincoln's Inn.
64   N.L.W., Wynnstay Rentals, 1820.
65   Harcourt Powell MSS: letter of 13 Aug. 1821 of H. Wilson to
     J. Harcourt Powell, in Howells, op. cit., p.95; Glansevern MS.
     2317: letter of 18 Oct. 1822 of E. Jones to R.O. Jones; Cawdor
     MSS, Box 136: letter of 29 June 1823 of R.B. Williams to Lord
     Cawdor; Longueville MSS, Bundle 1247: letter of 24 Aug. 1822
     of M. Lloyd.
66   Gregynog and Wynnstay Rentals.

67 As, for example, in Pembrokeshire - see Lucas MS.3240: letter
    of 20 July 1830 of J. Harvey to Lord Kensington.
68 Williams, op. cit.
69 P.R.O., H.O.45/1611: letter of 9 July 1843 of W. Day to G.C.
    Lewis, Esq.
70 Williams, op. cit.
71 N.L.W., Slebech MS.2409; see also N.L.W., Ashburnham MS.1352:
    letter of 20 Aug. 1850; Nanteos Rentals, Michaelmas 1848 and
    Lady Day 1849.
72 Howell, op. cit., pp.125-6.
73 N.L.W., Cilgwyn MS.44: letter of 26 Sept. 1872 of E.C.L. Fitz-
    williams to A. Lascelles, the estate steward.
74 N.L.W. MS.6642A.
75 Ashburnham MS.111: Report of the Llanddeusant estate, 1881;
    J.E. Thomas, The Agricultural Industry of Wales, 'Young Wales',
    vol.3 (1897), p.269.
76 P.P., XXXIV (1896), p.298; J.E. Vincent, 'The Land Question in
    South Wales' (London, 1897), p.84.
77 N.L.W., Picton Castle MS.3907: letter of 17 April.
78 Calculated from the estate Rentals.
79 P.P., XXXIV (1896), p.673.
80 W. Davies, 'A General View of the Agriculture and Domestic
    Economy of South Wales' (London, 1814), I, pp.161, 309-10;
    ibid., II, p.225 concerning the Vale of Glamorgan; B.H. Malkin,
    'The Scenery, Antiquities and Biography of South Wales' (2nd edn,
    1807), II, pp.417-18 concerning Radnorshire; J.W. Edwards,
    Enclosure and Agricultural Improvement in the Vale of Clwyd,
    1750-1875 (unpublished MA thesis, London, 1963), p.30.
81 P.P., XXXIV (1896), p.151.
82 J.M. Powell, The Economic Geography of Montgomeryshire in the
    Nineteenth Century (unpublished MA thesis, Liverpool, 1962),
    pp.84-5.
83 C.S. Read, On the farming of South Wales, 'J.R.A.S.E.', X (1849),
    p.132.
84 It was stated in the Introduction to the Agricultural Returns
    for 1869: 'corn crops have been grown more and more since 1867
    because of higher prices of corn in 1867 and 1868' - P.P., LXIII
    (1868-9).
85 E.L. Jones, The Changing Basis of English Agricultural Prosper-
    ity, 1853-73, 'Ag. Hist. Rev.', XII (1962).
86 'R.C. on Employment of Women and Children in Agriculture', P.P.,
    XIII (1870), Q. pp.166-7.
87 Ibid., Q. pp.170-1.
88 Ibid., Appendix A, part II, to Culley's Report, p.109.
89 T. Bowstead, Report on the Farm-Prize Competition of 1872, 'J.R.
    A.S.E.', 2nd ser., VIII (1872), p.288.
90 'Carmarthen Journal', 16 April 1875.
91 A.W. Ashby, The Place of Cereal Growing in Welsh Agriculture,
    'W.J.A.', II (1962), p.38.
92 D. Thomas, 'Agriculture in Wales during the Napoleonic Wars'
    (Cardiff, 1963), pp.79-95.
93 Calculations made from the Agricultural Returns.
94 Thomas, op. cit., pp.77, 87-9.
95 T. Rowlandson, The Agriculture of North Wales, 'J.R.A.S.E.', VII

(1846), p.582;   A. Fullarton, 'Parliamentary Gazeteer of England and Wales' (1840-4), part XI, p.405;   J. Darby, The Agriculture of Pembrokeshire, 'Jnl of the Bath and West of England
Soc.', 3rd ser., XIX (1887-8), p.94.

96   H.M. Customs and Excise Library, Kingsbeam House, Liverpool
Bills of Entry, 1847:   Records of imports of nitre and guano
into Welsh ports;   P.P., XXXIV (1896), p.728.

97   Lord Emlyn, 'Remarks and Suggestions on the System of Farming
adapted to the Climate and Soil of Carmarthen' (London, 1853),
pp.12-13;   Gibson, op. cit., pp.60-1.

98   D. Davies, op. cit., p.34.

99   Darby, op. cit., p.94.

100   W. Davies, op. cit., I, pp.577, 587-9, 591-6;   W. Davies,
'Agriculture of North Wales' (London, 1810), p.215.

101   'Cambrian News', 10 March 1876:   editorial on Progress of
Agriculture in Wales.

102   Figures calculated from the Agricultural Returns.

103   J.G. Williams, Changes in the Sheep Population of Wales,
'W.J.A.', VIII (1932), p.58;   A.W. Ashby and I.L. Evans, 'The
Agriculture of Wales and Monmouthshire' (Cardiff, 1944), p.13.

CHAPTER 2   The structure and distribution of landownership

1   'Return of Owners of Land, 1873', P.P., LXXII (1874), pt I for
Monmouthshire, pt II for Wales.

2   For example, G.C. Brodrick, 'English Land and English Landlords'
(London, 1881), pp.158-67.

3   J. Bateman, 'The Great Landowners of Great Britain and Ireland'
(London, 4th edn, 1883).

4   'Peers' include Peeresses and Peers' eldest sons.   'Great Landowners' include all estates held by commoners owning at least
3000 acres, if the rental reached £3000.   'Squires' include
estates of between 1000 and 3000 acres, and such estates as
would be included in the previous class if their rental reached
£3000, averaged at 1700 acres.   'Greater Yeomen' include
estates of between 300 and 1000 acres, averaged at 500 acres.
'Lesser Yeomen' include estates of between 100 and 300 acres,
averaged at 170 acres.   'Small proprietors' include lands above
1 acre and under 100 acres.   'Cottagers' include all holdings
of under 1 acre.

5   F.M.L. Thompson, 'English Landed Society in the Nineteenth Century' (London, 1963), pp.112-16.

6   Ibid., p.117.

7   See P. Roberts, The Landed Gentry in Merioneth, c. 1660 to 1832
(unpublished MA thesis, Wales, 1963);   D.W. Howell, The Landed
Gentry of Pembrokeshire in the Eighteenth Century (unpublished
MA thesis, Wales, 1965);   F. Jones, An Approach to Welsh Genea-
logy, 'Trans. Cymmr. Soc.' (1948), p.430.

8   P.P., XXXIV (1896), p.238.

9   For the law of strict settlement see H.J. Habakkuk, Marriage
Settlements in the Eighteenth Century, 'T.R.H.S.', 4th ser.,
XXXII (1950);   Thompson, op. cit., pp.64-70.

10   'Estates Gazette', 7 Jan. 1888, quoted by Thompson, op. cit.,

p.318. See also C. Morgan-Richardson, 'Does Wales require a
Land Bill?' (Cardiff, 1893), p.12: 'In valuing large estates
for sale it is usual, even in the present depression, to calcu-
late on getting for holdings, large and small, 30 years' purchase all through, but I have sold farms (in south-west Wales)
within the last five or six years for 40 or 50 years' purchase,
and the purchasers were generally the tenants themselves.'

11   'Departmental Committee on Tenant Farmers', Evidence, P.P.,
XLVII (1912-13), Q.3941.

12   'Estates Gazette', 23 Dec. 1911, p.995, quoted by S.G. Sturmey,
Owner Farming in England and Wales, 1900-1950, 'Manchester
School of Economic and Social Studies', XXIII, no.3 (1955),p.249.

13   J.H. Davies, The Social Structure and Economy of South-West
Wales in the Late Nineteenth Century (unpublished MA thesis,
Wales, 1967), p.154.

14   P.P., XLVII (1912-13), Report, p.5.

15   Ibid.: Thompson, op. cit., pp.323-5.

16   'Montgomeryshire Express', 21 Oct. 1919. For the boom in land
sales in Britain as a whole see Thompson, op. cit., pp.329-31.

17   J. Davies, The End of the Great Estates and the Rise of Freehold
Farming in Wales, 'The Welsh History Review', vol.7, no.2 (1974),
pp.208-11.

18   'S.C. on Land Revenues of the Crown', P.P., XV (1834), Report,
p.7.

19   Ibid., Q.2959: evidence of J. Wilkin.

20   'Attorney General v. Reveley and others in the Court of Exchequer, May 1868 and July 1869', H.M.S.O., 1870.

21   'Letter to the Chancellor of the Exchequer on the abuses stated
in the Petition of (Welsh) Landowners' (London, 1838); see also
the same letter in Glansevern MS.12507; N.L.W., Caerynwch MS.61:
letter of 9 Oct. 1838 of J. Jervis, Beaumaris, to R.W. Price,Esq.

22   'Reprint of the Report of J. Jervis on the Crown Rights in
Merionethshire, 30 May 1840' (printed by G. Evans, Pool St,
Caernarvon, 1911).

23   N.L.W., Wynnstay 110/45: letter of 24 March 1856 of H. Williams
to N. Wethell.

24   Wynnstay MS.L.652: letter of 3 Sept. 1864 of N. Burlinson to
the Office of Woods; Wynnstay MS.L.654.

25   P.P., XXXIV (1896), p.208.

26   'R.C. on Land in Wales and Monmouthshire', P.P., XXXVII (1894),
Evidence, pp.943-9.

27   'S.C. on Woods and Forests and Land Revenues of the Crown', P.P.,
XVI (1889), Qs 3504-6.

28   I have adopted the acreage taken by G.E. Mingay in his 'Enclosure and the Small Farmer in the Age of the Industrial Revolution' (London, 1968).

29   'Reports to the Board of Agriculture' (London, 1794).

30   'S.C. on Agriculture', P.P., V (1833), Evidence, Q.5820.

31   'S.C. on Commons' Inclosure', P.P., V (1844), pp.95-6.

32   P.P., V (1833), Evidence, Qs 6056-8; P.P., XXXIV (1896), p.550.

33   A.H. Dodd, 'The Industrial Revolution in North Wales' (2nd edn,
Cardiff, 1951), pp.73-4.

34   W. Davies, 'Agriculture of North Wales' (London, 1810), pp.266-7;
P.P., XXXIV (1896), p.549ff.

35 P.P., XXXIV (1896), p.550.
36 P.P., V (1844), Evidence, Qs 4601-2.
37 Ibid., Qs 2112 and 1238. The practice of stint of common ruled that a man could only keep as much stock upon the mountain in the summer as he could keep upon his farm in the winter.
38 P.P., V (1833), Evidence, Q.5821.
39 P.P., XV (1882), Report, p.7.
40 P.P., XXXIV (1896), p.553; see also Slebech MS.6423.
41 N.L.W., Llwyngwair MS.16699.
42 Ashburnham MS.1920.
43 P.P., XXXIV (1896), pp. 552-3; D. Jenkins, 'The Agricultural Community in South-West Wales at the turn of the Twentieth Century' (Cardiff, 1971), p.32; Anon., 'Letters from Wales'(London, 1889), pp.166-7.
44 'Final Report on Agricultural Depression', P.P., XV (1897), p.31.
45 'R.C. on Labour, The Agricultural Labourer, Wales', P.P., XXXVI (1893-4), Summary Report, p.6.
46 Jenkins, op. cit., p.32.
47 E.A. Lewis, Leet Proceedings of the Manor of Arwystli Uwchoed at the National Library of Wales, 'Montgom. Colls', XLVIII (1944), pp.11-29.
48 P.P., XXXIV (1896), p.576; R.U. Sayce, Popular Enclosures and the One-Night House, 'Montgom. Colls', XLVII (1942), p.111.
49 P.P., V (1844), p.211; Sayce, op. cit., p.112; P.P., XXXVI (1893-4), pp.85-6.
50 P.P., XXXIV (1896), p.592, quoting Lleuad yr Oes, vol.1 (1827); Dodd, op. cit., p.59.
51 Wynnstay 11/74: Humble Petition to Sir W.W. Wynn of the poor cottagers who dwell on the mountains of Llanllyfni, Garn and other parishes, Co. Caernarvon.
52 D.J.V. Jones, 'Before Rebecca' (London, 1973), pp.42-3.
53 G.A. Plume, The Enclosure Movement in Caernarvonshire (unpublished MA thesis, Wales, 1935), p.195. In the event of the sale of such waste land being insufficient to defray the expenses of enclosing (including here the heavy item of road construction) a rate would be levied upon the proprietors of allotments - see N.L.W., Plas yn Cefn MS.2406.
54 P.P., XXXIV (1896), p.587.
55 N.L.W. MS.821C.
56 Plume, op. cit., p.186.
57 Ibid., p.195.
58 Llwyngwair MS.15324: letter of 28 Dec. 1822 of G. Bowen to Thomas Lloyd of Bronwydd.
59 P.P., V (1844), p.211: evidence of Mr Banks, Crown Steward, and p.441: evidence of Col. Wood.
60 P.P., XV (1834), Qs 2956-7: evidence of J. Wilkin.
61 'Returns relating to Writs of Intrusion, Tack Notes and Inclosure Acts (Wales)', P.P., XLIII (1836); 'Letter to the Chancellor of the Exchequer ...', op. cit., p.62.
62 P.P., XVI (1889), Q.3593.
63 'Letter to the Chancellor of the Exchequer ...', p.47. Trouble was especially prevalent in the manor of Iscoed, bought off the Crown in 1826 by James Watt.
64 P.P., XVI (1889), Qs 3512-14; P.P., XXXIV (1896), p.591.

65   P.P., XXXIV (1896), p.590.
66   Ibid., pp.580-1.
67   Ibid., pp.582-7.
68   Ashburnham MS.62: Survey and Valuation, 1833.
69   J.H. Davies, The Social Structure and Economy of South-West
     Wales, op. cit., pp.7-9.
70   Ashburnham MS.111.
71   Nanteos MSS: letter book of 1863, letter of 15 Nov. 1863.

CHAPTER 3   Landowners and agriculture

1   P.P., XXXIV (1896), p.554.
2   Ibid., p.230; J. Gibson, 'Agriculture in Wales' (London,
     1879), p.20.
3   Cilgwyn MS.34: letter of 3 May of E.C.L. Fitzwilliams to
     O. Bowen; see also P.P., XXXIV (1896), p.231.
4   A.W. Ashby and I.L. Evans, 'The Agriculture of Wales and Mon-
     mouthshire' (Cardiff, 1944), p.92.
5   P.P., XIII (1870), P, pp.130-1.
6   Gibson, op. cit., p.73.
7   P.P., XIII (1870), P, p.54; P.P., XV (1882), p.7.
8   P.P., XIII (1870), P, pp.130-1.
9   Anon., 'Letters from Wales' (London, 1889), pp.160-7.
10   P.P., XXXIV (1896), p.232.
11   N.L.W., Aberpergwm MS.130: letter of 3 March 1856.
12   Ibid., MS.132: letter of 8 March 1856 of T. Williams to Mrs
     Williams.
13   J. Bateman, 'The Great Landowners of Great Britain and Ireland'
     (London, 4th edn, 1883), pp.2 and 69.
14   P.P., XXXIV (1896), p.232.
15   Picton Castle MSS: Farm Accounts, 1824, and Michaelmas Rental,
     1824; see also Llwyngwair MS.19: livestock account book,1825-7,
     and Nanteos MSS: home farm accounts, Feb. 1872 to Feb. 1873.
16   N.L.W., Hawarden MS.5449.
17   Picton Castle MS.4216: letter of 13 March 1869 of J. Longbourne
     to Messrs Goode and Owen.
18   Cawdor MSS, Box 141: letter of 16 June of T. Mousley to Lord
     Cawdor.
19   W. Davies, 'Agriculture of South Wales' (London, 1814), I,
     pp. 178-9.
20   Cawdor MSS, Box 135: letter of 11 May 1820 of J. Cooper to Lord
     Cawdor.
21   C.S. Read, On the Farming of South Wales, 'J.R.A.S.E.', X (1849),
     p.132.
22   It was entitled 'Remarks on the Advantages of the East Lothian
     System of Farming as Compared with the System Pursued in the
     Vicinity of Swansea' (London, 1850).
23   W. Little, The Agriculture of Glamorganshire, 'J.R.A.S.E.', 2nd
     ser., XXI (1885), p.184.
24   Ibid.
25   N.L.W., Tredegar Park 57/338-91: letters of the home farm
     bailiff to Sir Charles Morgan.
26   T. Rowlandson, The Agriculture of North Wales, 'J.R.A.S.E.', VII
     (1846), p.582.

27   Wynnstay Rental, 1890.
28   H. Edmunds, History of the Brecknockshire Agricultural Society, 'Brycheiniog', II (1956), p.45; Lucas MS.3239: report of the Cardiganshire and Tivyside Agricultural Society, 1839.
29   'Cambrian News', 24 July 1885.
30   'The Welshman', 21 Aug. 1874.
31   P.P., III (1882).
32   Cilgwyn MS.44: letter of 16 May 1872 to the secretary of the Tivyside Agricultural Society.
33   'Cambrian News', 11 Feb. 1871, concerning the North Cards. Agricultural Society.
34   Ibid., 8 April 1881, 22 Sept. 1882.
35   'Carnarvon and Denbigh Herald', 18 Oct. 1884.
36   Wynnstay 11/41: annual show of cattle and sheep at Wynnstay, 11 Sept. 1812; Tredegar Park 57/42: -advertisement for show of stock, 1825, and 72/139-41: cattle show bills, 1842 and 1851.
37   'Cambrian News', 22 April 1887.
38   Ibid., 10 April 1891; P.P., XXXIV (1896), p.744.
39   'The Welshman', 2 Feb. 1872; for prizes offered by other Cardiganshire owners see 'The Welshman', 19 June 1874.
40   D. Thomas, 'Agriculture in Wales during the Napoleonic Wars' (Cardiff, 1963), pp.79-95; J.M. Powell, The Economic Geography of Montgomeryshire in the Nineteenth Century (unpublished MA thesis, Liverpool, 1962), pp.26-8.
41   Thomas, op. cit., p.140.
42   P.P., XXXIV (1896), pp.209-13.
43   W. Davies, 'Agriculture of North Wales' (London, 1810), p.94.
44   J.W. Edwards, Enclosure and Agricultural Improvement in the Vale of Clwyd, 1750-1875 (unpublished MA thesis, London, 1963), pp.176-8, 184-6.
45   Thomas, op. cit., pp.134-8; W. Davies, 'Agriculture of North Wales', pp.256 and 271.
46   P.P., V (1844), Evidence, Q.1238; Powell, op. cit., p.38.
47   Edwards, op. cit., p.31; A.H. Dodd, 'The Industrial Revolution in North Wales' (2nd edn, Cardiff, 1951), p.59.
48   Rowlandson, op. cit., p.58.
49   P.P., V (1844), evidence of T. Davies, p.334; of R. Banks, p.205; of Edwards, p.215; of Rev. T. Williams, p.144, and of C. Mickleburgh, p.182.
50   For example, see Wynnstay 11/74.
51   Ibid., 110/45: letter of 24 March 1856 of H. Williams to N. Wethnell.
52   Cawdor MSS, Box 141: letter of 10 Jan. 1865 of T. Mousley to Lord Cawdor.
53   Rowlandson, op. cit., pp.581-2.
54   Edwards, op. cit., pp.201 and 62.
55   Tredegar Park 57/340; see also P.P., V (1844), evidence of Marston, p.174.
56   Thomas, op. cit., p.141.
57   P.P., XXXIV (1896), p.673.
58   P.P., V (1844), evidence of F. Lewis, pp.96-7, and evidence of Rev. T. Williams, p.145.
59   Ashburnham MS.111: report and valuation, 1881.
60   As, for example, of the Whitland and Cardigan railway - N.L.W. MS.5534C: directors' report, 31 Dec. 1879.

61 Ashburnham MS.1568: letter of 24 Dec. 1851 of the Secretary of
    the South Wales Railway Co. to Lord Ashburnham.
62 H.L.R.O., Minutes of Evidence, H. of C., 1862, vol.23, concern-
    ing the Cowbridge Railway Bill.
63 Cilgwyn MS.34: letter of 17 Feb. 1853 to the editor of 'The
    Welshman'.
64 H.L.R.O., Minutes of Evidence, H. of C., 1845, vol.50 (Towy
    Vale); Minutes of Evidence, H. of C., 1861, vol.1 (Aberystwyth
    and Welsh Coast); Minutes of Evidence, H. of C., 1853, vol.60
    (Llanidloes and Newtown); Minutes of Evidence, H. of C., 1862,
    vol.5 (Bala and Dolgellau).
65 Cilgwyn MS.34: letter of 4 Nov. 1853 to his brother.
66 N.L.W. MS.5534C.
67 H.L.R.O., Minutes of Evidence, H. of L., 1845, vol. 13, concern-
    ing the South Wales Railway Bill; Slebech MS.2111: letter of
    4 Dec. 1845 of de Rutzen; Glansevern MSS 6396 and 6397;
    Cilgwyn MS.34: letter of 21 April 1853 to the secretary of The
    Carmarthen and Cardigan Railway Co.
68 Quoted in translation in J.E. Vincent, 'The Land Question in
    North Wales' (London, 1896), p.15.
69 For the management of English landed estates see D. Spring, 'The
    English Landed Estate in the Nineteenth Century: Its Administra-
    tion' (1963) and F.M.L. Thompson, 'English Landed Society in the
    Nineteenth Century' (London, 1963), pp.151-83.
70 Cilgwyn MS.33: letter of 11 June 1836 of Hall of Cilgwyn to
    W.H. Yelverton.
71 For example, N.L.W., Margam/Penrice MSS: correspondence 1830-50
    between W. Llewellyn, the agent, and C.R.M. Talbot; Cawdor MSS,
    Boxes 135 and 136: letters of J. Cooper and R.B. Williams,
    estate agents, to Lord Cawdor during the 1820s, and Boxes 141
    and 142: letters of T. Mousley, agent, to Cawdor, in the 1860s
    and 1870s; Lucas MSS 3240 and 3241: letters of J. Harvey,
    agent, to Lord Kensington in the 1820s and 1830s; Cilgwyn MSS
    34-6, 39, 40-4: letters of E.C.L. Fitzwilliams from the 1850s
    to the 1870s.
72 Margam/Penrice MS.9240.
73 Ashburnham MS.1530: letter of 25 July 1850.
74 Lucas MS.3240: letter of 29 Aug. 1831.
75 N.L.W., Bute MSS, Corbett letters 1841-5: letter of 23 Jan.1843.
76 Thompson, op. cit., p.151.
77 Cawdor MSS, Box 141: letter of 8 July 1869.
78 Wynnstay 110/14: draft appointment to Agency, 1841.
79 Bute MSS, Box 104: Estate Report, Glamorganshire, 1842. A use-
    ful account of the management of the Margam estate is to be
    found in H.M. Thomas, Margam Estate Management, 1765-1860, in
    S. Williams (ed.), 'Glamorgan Historian', vol.6, pp.13-27.
80 Hawarden MS.4683: letter of 27 June 1843 of G. Robertson to
    J. Gladstone.
81 Cilgwyn MS.46: letter of 14 March 1887 to W. Hale.
82 P.P., XXXIV (1896), pp.251-9.
83 Thompson, op. cit., p.158.
84 As, for example, by S. Roberts, 'Farmer Careful of Cilhaul Uchaf'
    (2nd edn, Conway, 1881), p.31.
85 P.P., XXXIV (1896), p.250.

86   Glansevern MS.1053:   letter of 13 Feb. 1817;   Lucas MS.3089:
     letter of 8 Aug. 1822;   Wynnstay Rental for 1826;   Nanteos MS.3:
     letter of 18 Dec. 1832;   Cawdor MSS, Box 141:   letter of 3 April
     1867.
87   Tredegar Park 57/340:   letter of 7 May 1842 of T. Williams to
     Sir Charles Morgan;   see also P.P., XXXIV (1896), p.250.
88   Margam/Penrice MS.9245.
89   P.P., XXXIV (1896), p.252.
90   Cilgwyn MS.43:   letter of 6 Sept. 1863.
91   Quoted by Vincent, op. cit., p.25.
92   P.P., XXXIV (1896), pp.260-1.
93   N.L.W. MS.9060:   Prize Essay for the Rhuddlan eisteddfod 1850
     on The Advantages of a Resident Gentry.
94   Gibson, op. cit., p.19.
95   S. Roberts, 'Letters on Improvements addressed to Landlords and
     Road Commissioners' (Newtown, 1852):   letter one, Landlords and
     Tenants, pp.5-8.
96   'Parliamentary Debates', 4th ser., II (4 March 1892 to 25 March
     1892), Tenure of Land (Wales) Bill (no.27), 2nd Reading,
     16 March 1892.
97   P.P., XXXIV (1896), p.265.
98   C. Hassall, 'Agriculture of Pembrokeshire' (London, 1794), p.32;
     C. Hassall, 'Agriculture of Carmarthenshire' (London, 1794),
     pp.47-9.
99   Bute MSS, Corbett Letters, 1841-5:   letter of 23 Jan. 1843;
     N.L.W., Chirk Castle MS.12,533:   letter of 10 July 1827 of
     Wilson to R.A. Douglas;   Ashburnham MS.62:   Survey of 1832;
     Glynllivon MS.4665:   letter of 17 Feb. 1827.
100 P.P., XXXIV (1896), pp.387-9.
101 Tredegar Park 84/223.
102 N.L.W., Behrens MS.386A: letter of 6 March 1848 of D. Davies
     to Mrs Paynter.
103 Glansevern MS.1053:   letter of 13 Feb. 1817.
104 N.L.W., Mynachty MSS 103-5:   report by J. Harvey, 11 March 1836;
     Nanteos Rental 1836.
105 Margam/Penrice MS.9240:   letter of 26 June 1833 to Llewellyn;
     MS.9245:   letter of 19 June 1840.
106 Cilgwyn MS.32:   letter of Feb. 1825 of B. Hall.
107 Ibid., MS.34:   letter of 21 April 1853 to the Secretary of the
     Carmarthen and Cardigan Railway.
108 Cawdor MSS, Box 141:   letter of 16 June 1866 from Stackpole,
     Pembrokeshire.
109 Gregynog Hall, unscheduled MSS: historical summary, 14 July
     1893, by the fourth Lord Sudeley.
110 P.P., XXXIV (1896), p.246;   'Cambrian News', 11 Nov. 1892.
111 P.P., XIII (1870), p.50, para.74.   Mr Alan Bainbridge kindly
     provided me with this source.
112 Ibid., Report, p.14.
113 C.S. Orwin and E.H. Whetham, 'History of British Agriculture
     1846-1914' (2nd edn, Newton Abbot, 1971), pp.57-67.
114 Merioneth R.O., Rhagatt, DR.458:   squire Lloyd died 14 Sept.
     1859 aged 81.
115 C.R.O., Plas Llanstephan MS.442:   letter of 1 March 1862;
     'Cambrian News', 14 July 1905.

116 P.P., XXXIV (1896), pp.266-7.
117 Ibid., pp.270-2.
118 'Cambrian News', 13 Feb. 1903.
119 J.E. Vincent, 'Tenancy in Wales' (Caernarvon, 1889), p.84.
120 Gibson, op. cit., pp.17-18, 4.
121 Cawdor MSS, Box 141: letter of 14 May 1865 of T. Mousley to
     Cawdor.
122 For amounts borrowed by individual owners see P.R.O., I.R.3.
123 'The Welshman', 16 Feb. 1872.
124 P.P., XV (1882), pp.8-9.
125 Ashburnham MS.1804: letter of 27 July 1887.
126 For the situation on English estates see Thompson, op. cit.,
     pp.249-53.
127 P.P., XXXIV (1896), p.267.
128 Cawdor MSS, Box 141: letter of 16 June 1886. See also Cilgwyn
     MS.45: letter of 28 Aug. 1878 of J.R. Davies, clerk at Cilgwyn.
129 P.P., XXXIV (1896), pp.716-18.
130 Anon., 'Letters from Wales', p.195.
131 J. Davies, Glamorgan and the Bute Estate 1766-1947 (unpublished
     PhD thesis, Wales, 1969), vol.II, pp.377-8.
132 Anon., op. cit.
133 Davies, op. cit., vol.II, p.417.
134 P.P., XXXIV (1896), pp.699, 709, 713.
135 For example, Plas Llanstephan MS.507 and MS.511: estate sur-
     veys, 1872-3.
136 Gibson, op. cit., p.47.
137 Bute MSS, Box 70: letter book 1822-4; see also Lucas MS.3240:
     letter of 20 July 1829 of J. Harvey to Lord Kensington.
138 A point made in Nanteos MS.3: letter of 16 July 1831 of
     J. Hughes to Col. Powell.
139 Nanteos MS.3.
140 Wynnstay Rental for 1824.
141 N.L.W. MS.11,780E: letter of 26 March of D. Davies of Frood-
     vale to L.P. Jones of Glyneiddan; Aston Hall MS.628: letter
     of 26 April 1830 of J. Lee to Lloyd.
142 Slebech MS.2293: letter of 4 March 1852, MS.2269: letter of
     1 Feb. 1852.
143 N.L.W., Edwinsford MS.3057: letter of 2 June 1822 of D. Price
     to Sir J.H. Williams.
144 Wynnstay Rentals. For example, John Roberts of Diosc (father
     of Samuel) had a rent of £45 in 1821. In 1822-3 temporary
     abatements were given of £7 and in 1824 the rent was permanent-
     ly reduced to £30. In 1844 it was raised to £44.
145 Cilgwyn MS.32: letter of 2 Dec. 1825; D.W. Howell, The
     Economy of the Landed Estates of Pembrokeshire c.1680-1830,
     'The Welsh History Review', 3, no.3 (1967), p.278.
146 Behrens MS.501(a): letter of 9 Jan. 1844 to D. Davies of
     Froodvale.
147 P.P., XVI (1844), Q.53.
148 Ibid., Appendix 3.
149 Nanteos MSS: Particulars of Farms on the Nanteos estate, 1843.
150 P.P., XVI (1844), Q.1754: evidence of Capt. L. Evans.
151 Nanteos Rentals.
152 J.E. Vincent, 'The Land Question in North Wales', Appendix II;

J.E. Vincent, 'The Land Question in South Wales', Appendix;
'Final Report on Agricultural Depression', P.P., XV (1897), p.19.
153 J.E. Vincent, 'The Land Question in North Wales', Appendix II.
154 P.P., XXXIV (1896), p.270.
155 Quoted by J.H. Davies, The Social Structure and Economy of
South-West Wales in the Late Nineteenth Century (unpublished MA
thesis, Wales, 1967), p.55.
156 Quoted by P.J. Perry, 'British Farming in the Great Depression,
1870-1914' (Newton Abbot, 1974), p.174.
157 Gregynog Hall, unscheduled Gregynog MSS: letter of 4 Nov. 1892
of the fourth Lord Sudeley to G.M. Owen, Secretary of the North
Wales Landowners' Defence Association; P.P., XXXIV (1896),
p.396.
158 P.P., XV (1897), p.22.
159 J.H. Davies, op. cit., pp.59-60.

CHAPTER 4   Land occupancy and size of holdings

1 'Agricultural Returns', P.P., LXXXVIII (1887).
2 S.G. Sturmey, Owner Farming in England and Wales, 1900-1950,
'Manchester School of Economic and Social Studies', XXIII, no.3
(1955), pp.248-61.
3 A.W. Ashby and I.L. Evans, 'The Agriculture of Wales and Monmouthshire' (Cardiff, 1944), pp.91-3.
4 F.M.L. Thompson, 'English Landed Society in the Nineteenth
Century' (London, 1963), p.230.
5 W. Davies, 'Agriculture of North Wales' (London, 1810),
pp.98-100; P.P., XXXIV (1896), p.280.
6 W. Davies, 'Agriculture of South Wales' (London, 1814), I,
pp.170-3.
7 L. Kennedy and T.B. Grainger, 'Present State of the Tenancy of
Land in Great Britain' (London, 1828), pp.171, 212, 275.
8 D.W. Howell, The Landed Gentry of Pembrokeshire in the Eighteenth Century (unpublished MA thesis, Wales, 1965), ch.3. On
the Picton Castle estate, for example, leases for lives predominated down to 1840.
9 C.S. Read, On the Farming of South Wales, 'J.R.A.S.E.', X (1849),
p.147. The writer had farmed for many years in Pembrokeshire,
a circumstance which may have given him an exaggerated notion
of the extent of leases for lives over the whole area.
10 P.P., XXXIV (1896), p.281, quoting Dixon.
11 P.P., XXXIV (1896), p.283.
12 P.P., XV (1882), p.11.
13 P.P., XVI (1844), Q.2610.
14 P.P., XXXIV (1896), p.284.
15 Ibid.
16 J. Gibson, 'Agriculture in Wales' (London, 1879), p.21.
17 Ibid., p.1.
18 Ibid., p.285.
19 N.L.W., Glanranell Papers, bundle of letters 1824-37. Major
Francis Jones of Carmarthen kindly provided me with this source.
20 P.P., XXXIV (1896), p.280; T. Rees, 'South Wales', vol.XVIII
(London, 1815), p.276.

21 G.C. Brodrick, 'English Land and English Landlords' (London, 1881), p.205; P.P., XXXIV (1896), p.286; S. Roberts, 'Farmer Careful of Cilhaul Uchaf' (2nd edn, Conway, 1881), p.6.
22 P.P., XXXIV (1896), p.288.
23 'R.C. on Agriculture in Wales and Monmouthshire', P.P., XL (1895), Q.49,813.
24 P.P., XXXIV (1896), p.288.
25 'The Welshman', 26 July 1872.
26 P.P., XXXIV (1896), pp.288-9.
27 Ashburnham MS.1567: letter of 19 Nov. 1851.
28 'R.C. on Agriculture in Wales and Monmouthshire', P.P., XLI (1895), Q.70,030.
29 Gibson, op. cit., p.5.
30 D. Jenkins,'The Agricultural Community in South-West Wales at the Turn of the Twentieth Century' (Cardiff, 1971), pp.176-7.
31 P.P., XXXIV (1896), p.295.
32 P.P., XL (1895), Q.37,826; Jenkins, op. cit., pp.277-8.
33 P.P., XXXIV (1896), p.298; J.E. Vincent,'The Land Question in South Wales' (London, 1897), p.84.
34 P.P., XXXIV (1896), p.307.
35 D. Parry-Jones, 'My Own Folk' (Llandyssul, 1972), p.50. A good example of a small squire's social pursuits as noted in his diary is available in 'Narberth Weekly News', 10 Oct. 1946: the diary of John Thomas Beynon of Trewern, Llanddewi Velfrey, Pembrokeshire, 1837. Mr L. Owens kindly provided this source.
36 P.P., XXXIV (1896), pp.312-13.
37 Llwyngwair MS.16598.
38 Gibson, op. cit., pp.56-7; Anon., 'Letters from Wales' (London, 1889), p.15.
39 I.G. Jones, The Liberation Society and Welsh Politics, 1844 to 1868, 'The Welsh History Review', vol.I, no.2 (1961).
40 Cilgwyn MS.34.
41 Wynnstay Box 105/109.
42 K.O. Morgan, 'Wales in British Politics 1868-1922' (revised edn, Cardiff, 1970), pp.26-7. For evidence concerning evictions see 'S.C. on Parliamentary and Municipal Elections', P.P., VIII (1868-9), Qs 6541-616: evidence of Rev. Michael D. Jones.
43 Cawdor MSS, Box 141: letter of 31 March 1869.
44 Quoted by C.S. Orwin and E.H. Whetham, 'History of British Agriculture 1846-1914' (2nd edn, Newton Abbot, 1971), pp.169-70; Cawdor MSS, Box 141: letter of 21 May 1869 of T. Mousley to Lord Cawdor.
45 Cawdor MSS, Box 141. See also P.P., VIII (1868-9), Qs 5047-227 and 8455-94.
46 J.H. Davies, The Social Structure and Economy of South-West Wales in the Late Nineteenth Century (unpublished MA thesis, Wales, 1967), pp.118-19.
47 Picton Castle MS.3889.
48 Quoted in J.H. Davies, op. cit., p.100.
49 See Ellis's speech in the H. of C. in March 1892 in 'Parliamentary Debates', 4th ser., II (4 March 1892 to 25 March 1892).
50 N.L.W. MS.19462C (Rendel MS.14): letter of 9 April 1887 of R.C. Humphrey Owen to Rendel.
51 P.P., XXXIV (1896), p.313, quoting Col. Hughes, agent of the Wynnstay estate.

52 Anon., op. cit., p.10.
53 Dunraven MS.445: letter of 23 June 1822 of J. Collier to R. Webb.
54 Read, op. cit., p.147; Nanteos MSS: letter of 5 September 1865 of the agent to the South Wales Bank.
55 Margam/Penrice MS.9240.
56 P.P., XVI (1844), Appendix 3, p.446; see also Cawdor MSS, Box 136: letter of 23 Sept. 1824 of R.B. Williams to Lord Cawdor.
57 P.P., XXXIV (1896), pp.316-17.
58 Ibid., p.317.
59 Cilgwyn MS.41: letter of 9 April 1861.
60 P.P., XV (1882), p.8.
61 Cawdor MSS, Box 135.
62 Ashburnham MS.1674: letter of 25 Aug. 1863.
63 P.P., XL (1895), Q.43,343.
64 Picton Castle MS.3909: letter of 29 May 1886 and MS.3910.
65 T. Phillips, 'Wales' (London, 1849), p.30.
66 P.P., XXXIV (1896), p.335.
67 P.P., XIII (1870), N., p.30. D. Jenkins in his 'The Agricultural Community', p.30, puts the smallest unit that could be taken to constitute a farm in south-west Wales in the late century at 30 to 35 acres.
68 P.P., XXXIV (1896), pp.340-1.
69 P.R.O., H.O.107, 2475/590.
70 J.M. Powell, The Economic Geography of Montgomeryshire in the Nineteenth Century (unpublished MA thesis, Liverpool, 1962), p.73; C. Thomas, Rural Society in Nineteenth Century Wales, 'Ceredigion', VI, no.4 (1971), p.395.
71 A.H. John, 'The Industrial Development of South Wales' (Cardiff, 1950), p.66.
72 Cilgwyn MS.3.
73 Wynnstay Rental, 1875; P.P., XXXIV (1896), p.337.
74 Powell, op. cit., p.42; C.F. Cliffe, 'The Book of North Wales' · (2nd edn, London, 1851), p.214.
75 P.R.O., M.A.F.68/281; P.P., XXXIV (1896), pp.338-9.
76 M.A. Griffiths, Agricultural Development in South Wales 1830-75: the case of some Glamorgan parishes, 'Morgannwg', XVII (1973), pp.37-8.
77 W. Davies, 'Agriculture of North Wales', pp.92-3.
78 Hawarden MS.140. See also Wynnstay Rental for 1822 where the landlord directed that the three holdings of Pantygessel, Park-y-Rhiew and Pandy Rhos should be turned into two farms for 'it will ultimately save one lot of buildings'.
79 Cilgwyn MS.32: letter of Feb. 1825.
80 P.P., XIII (1870), Appendix A, I, p.101.
81 Ibid., N., p.30.
82 N.L.W., Glynllivon MS.4665.
83 'Cymru', 7 and 21 Oct. 1857, quoted in P.P., XXXIII (1896), pp.193-4; P.P., XXXIV (1896), p.350.
84 P.P., XXXIV (1896), pp.357-8.

CHAPTER 5   Tenurial relations

1   'S.C. on Agricultural Customs', P.P., VII (1847-8), Qs 197-8.
2   T. Bright, 'The Agricultural Valuer's Assistant' (London, 1910),
    pp.94-105.
3   J. Howells, The Land Question from a Tenant Farmer's Point of
    View, 'Red Dragon', II (1882), p.81. See also D. Owen, 'Tenant
    Right' (Cardiff, 1881); W. Little, The Agriculture of Glamorgan-
    shire, 'J.R.A.S.E.', 2nd ser., XXI (1885), pp.181-2; Anon.,
    'Letters from Wales' (London, 1889), pp.199-204; P.P., XXXIV
    (1896), pp.483-4.
4   P.P., XXXIV (1896), p.477.
5   Ibid., pp.496-8.
6   P.P., XLVII (1912-13), Report, pp.9-10, 12.
7   Ibid., Evidence, Q.3947.
8   Bright, op. cit., pp.106-9.
9   P.P., XXXIV (1896), p.499.
10 Ibid., p.900.
11 J. Clark, 'The Agriculture of Brecknockshire' (London, 1794),
    p.51.
12 Cawdor MSS, group I, Box 135: letter of 1821 of J. Cooper to
    Lord Cawdor.
13 Ibid.
14 P.P., XXXIV (1896), p.496.
15 Derwydd MS.CA.41.
16 Ibid., letter of 18 April 1856 of L. Jones to G. Brace.
17 J. Davies, Glamorgan and the Bute Estate 1766-1914 (unpublished
    PhD thesis, Wales, 1969), vol.II, p.421.
18 P.P., XXXIII (1896), Appendix F.
19 P.P., XXXIV (1896), p.496.
20 Ibid., p.492.
21 Bute letters, letter book 1845-6: Bute to J.S. Corbett, 22 Jan.
    1845.
22 Slebech MS.3822: letter of 4 March 1832.
23 P.P., XXXIV (1896), p.500.
24 Ibid., pp.509-10.
25 P.P., XL (1895), Q.38,769.
26 H.M. Vaughan, 'The South Wales Squires' (London, 1926), p.188.
27 Cilgwyn MS.44: letter of 29 Oct. 1872 to A. Lascelles.
28 P.P., XXXIV (1896), p.518.
29 Nanteos Rental for 1844.
30 P.P., XXXIV (1896), pp.510-13.
31 Ibid., pp.515-17.
32 J.H. Davies, The Social Structure and Economy of South-West
    Wales in the Late Nineteenth Century, pp.98-9; 'Pembrokeshire
    Herald', 11 Nov. 1870.
33 Cawdor MSS: letter of 11 Sept. 1869.
34 'Report of Commissioners into Salmon Fisheries in England and
    Wales', P.P., XXIII (1861), Qs 2592-3: evidence of Thomas Lewis
    Lloyd, Esq.
35 'Hereford Times', 18 Jan. 1879. This reference was kindly
    supplied by Dr David Jones.
36 W.H. Howse, Records of the Radnor General Sessions, 'Trans. Rads.
    Soc.', XIV (1944), p.14; Whiteface, Rebecca and the Salmon,

'Shooting Times', 7-13 Nov. (1974), p.14; A. Grimble, 'The
Salmon Rivers of England and Wales' (2nd edn, London, 1913),
p.98; D.J.V. Jones, Crime, Protest and Community in Nineteenth-
Century Wales, 'Llafur', I, no.3 (1974), p.7.

37   P.P., XXIII (1861), Q.2657: evidence of Rev. Edward Butler.
38   Ibid., Qs 2531, 2627; 'Hereford Times', 18 Jan. 1879.
39   P.P., XXIII (1861), Qs 4138-9: evidence of J. Beynon.
40   'Merioneth Standard', 18 Jan. 1868. This source was kindly pro-
     vided by Dr David Jones.
41   'Parliamentary Debates', 4th ser., II, Tenure of Land (Wales)
     Bill (no.27), pp.986-7.
42   S. Roberts, 'Farmer Careful of Cilhaul Uchaf' (2nd edn, Conway,
     1881), p.7.
43   O.O. Roberts, 'Protection a Pretext: or Home Truths for Tenant
     Farmers' (Caernarvon, 1850), located in Glynllivon MS.5438.
44   P.P., XXXIV (1896), pp.465-8.
45   P.P., XXXVII (1894), Q.28,660.
46   Cawdor MSS, Box 141.
47   P.P., XXXIV (1896), pp.467-8.
48   S. Roberts, op. cit., pp.9-10; P.P., XL (1895), Q.42,347:
     evidence of D.L. Price, land agent and solicitor.
49   'R.C. on Land in Wales and Monmouthshire', P.P., XLI (1895),
     Q.58,074.
50   Margam/Penrice MS.9237: letters of 31 Dec. 1829 and 10 Jan. 1831.
51   P.P., XLI (1895), Q.60,239.
52   P.P., XL (1895), Q.43,760.
53   Ibid., Q.40,258.
54   Ibid., Q.39,493.
55   Quoted in D. Ll. Thomas, 'The Welsh Land Commission: A Digest
     of its Report' (London, 1896), p.310.
56   P.P., XXXVII (1894), Q.28,655.
57   'Cambrian News', 11 Nov. 1892; P.P., XL (1895), Q.46,906: evi-
     dence of J. Humphreys Davies, a landlord in the parish of
     Llangeitho, Cardiganshire; Anon., op. cit., pp.148-51.
58   'Cambrian News', 11 Nov. 1892.
59   J.H. Davies, op. cit., p.101.
60   Gregynog Hall, unscheduled MSS: letter of 4 Nov. 1892.
61   P.P., XXXVII (1894), Q.30,636.
62   N.L.W. MS.11,774 (Behrens MS.15): letter of 12 March 1825 of
     L.P. Jones from Weston to D. Davies.
63   P.P., XXXIV (1896), pp.470-6; Roberts, op. cit., p.5.
64   In Wales, Walter Davies and Charles Hassall.
65   'Tithe Commissioners' Report', reproduced in 'The Welshman',
     10 May 1844; P.P., XVI (1844), Appendix 3, pp.444-6.
66   Nanteos MSS: letter of 15 Sept. 1843 to Col. Powell.
67   K.O. Morgan, 'Wales in British Politics 1868-1922' (revised edn,
     Cardiff, 1970), p.84.
68   P.R.O., H.O.45/454: letter of 23 July 1843.
69   'Inquiry as to the Disturbances connected with the levying of
     Tithe Rent Charge in Wales', P.P., XXXVIII (1887), Qs 1955-6:
     evidence of W. Jones.
70   Ibid., Q.2628: evidence of Owen Williams, secretary of the
     Tithe Defence Fund. He was a farmer and a cattle dealer.
71   Ibid., Q.2640: evidence of Owen Williams.

72 Ibid., Q.2646: evidence of Owen Williams.
73 Ibid., Q.2803.
74 J.P.D. Dunbabin, 'Rural Discontent in Nineteenth-Century Britain' (London, 1974), pp.227-8.
75 Picton Castle MS.3909: letter of 1886 to Philipps of Picton.
76 Dunbabin, op. cit., p.286.
77 Morgan, op. cit., p.90; 'The Times', 13 July 1893; J.H.Davies, op. cit., pp.91-4.
78 Samuel Roberts, op. cit.
79 P.R.O., H.O.45/1611: letter of 12 September 1846 of W. Day to Sir George Gray quoting a letter written him by Sir Edmund Head, 9 Oct. 1843.
80 T.J. Hughes, 'Landlordism in Wales' (1887), pp.3-4.
81 J.E. Vincent, 'The Land Question in North Wales' (London, 1896),· pp.48-9.
82 'House of Commons Debates', Tenure of Land (Wales) Bill, 16 March 1892. See N. Masterman, 'The Forerunner' (Llandybie, 1972).
83 Ibid., p.963.
84 Gregynog Hall, unscheduled MSS: letter of 4 Nov. 1892 to G.M. Owen, Secretary of the N.W. Landowners' Defence Association.
85 Picton Castle MS.3905 quoted by J.H. Davies, op. cit., p.86.
86 P.P., XXXIV (1896), p.461.
87 D. Lleufer Thomas, op. cit., pp.396-7.
88 Cawdor MSS, Box 141: letter of 5 June 1868 of Mousley to Cawdor.
89 'North Wales Chronicle', 1 Sept. 1860.
90 P.P., VII (1847-8), Q.848.
91 J. Davies, Glamorgan and the Bute Estate, II, pp.394-5.
92 P.P., XLI (1895), Q.58,269.
93 P.P., XXXVI (1894), Q.171.
94 P.P., XL (1895), Q.42,347: evidence of D.L. Price, agent for the Tanrallt estate; P.P., XLI (1895), Q.58,074: evidence of P.P. Pennant.
95 P.P., XL (1895), Qs 38,970-1.
96 P.P., XXXVI (1894), p.601.
97 J. Clark, 'General View of the Agriculture of Radnorshire' (London, 1794), p.25.
98 'North Wales Chronicle', 1 Sept. 1860.
99 J. Gibson, 'Agriculture in Wales' (London, 1879), p.5.
100 Cilgwyn MS.36: letter of 22 Oct. 1865 to Mr Lloyd, Esq.
101 'Cambrian News', 3 April 1874.
102 Ibid., 16 July 1880.
103 As argued in the 'Cambrian News', 16 July 1880: Fatstock or Stores.

CHAPTER 6 The agricultural labourer

1 P.P., XIII (1870), N., p.30.
2 D. Parry-Jones, 'My Own Folk' (Llandyssul, 1972), p.51.
3 D. Jenkins, 'The Agricultural Community in South-West Wales at the Turn of the Twentieth Century' (Cardiff, 1971), pp.100-1.
4 A.B. Williams, Courtship and Marriage in the nineteenth century, 'Montgom. Colls', 51 (1949), p.120; D. Parry-Jones, 'Welsh Country Upbringing' (London, 1948), pp.85-6.

183 Notes to chapter 6

5 P.P., XIII (1870), M., p.23: evidence of Rev. R.L. Venables concerning the Builth district of Brecknockshire.
6 P.P., XXXVI (1893-4).
7 J. Gibson, 'Agriculture in Wales' (London, 1879), p.47;
  P.P., XXXIV (1896), p.598; P.P., XXXVI (1893-4), p.6.
8 'Welsh Land: The Report of the Welsh Land Enquiry Committee,
  Rural' (1914), p.185.
9 P.P., XXXVI (1893-4), p.113.
10 'Little's Report on Scotland', P.P., XXXV (1894), p.230; H.J.
  Little, The Agricultural Labourer, 'J.R.A.S.E.', 2nd ser., XIV
  (1878), p.790.
11 G. Nicholls, On the condition of the agricultural labourer; with
  suggestions for its improvement, 'J.R.A.S.E.', VII (1846),
  pp.7-8; E.J. Hobsbawm and G. Rudé, 'Captain Swing' (London,
  1969), pt I, pp.44-6.
12 P.P., XIII (1870), Appendix, Part I, report by Boyle, p.59; P.P.,
  XXXVI (1893-4), report by Lleufer Thomas on the Llanfyllin Union,
  p.82; P.P., XIII (1870), Appendix, Part I, report by Norman,
  p.30, Appendix, Part II, Appendix A to report by Culley, p.101,
  and Appendix, Part I, report by Boyle, p.59.
13 P.P., XIII (1870), p.6; P.P., XXXIV (1896), p.608.
14 P.P., XXXVI (1893-4), pp.18-19.
15 Ibid., p.18; P.P., XXXIV (1896), p.607; 'Report on Wages and
  Earnings of the Agricultural Labourer in the U.K.', P.P., LXXXII
  (1900), p.55.
16 P.P., XXXIV (1896), p.599.
17 P.P., LXXXII (1900), p.55.
18 For an excellent statistical treatment of Welsh agriculturalists
  in these years see E. Williams, The Welsh Farm Labourer, 1850-
  1939 (thesis prepared but not submitted (owing to the writer's
  death) at the Dept of Agriculture, U.C.W., Aberystwyth).
19 J.H. Morris and L.J. Williams, 'The South Wales Coal Industry,
  1841-1875' (1958), pp.48-9.
20 'Report on the Decline in the Agricultural Population of Great
  Britain, 1881-1906', P.P., XCVI (1906), p.15; A.H. John, 'The
  Industrial Development of South Wales' (Cardiff, 1950), pp.53-66,
  for an analysis of migratory movements into the coalfield.
21 John, op. cit., pp.63-5.
22 D. Williams, Rural Wales in the Nineteenth Century, in A.J.
  Roderick (ed.), 'Wales through the Ages', II (2nd edn, 1965),
  p.150.
23 P.P., XIII (1870), p.12, and Appendix, Part I, report by Culley,
  p.48.
24 P.P., XCVI (1906), p.15 and pp.9-10.
25 P.P., XXXIV (1896), pp.601-2; 'Welsh Land: The Report of the
  Welsh Land Enquiry Committee, Rural' (London, 1914), p.195.
26 P.P., XXXVI (1893-4), p.10; P.P., XXXIV (1896), pp.605-7; 'Fifth
  Report of the Agricultural Labourer', P.P., XXXV (1894), Section
  B, p.217; on the gang system see Chambers and Mingay, op. cit.,
  p.193.
27 P.P., XXXIV (1896), p.601; P.P., XXXVI (1893-4), p.9.
28 P.P., XXXIV (1896), pp.610-11; P.P., XXXVI (1893-4), p.16.
29 Glansevern MS.8831: letter of Mrs Owen, 4 Dec. 1850.
30 P.P., XXXIV (1896), pp.607-11; P.P., XXXVI (1893-4), p.15.

Details of farm servants' leisure activities can be obtained
from farm account books as N.L.W. MS.12286A: account book of
J. Williams of Waunfawr farm, Tregaron, Cards., 1844-67; N.L.W.
MS.8691C: account book of Wern Mill farm, Llannarth, Cards.,
1875-84; N.L.W. MS.6986: account book of D. Harries of Penrhyw,
Goodwick, Pembs., 1842-58.

31 W. Davies, 'Agriculture of South Wales' (London, 1814), II,
pp.284-5.

32 'Replies as to the Agricultural Distress', 1816, quoted in P.P.,
XXXIII (1896), Appendix A, p.22.

33 P.R.O., M.H.32/12: letter of 30 Oct. 1837 to the Poor Law
Commissioners.

34 'Report of the Commissioners into the Administration and Practi-
cal Operation of the Poor Laws', P.P., XXIX (1834), Appendix A,
Part II, no.27, p.187a; 'S.C. of the H. of L. on the State of
Agriculture', P.P., V (1837), p.361.

35 'The Welshman', 10 Oct. 1845 and 20 Nov. 1846.

36 P.P., XIII (1870), Appendix, Part I, report by Culley, p.37.

37 Ibid., Third Report, p.9.

38 P.P., XXXVI (1893-4), pp.18 and 31.

39 Ibid., p.19.

40 W. Davies, op. cit., II, p.283; P.P., XIII (1870), Appendix,
Part I, report by Culley, p.40; P.P., XXXVI (1893-4), p.19.

41 P.P., XIII (1870), Appendix, Part I, report by Culley, pp.38-40.

42 P.P., XXXVI (1894), Evidence, Qs 1825 and 8937a.

43 P.P., XXXVI (1893-4), p.17.

44 W. Davies, op. cit., II, p.285; for the situation in Britain as
a whole see E.L. Jones, The Agricultural Labour Market in England, 1793-1872, 'Econ. Hist. Rev.', 2nd ser., XVII, no.2 (1964),
p.324; A.H. John, Farming in Wartime: 1793-1815, in E.L. Jones
and G.E. Mingay (eds), 'Land, Labour and Population in the
Industrial Revolution' (1968), pp.33-4; J.D. Chambers and G.E.
Mingay, 'The Agricultural Revolution 1750-1880' (London, 1966),
pp.118-19.

45 W. Davies, op. cit., II, pp.283-4.

46 'S.C. on Agriculture', P.P., V (1833), Qs 170 and 218.

47 As in 'First Report from the Commissioners on the Poor Law',
Appendix, P.P., XXX (1834), pp.635a-62a.

48 P.P., XVI (1844), Q.7749.

49 A.E. Davies, Some Aspects of the Old Poor Law in Cardiganshire,
1750-1834, 'Ceredigion', VI, no.1 (1968), p.13.

50 'Third Annual Report of the Commissioners under the Poor Law
Amendment Act', P.P., XXI (1837), pp.20-1.

51 A.E. Davies, op. cit., p.29.

52 'Number of Able-bodied Paupers receiving Relief in the Poor Law
Unions', P.P., XXXVI (1846), pp.12-13.

53 H.T.Evans,'The Gorse Glen' (Liverpool, 1948), ch.12; G. Evans,
On the Farm a Century Ago, 'Carmarthenshire Historian', vol.VIII
(1971), p.72; R. Samuel (ed.), 'Village Life and Labour'
(London, 1975): part II by D.H. Morgan is partly concerned with
gleaning.

54 O.M. Edward (ed.), 'Gwaith ap Vychan' (Llanuwchllyn, 1903), p.60.
This reference was kindly provided in translation by Dr Prys
Morgan.

55 'Reports of the Commissioners of Inquiry into the State of Educa-
    tion in Wales', P.P., XXVII (1847), part I; P.R.O., M.H.32/12:
    letter of 9 Dec. 1837 of Clive concerning south Wales: 'Many
    able men leave the country for the harvest in England'; M.I.
    Williams, Seasonal Migration of Cardiganshire Harvest Gangs to
    the Vale of Glamorgan in the Nineteenth Century, 'Ceredigion',
    III, no.2 (1957), pp.156-9; A. Redford, 'Labour Migration in
    England' (Manchester, 1926), p.122; A.H. John, 'The Industrial
    Development of South Wales' (Cardiff, 1950), p.66.
56 Gibson, op. cit., p.47; P.P., XXXVI (1893-4), p.29.
57 P.R.O., M.H.32/12: letter of 30 Oct. 1837 of Clive to the Poor
    Law Commissioners; C.S. Read, On the Farming of South Wales,
    'J.R.A.S.E.', X (1849), p.148; T. Rowlandson, The Agriculture
    of North Wales, 'J.R.A.S.E.', VII (1846), p.585.
58 P.P., XIII (1870), Appendix, Part II, A19, p.107: evidence of
    W. Philipps and Appendix, Part I, report by Norman, p.30.
59 P.P., XXXVI (1893-4), p.19.
60 P.P., XXXIV (1896), p.703.
61 Evans, op. cit., p.41; P.P., XXXVI (1893-4), pp.30-1.
62 D.C. Davies, The Present Condition of the Welsh Nation, 'Red
    Dragon', IV (1883), p.350.
63 W. Davies in 'Agriculture of South Wales', I, p.136, and
    'Agriculture of North Wales' (London, 1810), p.82.
64 Chambers and Mingay, op. cit., p.135; 'Cowbridge Tracts', no.2
    (1831), p.13.
65 Read, op. cit., p.149; Rowlandson, op. cit., p.585.
66 P.P., XXXVI (1893-4), pp.21-2.
67 Ibid., B.VIII, p.163.
68 P.P., XXXV (1894), Section B, p.220.
69 P.P., XXXIV (1896), p.579.
70 See M.E. Chamberlain, The Gower Farm Labourer: Vintage 1893,
    'Gower', 25 (1974), pp.38-9.
71 D.E. Williams, The payment of farm servants in the Towy valley,
    'Jnl of the Royal Welsh Ag. Soc.', XXIX (1960), pp.72-5.
72 P.P., XXVII (1847), Part I, Appendix to Report on Pembroke,
    p.466; P.P., XVI (1844), Q.5566: evidence of Lloyd Hall of
    Cilgwyn, who stated of the labourers' potato patch: 'no doubt
    it enables them to subsist upon wages which otherwise they would
    not do'.
73 For distress in the rural areas arising from the slump in the
    iron trade between 1841-3 see K.E.M. Skinner, Poor Law Adminis-
    tration in Glamorgan, 1750-1850 (unpublished MA thesis, Wales,
    1956), pp.322, 396-7; J.E. Thomas, Poor Law Administration in
    West Glamorgan from 1834 to 1930 (unpublished MA thesis, Wales,
    1951), pp.213-14.
74 D.W. Howell, The Agricultural Labourer in Nineteenth-Century
    Wales, 'The Welsh History Review', vol.6, no.3 (1973), p.280.
75 Slebech MSS 4794-7: Records of Great Sessions Suit re the
    poaching affray at Blackpool, 1830.
76 P.P., XIII (1870), p.18.
77 'Merioneth Standard', 18 Jan. 1868, under Game, The Farmers'
    Attitude. Dr David Jones kindly provided me with this source.
78 P.P., XXXVI (1893-4), pp.27-33.

79 Hobsbawm and Rudé, op. cit., part one.
80 D.J.V. Jones, 'Before Rebecca' (London, 1973), pp.58-9; 'Report
    on the Administration and Practical Operation of the Poor Laws',
    P.P., XXXIV (1834), Appendix B, Part V, replies from the Welsh
    Counties to Q.53; 'The Cambrian', 4, 11, 18 and 25 Dec. 1830;
    Lucas MS.3241: letter of 26 Nov. 1831 of J. Harvey to Lord
    Kensington.
81 Cardiff Central Library, MS.4.713, vol.2: letters of E.P.
    Richards to his employer, Lord Bute. Dr John Davies kindly pro-
    vided me with this source; Margam/Penrice MS.9237; P.P., XXXIV
    (1834), Appendix B, Part V, p.648c: reply to Q.53.
82 Included in 'Cowbridge Tracts', op. cit., no.3, p.11. See also
    'The Cambrian', 22 Jan. 1831 under Glamorganshire Agricultural
    Report, and 'The Cambrian', 11 Dec. 1830 under editorial General
    State of the Country (Monmouthshire).
83 P.P., XXXIV (1834), Appendix B, Part V: reply to Q.53 from the
    parish of Llanarrion yn Tal, Denbighshire.
84 D. Williams, 'The Rebecca Riots' (Cardiff, 1955), p.243.
85 Evans, op. cit., p.31.
86 P.P., XXXVI (1893-4), pp.29-30, and under Poor Law Unions of
    Anglesey and Pwllheli; C. Parry, 'The Radical Tradition in
    Welsh Politics: a Study of Labour and Liberal Politics in
    Gwynedd, 1900-20' (Hull, 1970), pp.11-13.
87 J.P. Dunbabin, The Revolt of the Field: The Agricultural Labour-
    ers' Movement in the 1870s, 'Past and Present', vol.26 (1963),
    p.72.
88 J.P. Dunbabin, The Incidence and Organisation of Agricultural
    Trade Unionism in the 1870s, 'Ag. Hist. Rev.', vol.16, part II
    (1968), p.124.
89 P.P., XXXVI (1893-4), p.15; P.P., XXXIV (1896), pp.608-10;
    W. Sikes, 'Old South Wales' (London, 1881), pp.194-201.
90 P.P., IX (1919), General Report, p.24.

CHAPTER 7 Marketing

 1 W. Davies, 'Agriculture of North Wales' (London, 1810), p.310;
    British Transport Historical Records, CHH 4/1: Edward Parry's
    Report of 1848 concerning the Chester and Holyhead Railway;
    H.L.R.O., Minutes of Evidence, H. of C., 1845, vol.69, concern-
    ing the North Wales Railway Bill (8-9 Vic., CVI): evidence of
    Daniel Priest; J. Lloyd, 'Historical Memoranda of Breconshire'
    (Brecon, 1903), I, p.56; S. Lewis, 'A Topographical Dictionary
    of Wales' (4th edn, London, 1849), I, p.41.
 2 H.M. Customs and Excise Library, Kingsbeam House, London: Bristol
    and Liverpool Bills of Entry. Mr R. Craig indicated this source.
 3 G.A. Cooke, 'Topographical and Statistical Description of the
    Principality of Wales' (London, 1818), pt I, North Wales, pp.51-6,
    pt II, South Wales, pp.31-7, Monmouthshire, p.9; W. Davies,
    'Agriculture of South Wales' (London, 1814), II, pp.412-14;
    J. Ll. Davies, The Livestock Trade in West Wales in the Nine-
    teenth Century, 'Aberystwyth Studies', XIV (1936), pp.99 and 108.
 4 For county fair-areas see my Welsh Agriculture 1815-1914 (unpub-
    lished PhD thesis, London, 1969), p.202.

5   N.L.W. MS.4560D: account book of David Thomas;   N.L.W. MS.3110A:
    account book of Market Gate Farm.
6   The most useful works dealing with the droving trade include
    C. Skeel, The Cattle Trade between England and Wales from the
    Fifteenth to the Nineteenth Centuries, 'T.R.H.S.', 4th ser., IX
    (1926);   J.Ll. Davies, The Livestock Trade in West Wales in the
    Nineteenth Century, 'Aberystwyth Studies', XIII (1934) and XIV
    (1936);   H.R. Rankin, Cattle Droving from Wales to England,
    'Agriculture' (1955);   R. Phillips, The Last of the Drovers,
    'Trans. Cymmr. Soc.', pt I (1969);   P.G. Hughes, 'Wales and the
    Drovers' (London, c.1944);   K.J. Bonser, 'The Drovers' (London,
    1970);   the most recent and fully researched are: R. Colyer,
    The Welsh Cattle Drovers in the Nineteenth Century, pt I, 'N.L.W.
    Jnl', XVII, no.4 (1972), pt II, 'N.L.W. Jnl', XVIII, no.3 (1974).
7   Colyer, op. cit., pt II, pp.329-30.
8   For further details see ibid., pp.312-16, and Bonser, op. cit.,
    ch.15.
9   Colyer, op. cit., pt I, p.398.
10 These valuable accounts based on N.L.W. MSS 9600-14 are closely
    examined in the articles quoted above of J.Ll. Davies and
    R. Colyer. My calculations are based on figures provided by
    Davies.
11 N.L.W. MS.11,706A: account book of 1838-9 of R.R. containing
    records of cattle sales and of expenses incurred on visits from
    Lampeter to south-east England.
12 Strictly, 'drovers' should be confined to the men who actively
    drove the cattle, and, in discussing business activities, by
    'drovers' is meant dealers.
13 O. Parry, The Financing of the Welsh Cattle Trade in the Eight-
    eenth Century, 'Bulletin of the Board of Celtic Studies', vol.8,
    pt I, 1935.
14 R.O. Roberts, The Operations of the Brecon Old Bank of Wilkins
    and Co., 1778-1890, 'Business History', I, no.1 (1958), p.35;
    R.O. Roberts, The Brecon Old Bank, 'Brycheiniog', VII (1962),
    pp.65-6.
15 'Report of the Bank of England Charter', 1832, P.P., VI (1831-2),
    Qs 1614-15.
16 T. Rowlandson, The Agriculture of North Wales, 'J.R.A.S.E.', VII
    (1846), p.569.
17 P.R.O., B1/86:   Bankruptcy hearing, 20 March 1793. Mr Christo-
    pher Chalklin of Reading University kindly directed me to this
    source.
18 N.L.W. MS.822C.
19 Bonser, op. cit., p.44.
20 J.Ll. Davies, op. cit., XIV (1936), pp.111-13.
21 Lewis, op. cit., I, pp.171, 198 and 290.
22 Rowlandson, op. cit., pp.569-70;   R.T. Jenkins, A Drover's
    Account Book, 'Trans. Caerns. Hist. Soc.', VI (1945), pp.46-9.
23 Rowlandson, op. cit., p.571;   W. Davies, 'Agriculture of North
    Wales', p.315;   British Transport Historical Records, CHH 4/1:
    E. Parry's Report of 1848;   Lewis, op. cit., I, pp.171 and 198.
24 'Pigot's National Commercial Directory' (1830), 'South Wales';
    'Pigot's Directory' (4th Survey), 'South West and Wales' (1844).
25 H.L.R.O., Minutes of Evidence, H. of C., 1846, vol.73, concerning

the Vale of Neath Railway Bill (9-10 Vic., CCCXLI): evidence of
Edward Purchase. Mr R. Craig kindly directed me to these Bills.

26 Ibid., Minutes of Evidence, H. of C., 1862, vol.23, concerning
the Cowbridge Railway Bill: evidence of J. Nixon.

27 Ibid., Minutes of Evidence, H. of L., 1845, vol.13: evidence of
J. Buckland.

28 Ibid., Minutes of Evidence, H. of C., 1845, vol.80: evidence of
J. Buckland and Joseph Fisher.

29 Ibid., Minutes of Evidence, H. of C., 1846, vol.73, concerning
the Vale of Neath Railway Bill.

30 J. Williams, On the Connection between the West of England and
South Wales, 'Jnl of the Bath and West of England Soc.', VIII
(1860), p.62.

31 Lewis, op. cit., I, p.376.

32 H.L.R.O., Minutes of Evidence, H. of C., 1846, vol.73.

33 Dewi Davies, 'Stories of Breconshire' (printed by W. Walters,
Clydach, Swansea, 1974), pp.32-4.

34 J.Ll. Davies, op. cit., pp.93-4.

35 W. Davies, 'Agriculture of South Wales', II, p.225, and I, p.480.

36 H.L.R.O., Minutes of Evidence, H. of C., 1862, vol.23: evidence
of Daniel Thomas, cattle dealer, and Jenkin Thomas, farmer and
cattle jobber.

37 Ibid., Minutes of Evidence, H. of C., 1846, vol.73: evidence of
Edward Morgan and Weston Young.

38 Ibid., Minutes of Evidence, H. of C., 1859, vol.8, concerning
the Brecon and Merthyr Railway Bill (22-3 Vic., LXVIII): evidence of G.T. Clark.

39 Ibid., Minutes of Evidence, H. of C., 1846, vol.73: evidence of
Edward Morgan.

40 Ibid., Minutes of Evidence, H. of C., 1862, vol.23: evidence of
J. Nichol Carne, Daniel Edwards and Daniel Thomas.

41 Ibid.: evidence of J. Nichol Carne and T. Wilson.

42 Lewis, op. cit., II, pp.435-6; British Transport Historical
Records, CHH 4/1: Edward Parry's Report of 1848.

43 Lewis, op. cit., I, p.121; H. Pollins, Transport in Brecknock,
'Brycheiniog', VII (1962), p.49.

44 A.H. Dodd, 'The Industrial Revolution in North Wales' (2nd edn,
Cardiff, 1951), p.122; A.S. Davies, The River Trade of Montgomeryshire and its Borders, 'Montgom. Colls', XLIII, no.1
(1933), pp.43-5.

45 M.I. Harries, The Railway Network of Wales (unpublished MA
thesis, Wales, 1953), pp.45-103; P.P., XXXIV (1896), p.374.

46 J.D. Chambers and G.E. Mingay, 'The Agricultural Revolution
1750-1880' (London, 1966), p.171; C.S. Orwin and E.H. Whetham,
'History of British Agriculture 1846-1914' (2nd edn, Newton
Abbot, 1971), pp.97-9.

47 Ap Adda, The Welsh Drover, 'Red Dragon' (July-Dec. 1883), p.453.

48 G.R. Hawke, 'Railways and Economic Growth in England and Wales,
1840-1870' (Oxford, 1970), p.145.

49 'The Welshman', 29 Sept. 1871.

50 Hawke, op. cit., pp.143-4.

51 J.E. Jones, Cardiganshire Fairs, 'Trans. Cards. Antiq. Soc.'
(1930), pp.99-100; H.L.R.O., Minutes of Evidence, H. of C.,
1862, vol.23: evidence of J. Nichol Carne.

52 'R.C. on Market Rights and Tolls', P.P., LIV (1888), 6: evidence of Sumner Toms.
53 'North Wales Chronicle', 22 April 1854.
54 'Cambrian News', 11 April 1913.
55 Anon. (styled 'A Practical Farmer'), Selling Storestock at Home, 'Welsh Nat. Ag. Soc. Jnl', no.4 (July 1905), pp.181-2.
56 'Cambrian News', 26 Dec. 1913.
57 J. Gibson, 'Agriculture in Wales' (London, 1879), p.29.
58 P.P., LIV (1888), p.6: evidence of Sumner Toms and p.16: evidence of W.B. Mildon concerning Wellington; R.H. Rew, English Markets and Fairs, 'J.R.A.S.E.', 3rd ser., III (1892), pp.101-2.
59 D. Alexander, 'Retailing in England during the Industrial Revolution' (London, 1970), p.34.
60 Gibson, op. cit., pp.29-30.
61 Gibson, op. cit., p.139; P.P., LIV (1888), p.36: evidence concerning Hitchin market, Hertfordshire.
62 Orwin and Whetham, op. cit., p.99.
63 Gibson, op. cit., p.56.
64 'Cambrian News', 16 July 1880.
65 'The Welshman', 22 Nov. 1872, 2 June 1876, 13 Dec. 1878; J. Darby, The Agriculture of Pembrokeshire, 'Jnl of the Bath and West of England Soc.', 3rd ser., XIX (1887-8), p.94.
66 S. Thomas, Changing Land Utilisation, Occupation and Ownership in south-west Carmarthenshire (unpublished PhD thesis, London, 1965), p.168.
67 W. Little, The Agriculture of Glamorganshire, 'J.R.A.S.E.', 2nd ser., XXI (1885), pp.172-9.
68 Ibid., p.177.
69 'The Welshman', 29 Sept. 1871.
70 'Carnarvon and Denbigh Herald', 23 Sept. 1882.
71 'Cambrian News', 9 Nov. 1888.
72 Ibid., 12 April 1878, 21 Jan. 1876; 'Brecon County Times', 3 April 1875.
73 Gibson, op. cit., p.25.
74 'The Milk Journal', 1 March 1871.
75 'The Welshman', 7 March 1879; P.P., XXXIV (1896), p.766.
76 Anon., Agriculture in Montgomeryshire, 'Welsh Nat. Ag. Soc. Jnl', no.16 (July and Oct. 1908), p.23.
77 'The Welshman', 16 Jan. 1891, 31 Oct. 1902.
78 P.P., XL (1895), Qs 44,782-91.
79 'The Welshman', 20 Sept. 1872, 7 March 1879.
80 Orwin and Whetham, op. cit., p.144.
81 Cawdor MSS, Box 141: letter of 23 March 1868 of T. Mousley to Lord Cawdor.
82 P.P., XXV (1896), Q.78,145.
83 Ibid., 77,527; W. Little, op. cit., p.187; 'The Welshman', 24 Jan. 1902.
84 'Cambrian News', 7 Dec. 1909.
85 Orwin and Whetham, op. cit., p.262; 'Cambrian News', 11 Sept. 1903: a report of the Cambrian Railways Co. advising Welsh farmers to market co-operatively.
86 Orwin and Whetham, op. cit., pp.146-7.
87 Picton Castle MS.4829: St Clears Farmers' Butter Factory Ltd: Half Year Reports ... 1891-7; P.P., XXXIV (1896), p.767; 'The Welshman', 7 April 1905.

88 'Cambrian News', 16 Jan. 1903.
89 The contrast here between Wales and Ireland was often drawn by the 'Cambrian News' as, for instance, in its issue of 30 Jan. 1903.
90 Chambers and Mingay, op. cit., p.171; Orwin and Whetham, op. cit., pp.147-50, 362-6.
91 R. Howells, 'Farming in Wales' (new edn, London, 1967), pp.40-1; A.W. Ashby and I.L. Evans, 'The Agriculture of Wales and Monmouthshire' (Cardiff, 1944), p.60.
92 P.P., XXXIV (1896), p.764.
93 Little, op. cit., p.182; P.P., XXXVII (1894), Q.36,354: evidence of Mr Pilliner.
94 N.L.W., Glyneiddan MS.: 'Farming in the Vale of Towy, 1870-1950', fo.145.
95 Ibid., fo.147; A.D. Hall, 'A Pilgrimage of British Farming, 1910-12' (London, 1913), p.318.

CHAPTER 8   Farming practices

1 P.P., XIII (1870), O, p.49, and N, p.30; P.P., XV (1882), p.7.
2 P.P., XXXIV (1896), p.728; W. Davies, 'Agriculture of South Wales' (London, 1814), II, p.167; W. Davies, 'Agriculture of North Wales' (London, 1810), p.298; Anon., 'Geological Facts and Observations with Hints for Improvements' (London, 1831), p.31; S. Lewis, 'A Topographical Dictionary of Wales' (4th edn, London, 1849), II, p.339, concerning Radnorshire.
3 P.P., XXXIV (1896), pp.728 and 731.
4 Ibid., pp.728-9; 'Cambrian News', 12 Dec. 1873; J. Gibson, 'Agriculture in Wales' (London, 1879), p.115; Anon., Agriculture in Montgomeryshire, 'Welsh Nat. Ag. Soc. Jnl', no.16 (July and Oct. 1908), p.168; A.D. Hall, 'A Pilgrimage of British Farming, 1910-12' (London, 1913), p.315; W. Barrow Wall, Agriculture in Pembrokeshire, 'J.R.A.S.E.' (1887), p.92; 'Carnarvon and Denbigh Herald', 19 Sept. 1894.
5 Gibson, op. cit., pp.112-15.
6 R. Phillips, The Diary of a Cardiganshire Farmer, 'W.J.A.', X (1934), pp.17-18.
7 'Cambrian News', 12 Oct. 1883.
8 'The Welshman', 5 Aug. 1859, quoted by S. Thomas, Changing Land Utilisation, Occupation and Ownership in south-west Carmarthenshire (unpublished PhD thesis, London, 1966), p.149.
9 'The Farmers' Magazine', 3rd ser., 14 (1858), p.118, under The Agriculture of North Wales.
10 R.H. Jackson, 'Welsh Highland Farming' (Denbigh, 1852), pp.15-17.
11 'The Welshman', 26 July 1872.
12 J. Darby, The Agriculture of Pembrokeshire, 'Jnl of the Bath and West of England Soc.', 3rd ser., XIV (1887-8), p.97; P.P., XXXVI (1894), Q.8185: evidence concerning Merioneth.
13 P.P., XXXIV (1896), p.736.
14 Darby, op. cit., pp.104-5; W. Davies, 'Agriculture of South Wales', I, pp.544-7.
15 Quoted in A. Fullarton, Parliamentary Gazeteer of England and Wales, pt XI (1840-4), p.405.

16 Gibson, op. cit., p.98; H.T. Evans, 'The Gorse Glen' (Liverpool, 1948), p.130.

17 P.P., XXXIV (1896), pp.726 and 736; C.S. Read, On the Farming of South Wales, 'J.R.A.S.E.', X (1849), p.139; T. Rowlandson, The Agriculture of North Wales, 'J.R.A.S.E.', VII (1846), p.582; Glyneiddan MS.fo.134.

18 P.P., XXXIV (1896), p.726; W. Davies, op. cit., I, p.201.

19 D. Parry-Jones, 'Welsh Country Upbringing' (1st impn, Liverpool, 1974), p.59; P.P., XXXIV (1896), p.726; C.B. Jones, Agricultural Implements and Machinery, 'Welsh Nat. Ag. Soc. Jnl', no.9 (1906), p.7.

20 Gibson, op. cit., pp.98 and 103; P.P., XXXIV (1896), p.737; Jones, op. cit., pp.8-9.

21 There were two basic types, namely, the Sled (Car Llusg) and the Slide-Car (Car Cefn). The Car Llusg was drawn by a trace horse and the Car Cefn by a shaft horse with a cart saddle. The Car Cefn was easier to draw than the Car Llusg as only a part of the body was dragged along the grass and, in addition, it was more easily turned around - see Evans, op. cit., p.130; G. Jenkins, 'Agricultural Transport in Wales' (Cardiff, 1962), pp.14-15; W. Davies, op. cit., I, p.205; W. Davies, 'Agriculture of North Wales', p.121.

22 I.C. Peate, Some Aspects of Agricultural Transport in Wales, 'Arch. Camb.', XC (1935), pp.224-5.

23 Jenkins, op. cit., pp.20, 33-5; P.P., XXXIV (1896), p.727.

24 W. Davies, 'Agriculture of South Wales', I, pp.426-7; J. Evans, 'South Wales', p.426; Parry-Jones, op. cit., p.63; D. Jenkins, 'The Agricultural Community in South-West Wales at the Turn of the Twentieth Century' (Cardiff, 1971), p.49; H.T. Evans, op. cit., p.111; P.P., XXXIV (1896), p.737; Jones, op. cit., p.11.

25 Parry-Jones, op. cit., pp.64-5.

26 D.J. Williams, 'The Old Farmhouse' (London, 1961), p.104; Evans, op. cit., pp.114-15.

27 'Brecon County Times', 2 Oct. 1875; Gibson, op. cit., p.99; Evans, op. cit., pp.116-17; P.P., XXXVI (1893-4), p.96, concerning the Dolgellau Union, Merioneth; P.P., XXXIV (1896), p.727.

28 'The Welshman', 25 Oct. 1872; Cilgwyn MS.35: letter of 27 March 1868 and MS.44: letter of 9 Feb. 1870;S.Thomas, op. cit., p.185; P.P., XXXIV (1896), p.727.

29 'Brecon County Times', 2 Oct. 1875; P.P., XXXVI (1893-4), p.7 and, for example, p.72 concerning small farmers in north Pembrokeshire.

30 Gibson, op. cit., p.98.

31 Jones, op. cit., p.15.

32 D. Jenkins, op. cit., p.257; D. Parry-Jones, 'My Own Folk', pp.69-70.

33 A.W. Ashby and J.Ll. Davies, The Work Efficiency of Farm Organisation in Wales, 1871-1921, 'W.J.A.', V (1929), pp.54-7.

34 J. Ll. Davies, Horse Labour on Welsh Farms, 1871-1927, 'W.J.A.', VI (1930), p.44; Ashby and Davies, op. cit., p.59.

35 D. Parry-Jones, 'Welsh Country Upbringing', p.59.

36 P.P., IX (1919), Brecknockshire, par.14, p.35.

37 Ibid., Radnorshire, par.13, p.133; P.P., XXXVI (1893-4), par.35, p.165, and par.61, p.168.

38 P.P., XXXVI (1893-4), par.13, p.97.
39 D.Jenkins,op.cit., p.88; Parry-Jones, op. cit., p.60; G. Jen-
    kins, Technological Improvement and Social Change in South
    Cardiganshire, 'Ag. Hist. Rev.', XIII, pt II (1965), pp.97-8.
40 P.P., IX (1919), par.14, p.57.
41 D. Jenkins, 'The Agricultural Community in South West Wales',
    pp.48-9.
42 P.P., IX (1919), Carmarthenshire, par.28, p.61; D. Jenkins, op.
    cit., pp.51-3.
43 D. Jenkins, op. cit., pp.54-5; G. Jenkins, Technological Im-
    provement and Social Change in South Cardiganshire, pp.99-100;
    P.P., XXXVI (1893-4), par.28, pp.62-3, concerning Narberth Union;
    P.P., IX (1919), Carmarthenshire, par.28, p.61.
44 P.P., XXXVI (1893-4), par.40, p.150; J.H. Evans, Derwenlas,
    'Montgom. Colls', vol.51 (1949), p.84.
45 D. Jenkins, 'The Agricultural Community in South West Wales',
    p.43; I am indebted to Rev. Samuel Thomas for information about
    the prevalence of these small holdings around the area of
    Eglwyswrw, north Pembrokeshire, in the early years of this
    century.
46 P.P., XXXVI (1893-4), par.35, p.165.
47 D. Jenkins, op. cit., p.43; Parry-Jones, op. cit., p.63.
48 D. Jenkins, op. cit., pp.47-8; G. Jenkins, Technological Im-
    provement and Social Change in South Cardiganshire, p.96.
49 C.B. Jones, Welsh Black Cattle, 'J.R.A.S.E.', vol.77 (1916),
    p.45; M. Evans, On the Black Cattle of South Wales', 'Jnl of
    the Bath and West of England Soc.', 3rd ser., XIII (1881),
    p.103.
50 Rowlandson, op. cit., pp.572 and 574.
51 S. Thomas, op. cit., p.165.
52 'Cambrian News', 27 Feb. 1874.
53 Ibid., 13 Dec. 1878; Anon., 'North Wales Black Cattle Herd Book'
    (Bangor, 1883), I, p.18; Gibson, op. cit., p.66.
54 Anon., 'North Wales Black Cattle Herd Book', I, p.15; W. Youatt,
    'Cattle: Their Breeds, Management and Diseases' (London, 1834),
    p.59; Jones, op. cit., p.45.
55 'The Welshman', 6 Oct. 1871. See also 'The Welshman', 1 Sept.
    1871, 11 Sept. 1874 and 25 Jan. 1878.
56 Evans, op. cit., p.105; Llwyngwair MS.16,668: letter of 14 Dec.
    1870 of M. Evans to Mr Bowen; 'The Welshman', 1 and 15 Sept.
    1871, 20 Feb. and 11 Sept. 1874; M. Evans, Pembrokeshire or
    Castlemartin Cattle, in J. Coleman (ed.), 'The Cattle, Sheep and
    Pigs of Great Britain' (London, 1887), ch.XVII, p.203.
57 'Cambrian News', 13 Dec. 1878, 18 March 1887; 'The Welshman',
    1 Nov. 1878, 27 Oct. 1882, 12 Dec. 1884; 'Carnarvon and Denbigh
    Herald', 30 Dec. 1882.
58 'The Welshman', 25 Jan. 1878, 2 Jan. 1885; C.R.O., Castell
    Gorfod MSS, Buckley Papers, B.178: letter of 1 May 1879 of Lord
    Cawdor to Mr Buckley.
59 Jones, op. cit., p.40; P.P., XXXIV (1896), p.748; 'Carnarvon
    and Denbigh Herald', 25 Sept. 1880, 17 Feb. 1883; J.B. Owen,
    The Welsh Black Cattle Society, 'Welsh Nat. Ag. Soc. Jnl', no.4
    (July 1905), p.169; N.L.W. MS.11,180E.
60 Jones, op. cit., pp.43-4; Hall, op. cit., pp.318, 323.

61 H.T. Evans, op. cit., pp.131-5.
62 R. Phillips, Some Aspects of the Agricultural Conditions in Car-
    diganshire in the Nineteenth Century, 'W.J.A.', vol.I, no.I
    (1925), p.24; Barrow Wall, op. cit., p.76.
63 P.P., XXXIV (1896), pp.760, 764-5.
64 Cawdor MSS, Box 141: letter of 23 March 1868 of T. Mousley;
    Phillips, op. cit., p.25.
65 W. Davies, 'Agriculture of South Wales', II, pp.227-8.
66 Evans, op. cit., p.131.
67 P.P., XXXIV (1896), p.757.
68 Thos. Jones, Mountain Sheep Farming, 'Wales', vol.I (1894), p.80.
69 'Cambrian News', 18 April 1879, 30 March 1883.
70 See also W. Fothergill, The Farming of Monmouthshire, 'J.R.A.S.E.',
    2nd ser., VI (1870), p.289; Tredegar Park 57/340: letter of
    7 May 1842 of T. Williams to Sir Charles Morgan.
71 Jones, op. cit., p.81; P.P., XXXIV (1896), p.754.
72 E. Davies, Sheep Farming in Upland Wales, 'Geography', XX (1935),
    pp.108-9; E. Davies, Hendre and Hafod in Merioneth, 'Jnl of the
    Merioneth Hist. and Rec. Soc.', VII, pt I (1973), pp.16-26;
    R.U. Sayce, The Old Summer Pastures, 'Montgom. Colls', vol.54
    (1955-9), p.119.
73 Gibson, op. cit., p.34.
74 W. Little, The Agriculture of Glamorganshire, 'J.R.A.S.E.', 2nd
    ser., XXI (1885), p.186.
75 J.E. Thomas, Welsh Agricultural Industry, 'Young Wales' (1897),
    p.267.
76 Gibson, op. cit., pp.42-4; 'Cambrian News', 19 June 1869; P.P.,
    XXXIV (1896), p.756.
77 Read, op. cit., p.141; 'The Welshman', 3 April 1860 and 11
    March 1864, quoted by S. Thomas, op. cit., p.174.
78 Anon., Agriculture in Montgomeryshire, 'Welsh Nat. Ag. Soc. Jnl',
    no.16 (July and Oct. 1908), p.26.
79 'Cambrian News', 1 June 1877; P.P., XXXIV (1896), p.744.
80 P.P., XXXVI (1893-4), p.163.
81 Sir R.D. Green-Price, Welsh Cobs and Ponies, 'Welsh Nat. Ag. Soc.
    Jnl', no.1 (1904).
82 'Cambrian News', 5 March 1875, 27 April 1877, 7 Feb. 1879, 14
    March 1879; Gibson, op. cit., p.118.
83 'Cambrian News', 7 March 1890; P.P., XXXIV (1896), p.745.
84 D.C. Davies, The Present Condition of the Welsh Nation; V, Indus-
    trial and Agricultural, 'Red Dragon', vol.4 (1883), p.535;
    Gibson, op. cit., p.122; P.P., XXXIV (1896), p.745.
85 J. Darby, The Agriculture of Glamorganshire, 'Jnl of the Bath
    and West of England Soc.', 3rd ser., XVII (1885-6), p.141;
    Little, op. cit., p.172; Fothergill, op. cit., p.290.
86 Read, op. cit., pp.150-4.
87 Little, op. cit., p.176.
88 Bute MSS: letter of 9 May 1844 of Corbett to Bute; Margam/Pen-
    rice MS.9278: letter of 2 May 1845 of C.R.M. Talbot to Messrs
    Gibbs, Bright and Co., Bristol.
89 N.L.W. MS.3112E: Accounts of M.G. Farm, 1850-5.
90 T. Bowstead, Report on the Farm Prize Competition of 1872,
    'J.R.A.S.E.', 2nd ser., VIII (1872), pp.286-90.
91 Ibid., pp.281-325.

92   'North Wales Chronicle', 8 June 1861;   'Cambrian News', 26 March 1875.

93   Darby, op. cit., pp.140-1.

94   Chirk Castle E/1735:   letter of 26 May 1884;   P.P., XXXVI (1893-4), p.7.

95   Bowstead, op. cit., p.315;   Fothergill, op. cit., pp.292-3.

96   C.B. Jones, Agricultural Implements and Machinery, 'Welsh Nat. Ag. Soc. Jnl', no.9 (Oct. 1906), pp.4-5;   Barrow Wall, op. cit., p.83.

97   Bowstead, op. cit., p.315;   Little, op. cit., p.174.

98   Darby, op. cit., pp.140-1.

99   N.L.W., Peniarth MS.623:   letter of 25 Aug. 1853;   see also Read, op. cit., p.145;   N.L.W. MS.3110A: Account Book of Market Gate Farm;   N.L.W. MS.16473B: letter book of W.Williams of Carne, parish of Llanwnda, Pembrokeshire, letter of 27 March 1845.

100 Bowstead, op. cit., p.319;   P.P., XXXVI (1893-4), p.7;   Barrow Wall, op. cit., p.86.

101 Darby, op. cit., pp.140-1.

102 Tredegar Park MS.57/336:   letter of 9 June 1842;   P.P., XXXIV (1896), p.747; S.Thomas, op. cit., p.165.

103 Bowstead, op. cit., pp.292, 306 and 311.

104 Barrow Wall, op. cit., p.77.

105 P.P., XXXIV (1896), p.685.

106 N.L.W. MS.6642A.

107 W. Youatt, 'Sheep: Their Breeds, Management and Diseases' (London, 1837), p.267 (Glamorgan), p.269 (Carmarthenshire), p.270 (Pembrokeshire), p.273 (Anglesey) and p.276 (Montgomery-shire);   Read, op. cit., p.141.

108 P.P., XXXIV (1896), pp.751-2;   Bowstead, op. cit., p.320;   M. Evans, Welsh Mountain Sheep, in J. Coleman (ed.), op. cit., ch.XXIII, p.408.

109 P.P., XXXIV (1896), p.753.

110 Bowstead, op. cit., p.320. Again, sheep were folded upon turnips in the Vale of Clwyd - P.P., XXXIV (1896), p.683.

111 P.P., XXXVI (1893-4), p.58;   D.C. Davies, op. cit., p.535.

CHAPTER 9   Conclusion

1   Rev. William Jones, 'A Prize Essay on the Character of the Welsh as a Nation' (London, 1841), p.157.

2   This was stressed in conversations with Mr Emrys Williams of the MSS Dept, N.L.W., and Rev. Samuel Thomas.

3   Quoted in D. Parry-Jones, 'My Own Folk' (Llandyssul, 1972), pp.49-50.

4   N.L.W. MS.6733: an account of farming in north Wales in the late nineteenth century by Gomer Roberts. I am indebted to Miss Menna Jones of the N.L.W. MSS Dept for this reference.

5   Parry-Jones, op. cit., pp.56-7.

6   See J.P.D. Dunbabin, 'Rural Discontent in Nineteenth Century Britain' (London, 1974), D.J.V. Jones, 'Before Rebecca' (London, 1973) and D. Williams, 'The Rebecca Riots' (Cardiff, 1955).

7   D.J.V. Jones, Crime, Protest and Community in Nineteenth-Century Wales, 'Llafur', I, no.3 (1974), p.10.

8 Dunbabin, op. cit., p.296.
9 'Western Mail', 29 Jan. 1886.
10 D.J.V. Jones, op. cit., p.7.
11 As in Henry Richard, 'Letters on the Social and Political Con-
    dition of the Principality of Wales' (London, 1867) and P.P.,
    XXXIV (1896), p.642.
12 'R.C. on Land in Wales and Monmouthshire', P.P., XXXIII (1896),
    Appendix E.
13 S.H. Jones-Parry, Crime in Wales, 'Red Dragon', vol.IV (1883).
14 H.J. Owen, 'From Merioneth to Botany Bay' (Bala, 1952), p.73.
15 D. Parry-Jones, 'Welsh Country Upbringing' (London, 1948), p.134.
16 D.E. Jones, 'Hanes Plwyfi Llangeler a Phenboyr' (Llandyssul,
    1899), p.332. I am indebted to Mrs Nia Henson of the N.L.W. MSS
    Dept for translating parts of this work.

BIBLIOGRAPHY

This bibliography is not meant to be exhaustive. It includes the main MS collections and printed works found useful in the preparation of this book, but many specialised sources contained in the footnotes are omitted.

A MANUSCRIPT COLLECTIONS

1 National Library of Wales: Aberpergwm, Ashburnham, Aston Hall, Behrens, Bronwydd, Bute, Caerynwch, Chirk Castle, Cilgwyn, Crosswood, Dunraven, Edwinsford, Glanranell, Glansevern, Glyneiddan, Glynllivon, Hawarden, Llwyngwair, Longueville, Lucas, Margam/Penrice, Mynachty, Nanteos, N.L.W. MSS, Peniarth, Picton Castle, Plas yn Cefn, Slebech, Tredegar Park, Trenewydd, Wynnstay.

2 Public Record Office (London): H.O.45: Registered Papers, H.O.107: Population Returns, M.A.F.66/1-9: Land Improvement, Register of Loans, M.H.32: Correspondence of Assistant Poor Law Commissioners and Inspectors, Customs 23: Articles Imported, I.R.3: Advances under the Drainage Acts.

3 House of Lords Record Office: Minutes of Evidence before the House of Commons and the House of Lords concerning the various Welsh Railway Bills.

4 British Transport Commission Record Office (Royal Oak): CHH 4/1: Edward Parry's Report of 1848 concerning the Chester and Holyhead Railway.

5 Carmarthen Record Office: Cawdor, Plas Llanstephan, Derwydd, Castell Gorfod.

6 Merioneth Record Office: Rhagatt DR.458: instruction of Edward Lloyd (d. 14 September 1859) to his son.

7 Gregynog Hall (Montgomeryshire): Unscheduled Gregynog MSS.

8   Cardiff Central Library: MS 4.713, vol.II: letters of
E.P. Richards to Lord Bute in the 1830s.

B   PRINTED PRIMARY SOURCES

1   British Parliamentary Papers
1833, V, 'S.C. on Agriculture'.
1834, XV, 'S.C. on Land Revenues of the Crown'.
1834, XXIX, 'Report of the Commissioners into the Administration and
Practical Operation of the Poor Laws'.
1834, XXXIV, 'Report on the Administration and Practical Operation
of the Poor Laws'.
1836, XLIII, 'Returns relating to Writs of Intrusion, Tack Notes and
Inclosure Acts (Wales)'.
1844, V, 'S.C. on Commons' Inclosure'.
1844, XVI, 'R.C. of Inquiry for South Wales'.
1847, XXVII, 'Reports of the Commissioners of Inquiry into the State
of Education in Wales'.
1847-8, VII, 'S.C. on Agricultural Customs'.
1861, XXIII, 'Report of Commissioners into Salmon Fisheries in
England and Wales'.
1868-9, VIII, 'S.C. on Parliamentary and Municipal Elections'.
1870, XIII, 'R.C. on Employment of Women and Children in Agriculture'.
1874, LXXII, 'Return of Owners of Land, 1873'.
1882, XV, 'R.C. on Agriculture'.
1887, XXXVIII, 'Inquiry as to the Disturbances connected with the
levying of Tithe Rent Charge in Wales'.
1888, LIV, 'R.C. on Market Rights and Tolls'.
1889, XVI, 'S.C. on Woods and Forests and Land Revenues of the Crown'.
1893-4, XXXVI, 'R.C. on Labour, The Agricultural Labourer, Wales'.
1894, XXXVII; 1895, XL; XLI, 'R.C. on Land in Wales and Monmouthshire', Evidence.
1896, XXXIV, 'Report of the Royal Commission on Land in Wales and
Monmouthshire'.
1897, XV, 'Final Report on Agricultural Depression'.
1900, LXXXII, 'Report on Wages and Earnings of the Agricultural
Labourer in the U.K.'
1906, XCVI, 'Report on the Decline in the Agricultural Population of
Great Britain, 1881-1906'.
1912-13, XLVII, 'Departmental Committee on Tenant Farmers'.

2   Newspapers and periodicals
'Brecon County Times', 'Cambrian News', 'Carmarthen Journal',
'Carnarvon and Denbigh Herald', Montgomeryshire Express', 'North
Wales Chronicle', 'The Cambrian', 'The Farmers' Magazine', 'The
Times', 'The Welshman'.

3   Works of reference
J. Bateman, 'The Great Landowners of Great Britain and Ireland'
(London, 4th edn, 1883).
Hansard, 'Parliamentary Debates', 4th ser., II (4 March 1892 to
25 March 1892).
'The London Gazette', 1814-63 and 1885-1914.

4 H.M. Customs and Excise Library, Kingsbeam House, London
Bristol and Liverpool Bills of Entry.

5 Contemporary books
Anon., 'Letters from Wales' (London, 1889).
W. Davies, 'Agriculture of North Wales' (London, 1810).
W. Davies, 'A General View of the Agriculture and Domestic Economy
of South Wales' (2 vols, London, 1814).
A. Fullarton, 'Parliamentary Gazeteer of England and Wales' (1840-4),
part XI.
J. Gibson, 'Agriculture in Wales' (London, 1879).
A.D. Hall, 'A Pilgrimage of British Farming, 1910-12' (London, 1913).
T.J. Hughes (Adfyfr), 'Landlordism in Wales' (Cardiff, 1887).
R.H. Jackson, 'Welsh Highland Farming' (Denbigh, 1852).
L. Kennedy and T.B. Grainger, 'Present State of the Tenancy of Land
in Great Britain' (London, 1828).
S. Lewis, 'A Topographical Dictionary of Wales' (4th edn, London,
1849).
S. Roberts, 'Letters on Improvements addressed to Landlords and Road
Commissioners' (Newtown, 1852).
S. Roberts, 'Farmer Careful of Cilhaul Uchaf' (2nd edn, Conway, 1881).
J.E. Vincent, 'Tenancy in Wales' (Caernarvon, 1889).
J.E. Vincent, 'The Land Question in North Wales' (London, 1896).
J.E. Vincent, 'The Land Question in South Wales' (London, 1897).
W. Youatt, 'Cattle: Their Breeds, Management and Diseases' (London,
1834).
W. Youatt, 'Sheep: Their Breeds, Management and Diseases' (London,
1837).

6 Contemporary articles
J. Darby, The Agriculture of Glamorganshire, 'Jnl of the Bath and
West of England Soc.', 3rd ser., XVII (1885-6).
J. Darby, The Agriculture of Pembrokeshire, 'Jnl of the Bath and
West of England Soc.', 3rd ser., XIX (1887-8).
M. Evans, On the Black Cattle of South Wales, 'Jnl of the Bath and
West of England Soc.', 3rd ser., XIII (1881).
M. Evans, Welsh Mountain Sheep, in J. Coleman (ed.), 'The Cattle,
Sheep and Pigs of Great Britain' (London, 1887).
J. Howells, The Land Question from a Tenant Farmer's Point of View,
'Red Dragon', II (1882).
C.B. Jones, Agricultural Implements and Machinery, 'Welsh Nat. Ag.
Soc. Jnl', no.9 (1906).
W. Little, The Agriculture of Glamorganshire, 'J.R.A.S.E.', 2nd ser.,
XXI (1885).
C.S. Read, On the Farming of South Wales, 'J.R.A.S.E.', X (1849).
T. Rowlandson, The Agriculture of North Wales, 'J.R.A.S.E.', VII
(1846).
J.E. Thomas, The Agricultural Industry of Wales, 'Young Wales',
vol.3 (1897).
W. Barrow Wall, Agriculture in Pembrokeshire, 'J.R.A.S.E.' (1887).

C   SECONDARY SOURCES

1   Books

A.W. Ashby and I.L. Evans, 'The Agriculture of Wales and Monmouth-shire' (Cardiff, 1944).

J.D. Chambers and G.E. Mingay, 'The Agricultural Revolution 1750-1880' (London, 1966).

J.P.D. Dunbabin, 'Rural Discontent in Nineteenth-Century Britain' (London, 1974).

H.T. Evans, 'The Gorse Glen' (Liverpool, 1948).

R. Howells, 'Farming in Wales' (new edn, London, 1967).

D. Jenkins, 'The Agricultural Community in South-West Wales at the turn of the Twentieth Century' (Cardiff, 1971).

A.H. John, 'The Industrial Development of South Wales' (Cardiff, 1950).

D.J.V. Jones, 'Before Rebecca' (London, 1973).

E.L. Jones, 'The Development of English Agriculture 1815-1873' (London, 1968).

G.E. Mingay, 'Enclosure and the Small Farmer in the Age of the Industrial Revolution' (London, 1968).

K.O. Morgan, 'Wales in British Politics 1868-1922' (revised edn, Cardiff, 1970).

C.S. Orwin and E.H. Whetham, 'History of British Agriculture 1846-1914' (2nd edn, Newton Abbot, 1971).

D. Parry-Jones, 'My Own Folk' (Llandyssul, 1972).

D. Parry-Jones, 'Welsh Country Upbringing' (1st impn, Liverpool, 1974).

P.J. Perry (ed.), 'British Agriculture 1875-1914' (London, 1973).

D. Thomas, 'Agriculture in Wales during the Napoleonic Wars' (Cardiff, 1963).

F.M.L. Thompson, 'English Landed Society in the Nineteenth Century' (London, 1963).

H.M. Vaughan, 'The South Wales Squires' (London, 1926).

D. Williams, 'The Rebecca Riots' (Cardiff, 1955).

2   Articles

R. Colyer, The Welsh Cattle Drovers in the Nineteenth Century, pt I, 'N.L.W. Jnl', XVII, no.4 (1972);   pt II, 'N.L.W. Jnl', XVIII, no.3 (1974).

E. Davies, Sheep Farming in Upland Wales, 'Geography', XX (1935).

E. Davies, Hendre and Hafod in Merioneth, 'Jnl of the Merioneth Hist. and Rec. Soc.', VII, pt I (1973).

J. Davies, The End of the Great Estates and the Rise of Freehold Farming in Wales, 'The Welsh History Review', vol.7, no.2 (1974).

J.Ll. Davies, The Livestock Trade in West Wales in the Nineteenth Century, 'Aberystwyth Studies', XIII (1934) and XIV (1936).

J.P.D. Dunbabin, The Revolt of the Field: The Agricultural Labourers' Movement in the 1870s, 'Past and Present', vol.26 (1963).

T.W. Fletcher, The Great Depression in English Agriculture 1873-1896, 'Econ. Hist. Rev.', 2nd ser., XIII (1960-1).

G. Jenkins, Technological Improvement and Social Change in South Cardiganshire, 'Ag. Hist. Rev.', XIII, pt II (1965).

D.J.V. Jones, Crime, Protest and Community in Nineteenth-Century Wales, 'Llafur', I, no.3 (1974).

I.G. Jones, Merioneth Politics in the mid-Nineteenth Century, 'Jnl
of the Merioneth Hist. and Rec. Soc.' (1968).
Jane Morgan, Denbighshire's 'Annus Mirabilis': The Borough and
County Elections of 1868, 'The Welsh History Review', vol.7, no.1
(1974).
I.C. Peate, Some Aspects of Agricultural Transport in Wales, 'Arch.
Camb.', XC (1935).
R.O. Roberts, The Operations of the Brecon Old Bank of Wilkins and
Co., 1778-1890, 'Business History', I, no.1 (1958).
S.G. Sturmey, Owner Farming in England and Wales, 1900-1950,
'Manchester School of Economic and Social Studies', XXIII, no.3
(1955).

INDEX